Courts and Power in
Latin America and Africa

Also by Siri Gloppen:
South Africa: The Battle over the Constitution
Democratization and the Judiciary: The Accountability Function of Courts in New Democracies (coeditor with Roberto Gargarella and Elin Skaar)
Roads to Reconciliation (coeditor with Elin Skaar and Astri Suhrke)
Globalization and Democratization: Challenges for Political Parties (coeditor with Lise Rakner)

Also by Bruce M. Wilson:
Costa Rica: Politics, Economics, and Democracy

Also by Roberto Gargarella:
The Legal Foundations of Inequality. Constitutionalism in the Americas, 1776–1860
El derecho a la igualdad (coeditor with Marcelo Alegre)
Social Transformation and the Judiciary (coeditor with Pilar Domingo and Theunis Roux)
Carta abierta sobre el derecho y la protesta
Los fundamentos legales de la desigualdad
Derecho a protestar. El primer derecho
El derecho a resistir el derecho
Democratization and the Judiciary (coeditor with Siri Gloppen and Elin Skaar)
Nuevas ideas republicanas (coeditor with Felix Ovejero and José Luis Martí)
Crítica de la Constitución
Razones para el socialismo (coeditor with Felix Ovejero)

Also by Elin Skaar:
Judicial Independence and Human Rights in Latin America: Violations, Politics, and Prosecution (forthcoming 2010)
Roads to Reconciliation (coeditor with Siri Gloppen and Astri Suhrke)
Democratization and the Judiciary: The Accountability Function of Courts in New Democracies (coeditor with Siri Gloppen and Roberto Gargarella)
Reconciliation or Justice? Protecting Human Rights Through Truth Commissions and Trials (in Norwegian) (coeditor with Bård-Anders Andreassen)

Also by Morten Kinander:
Power and Law (in Norwegian)
Legal Philosophy—an Introduction (in Norwegian)

Courts and Power in Latin America and Africa

Siri Gloppen
Bruce M. Wilson
Roberto Gargarella
Elin Skaar
Morten Kinander

palgrave
macmillan

COURTS AND POWER IN LATIN AMERICA AND AFRICA
Copyright © Bruce M. Wilson, 2010.

First published in 2010 by
PALGRAVE MACMILLAN®
in the United States—a division of St. Martin's Press LLC,
175 Fifth Avenue, New York, NY 10010.

Where this book is distributed in the UK, Europe and the rest of the
world, this is by Palgrave Macmillan, a division of Macmillan Publishers
Limited, registered in England, company number 785998, of Houndmills,
Basingstoke, Hampshire RG21 6XS.

Palgrave Macmillan is the global academic imprint of the above companies
and has companies and representatives throughout the world.

Palgrave® and Macmillan® are registered trademarks in the United States,
the United Kingdom, Europe and other countries.

ISBN: 978–0–230–62100–8

Library of Congress Cataloging-in-Publication Data is available from the
Library of Congress.

A catalogue record of the book is available from the British Library.

Design by Newgen Imaging Systems (P) Ltd., Chennai, India.

First edition: March 2010

10 9 8 7 6 5 4 3 2 1

Printed in the United States of America.

Contents

Tables and Figure

Tables

Figure

Preface and Acknowledgments

S ince the authors of this volume got together at Café Rustique in Bergen in 2002 to discuss approaches to studying the phenomenon of accountability in new democracies, this project has gone a long way. Our overriding concern was with how courts, power, and politics could be understood in an interregional context. The ongoing intellectual struggle to integrate our different disciplinary insights and approaches to power and law has made the process unusually rewarding: the political scientists' fascination with institutions and power has been challenged by the legal scholars' insistence on legal text and interpretation and the moral-philosophical and ethical concerns of appropriate court action of the philosopher. Our theoretical journey was also influenced by the varied empirical background of the team members—from studies of Latin America, Africa, Europe, and the United States—providing a rich empirical grounding of the discussions. The concept of accountability, which lies at the core of this book, has been fiercely debated, beaten up, torn apart, and reconstructed innumerable times in the thinking and writing process. The result, we hope, is a book that reflects many different ways of understanding how courts manage to hold power holders in democratic countries to account when they override the law or overstep their constitutionally vested powers. And what happens to democracy when they do not.

This project builds on a long-standing intellectual cooperation, which has previously resulted in two edited volumes on the subject of courts and politics in new democracies, as well as a number of articles. The authors have brought to the project a wealth of empirical expertise and have collected original data in all the countries analyzed. However, others have greatly assisted in the processes and must be acknowledged here: Data collection for the African cases was carried out in collaboration with Fidelis Kanyongolo (Faculty of Law, University of Malawi), Emmanuel Kazimbasi and Alexander Kibandama (both Faculty of Law, Makerere University, Uganda), and Chris x • Preface and Acknowledgments

Maina Peter (Faculty of Law, University of Dar es Salam, Tanzania), all of whom have also contributed to the analysis. Ingrid Birkelund collected additional material in Mozambique, while Jorge Contesse and Oscar Javier Parra assisted in the data collection for the Latin American chapter. We want to thank you all. The authors are jointly responsible for the theoretical framework, analysis, and conclusions drawn from the empirical analyses—and for any errors.

We are thankful to a number of funding agencies, institutions, and persons who have assisted us materially and intellectually at different stages of the writing process. The Research Council of Norway has generously funded the main bulk of the project. Supplementary funding was provided by the Chr. Michelsen Institute and the University of Bergen. Institutions and informants in all ten countries—far too numerous to be mentioned individually—generously provided information and support during the data collection stages. Thanks also to colleagues who have contributed valuable comments on various drafts and to Racine Altif, Kerri Milita, María Luisa Piqué, and Kieran Wilson for editorial assistance. Particular thanks are due to Kerstin Hamann, who has earned our gratitude and respect for the way she has edited the manuscript and steered the process towards submission.

BERGEN, ORLANDO, BUENOS AIRES, OSLO
December 2009

Contributors

Siri Gloppen (PhD, University of Bergen) heads the "Courts in Transition" program at the Chr. Michelsen Institute, Bergen and is Professor of Comparative Politics, University of Bergen, and a former Visiting Fellow at the Harvard Law School. Her research focuses on the role of African judiciaries in democratization processes and social transformation, South African constitution-making and constitutionalism, election processes, human rights, and reconciliation. Publications include *South Africa: The Battle over the Constitution* (Ashgate) and *Democratization and the Judiciary* (coedited, Frank Cass).

Bruce M. Wilson (PhD, Washington University, St. Louis) is Professor of Political Science at the University of Central Florida and Research Professor II at the Chr. Michelsen Institute, Bergen, Norway. He was editor of *The Latin Americanist*. His research on political parties, policymaking, and judicial reform in Latin America has been published in numerous journals including *Comparative Political Studies*, *Comparative Politics*, the *International Journal of Constitutional Law*, and *Electoral Studies*. His book *Costa Rica: Politics, Economics and Democracy*, was published by Lynne Rienner. He has published his research on the Scholarship of Teaching and Learning in journals such as *PS: Political Science & Politics* and the *Journal of Political Science Education*.

Roberto Gargarella (Doctor of Law, University of Buenos Aires, 1991; Ll.M., University of Chicago, 1992; J.D. University of Chicago, 1993) is a researcher at Argentina's National Research Council (CONICET), Senior Researcher at the Chr. Michelsen Institute, Bergen, Norway and Professor of Constitutional Theory at the Universities of Torcuato Di Tella and UBA in Buenos Aires, Argentina. He has conducted postdoctoral studies at Balliol College, Oxford and was awarded a John Simon Guggenheim Fellowship and a Harry Frank Guggenheim Fellowship. He was a visiting professor at the following universities: University of Oslo and University of Bergen, Norway; Pompeu Fabra, Barcelona; and Columbia and New School in New York. He has published extensively on issues of legal and political philosophy, as well as on U.S. and Latin American constitutionalism.

Elin Skaar (PhD, University of California, Los Angeles) is Research Director at the Chr. Michelsen Institute, Bergen, Norway. Her main areas of research include human rights, transitional justice, and judicial reform. Geographically, her work focuses on Latin America and Southern Africa. Among her recent publications is *Roads to Reconciliation* (coedited, Lexington Books).

Morten Kinander (PhD, University of Bergen) is former Associate Professor of Law at the University of Bergen and is currently working as a lawyer in the law firm Wiersholm, Mellbye & Bech. A former Fulbright Scholar at Columbia University New York, he has published on subjects including legal philosophy, democratic theory, judicialization, law, and power. His most recent books are *Makt og Rett* (*Law and Power*) and *Rettsfilosofi—en innføring* (*Legal Philosophy—an Introduction*).

CHAPTER 1

Introduction: Power and Accountability in Latin America and Africa

The last two decades have witnessed a transformation of superior court behavior in many less developed countries. These courts have metamorphosized from being moribund, rubber-stamping institutions with little importance in political matters to more forceful, assertive institutions that constrain the behavior of popular branches of government and that hold them responsible when they break the law. In short, in recent decades, many superior courts have emerged as more independent, assertive, and powerful accountability agents. But, this has not been universally true. While some courts have exercised strong accountability functions, others have either remained passive or have inconsistent track records of holding popular branches to account. The puzzle that motivates this book, then, concerns the variation in the exercise of accountability functions of superior courts in Latin America and Africa over the last two decades. Why and when are courts able and willing to exercise accountability functions vis-à-vis power holders?

The book makes three major contributions: First, it develops a refined concept of accountability functions of courts through an exploration of the often blurry connections between vertical and horizontal accountability in a context of what role courts should, could, and do play in a democratic setting. Second, it offers a conceptual framework for an exploration of the behavior of courts while testing and challenging existing explanations of judicial behavior. Third, it offers empirical evidence for an explanation of judicial behavior through a systematic examination of a set of explanatory factors across ten countries. The synthesis of these empirical data, in turn, helps refine theories of judicial behavior.

Courts' Accountability Functions

Courts are not the only "institution of restraint" in contemporary democracies. In addition to the "vertical," or internal, accountability functions that voters exercise over their representatives through elections and other forms of political mobilization, several state agencies exercise "horizontal" accountability functions. Mapping out the connections between vertical and horizontal accountability functions, the first aim of this book is *to provide a useful working concept of the accountability functions of courts.* A host of bodies is charged with an accountability mandate: human rights commissions, ombudspersons, election tribunals and commissions, supreme audit institutions, and anticorruption bodies. The division of labor between such institutions and the courts varies from case to case. Yet, as much of the democratization and democratic governance literature stresses, a strong, independent judicial branch to protect constitutional rights and restrain the actions of popularly elected politicians, attempting to close political space, is required for these accountability structures to function (Carothers 2006; Domingo 1999, 2001; Linz et al. 1996). Therefore, it is important from the perspective both of democratic theory and judicial politics to improve our understanding of how and under which conditions courts develop such a significant accountability function.

Explaining Variations in Courts' Accountability Functions

Until the onset of a wave of judicial reforms in the late 1980s fostered by international financial institutions and NGOs, inactive superior courts were the norm for much of Latin America and Africa. None of the existing literatures on democracy, democratization, rule of law, judicial reform, or judicialization offers satisfactory explanations for shifts in the accountability functions of courts. In part, these analyses offer incomplete explanations because they rely on monocausal approaches that focus on single variables to explain judicial behavior. For example, they focus primarily or exclusively on the structures in which judges operate (institutional approaches) or on the judges and their mindset (attitudinal models).

The second aim of this book is therefore *to offer a multifaceted conceptual framework for exploring the behavior of courts* by testing and building on existing explanations of judicial behavior. In doing so, we take the current debate a step further suggesting that monocausal explanations inadequately explain the complex phenomenon of why some courts exercise a higher accountability function than others. We can further our understanding of different legal outcomes by combining a series of explanatory factors: (a) the historical and political context; (b) institutional variables (such as the structure of the courts and procedures, the constitutional and legal framework); and (c) the nature of the actors: in this case, judges.

Our analysis thus assesses the effects of different historical, political, and institutional factors that combine to shape the opportunity structure within which judges act. For instance, does a country's legal tradition (common law or civil law) have an impact on judicial behavior? Does it matter whether the country has a history of a multiparty system as opposed to a recent transition from a one-party state? To what extent do appointment procedures for judges or the resource situation of courts matter? Do different rules of standing and access influence what type of actors bring what types of cases to court? By addressing the so-called demand-side factors, we also ask what role civil society plays.

In addition to external factors, we accept that much of the decision-making of judges is based on their ideological preferences, ethical norms, professional training, and other personal factors. The decisions made by judges are influenced, for instance, by their ideological proximity to executives, career interests, or concern for the political life of their country. We examine these different variables in the case studies drawn from Latin America and Africa.

The Country Case Studies

Obviously, courts will vary from country to country, as will the actions taken by these courts. This book describes these experiences, analyzes the reasons for their variations, and generates more secure knowledge about what conditions favor the ability of courts to exercise an effective accountability function. We approach this task through a systematic comparison of ten judiciaries in Latin America and Africa: Argentina, Chile, Colombia, Costa Rica, Malawi, South Africa, Tanzania, Uganda, Zambia, and Mozambique. Since many of these countries are underexamined in the literature, our analyses bring new empirical knowledge to the field.

The cases were selected using three main criteria. First, the book focuses on superior courts in Latin America and Africa—regions where accountability problems appear to be particularly important and legal traditions vary largely by region. However, the areas of primary concern to the courts vary between the regions. What might present pressing accountability issues in one region might not be relevant in another. For example, many Latin American courts have become concerned with curbing presidential power and enforcing social and economic rights, while in Africa electoral issues and corruption cases frequently dominate.

Second, since legal culture has been assumed to influence the accountability functions of courts, we selected cases from different legal traditions. Latin America is dominated by the civil law tradition, while the African cases chosen are largely in the British common law tradition, with the exception of Lusophone Mozambique.

Third, our case selection targets superior courts that vary in the extent to which they exercise an accountability function. Two of the world's most assertive courts are found in Latin America (Costa Rica and Colombia) and so are some of the most deferential ones (Chile). This pattern is repeated in our African cases, which include relatively assertive judiciaries (Malawi and South Africa) as well as rather passive ones (Mozambique and Tanzania). The ten countries also display different patterns of within-country variance; Some (Colombia and South Africa) have a strong and relatively stable track record regarding their accountability function, whereas others (Uganda and Argentina) display great variation across time. Some of this variation is illustrated in Table 1.1.

The book's ten country case studies include six relatively proximate southern and eastern African countries and four Central and South American states. The countries vary in size and socioeconomic development, as indicated in Table 1.2, but they share important characteristics that make comparisons interesting. Most importantly, during a short period from the mid-1980s through the early 1990s, all the countries experienced a critical juncture, significantly changing in their constitutional and/or legal frameworks (a *constitutional moment*).[1] Prior to the reform process, all the countries shared a relatively similar experience of judicial inactivity. This similarity in superior court behavior and the similar nature of the reforms allows us to study the effects of changing constitutional context on court behavior.

Furthermore, there are commonalities presenting similar challenges for courts' exercise of their accountability function, most importantly in terms of controlling dominant executives. All the six African countries emerged from an extended period of authoritarian rule with strong executive presidents, and in every case, the new electoral politics have failed to end executive dominance. The new political systems have, to varying degrees, yielded polities with a weak and fragmented opposition. With the partial exception of post-2004 Malawi, either the old ruling party, which opened for competition, or the opposition, which forced the constitutional changes, have won all subsequent elections and controlled the levers of political power to the extent of blurring the boundaries between the party and the state.

In the African cases of Malawi, Uganda, Tanzania, and Zambia, British colonial rule left not only a common law heritage, but also the influence of the Westminster tradition where political (parliamentary) rather than

Table 1.1 Postreform accountability levels exercised by superior courts

Country	Overall accountability function in post-reform period	Direction and consistency of change.	Central areas for exercise of accountability function.
Costa Rica	High	Increased rapidly, remained high over time.	Broad: social rights (health), political succession, foreign policy.
Colombia	High	Consistently high in social rights, decreasing on executive power.	Broad: social rights/public policy, states of emergency, political succession.
Malawi	Medium/high	Variable, but consistently significant. Strengthens over time.	Broad: political space, democratic principles, succession.
South Africa	Medium/high	Consistently significant, but more cautious over time.	Broad: social rights/public policy, political space, corruption.
Argentina	Medium	Inconsistent, variable. Increasing more recently.	Political space, social rights.
Uganda	Medium	Starts weak, increasing but inconsistent.	Political space, democratic principles, succession.
Chile	Low/medium	Consistent, gradually increasing, relevant in routine cases.	Property rights, freedom of expression.
Zambia	Low/medium	Variable, strongest in first post-reform period.	Political space, democratic principles, succession.
Tanzania	Low	Consistently low, increasing somewhat, relevant in routine cases.	Political space.
Mozambique	Low	Very low, but gradually increasing.	Political space, democratic principles, corruption.

Table 1.2 Basic country data

Country	Population millions	GDP/Capita (PPP) $	World HDI rank (2008)	Gini coefficient
Malawi	14.3	800	162	0.503
Mozambique	21.7	900	175	0.473
South Africa	49	10,400	125	0.578
Tanzania	41	1,400	152	0.382
Uganda	32.3	1,100	156	0.430
Zambia	11.6	1,500	163	0.526
Argentina	40.9	14,200	46	0.513
Chile	16.6	14,900	40	0.549
Colombia	45.6	8,900	80	0.586
Costa Rica	4.3	11,600	50	0.498

Sources: CIA World Factbook (2009a, b, c); UNDP (n.d.).

constitutional supremacy lies at the core. Save for South Africa, they gained independence in the early 1960s, with similar constitutions that attempted—but failed—to curb the centralization of political power and the emergence of a single-party state.[2] The case study of Mozambique, a former Portuguese colony, illustrates that factors other than its civil law legal tradition have been responsible for limiting the willingness and capacity of superior courts to exercise their accountability functions.

The Latin American cases, too, experienced similar colonial and independence histories, long experiences with dominant executives and weak, moribund courts, and these countries have adopted similar constitutional documents and political institutional designs. These similarities are particularly true for three cases jointly examined in Chapter 3. Each country experienced major political transitions in the late 1980s and early 1990s. For Argentina and Chile, the 1980s marked a return of democratic governance after many years of dictatorial rule by military juntas that routinely trampled individual rights. Democratic governance, new constitutional documents, and formally strengthened courts characterized the new regimes. Colombia transitioned into a more democratic period when the old political structure of dominant parties was replaced by a new political system, a new, rights-rich constitutional document, and the creation of a strong, independent constitutional court. In response to the new constitutional order, the courts in Chile remained passive; those of Argentina initially maintained their role as political ciphers, before becoming somewhat more assertive in recent years, whereas the Colombian Constitutional Court became one of the most assertive courts in the region.

The Costa Rican Supreme Court was similarly an insignificant institution in terms of accountability before the 1989 constitutional amendment created the Constitutional Chamber of the Supreme Court. Unlike the other Latin American cases, this simple constitutional amendment was the only significant change in the country's political life, and it allows a clearer view of the impact of the relevant factors for the Costa Rican case. Everything else in the Costa Rican polity remained as it was before the creation of the court; political parties, party system, economic policies, and civil society incurred no major changes during the time the court was reformed.

Using the "constitutional moment" for each country as a point of departure, we use a combination of comparative chapters and in-depth case studies to systematically assess the various groups of explanatory factors across the ten countries. The two single case studies of Costa Rica and Mozambique allow us to explore some of the explanatory factors in more detail. The study of the hyperactive and assertive Constitutional Chamber of the Supreme Court in Costa Rica demonstrates that the court has been able to assume its function in the context of weak political parties and a president with limited powers, thereby illustrating the significance of the institutional setup in a country. The study of the high courts in Mozambique explores the significance of a civil law tradition in an African context and illustrates how the interaction between the legacy of the one-party state, the institutional setup of the courts, and strong personalities at the top of the judicial hierarchy restrict the courts in exercising their accountability functions. Combined, the chapters show that it is useful to move beyond explanations that focus on a single variable in order to understand the accountability functions of courts. Combining explanations, grounded in a variety of analytical approaches, generates new knowledge about why some courts exercise their accountability function more prominently than others.

Methods and Data Collection

The comparison of the ten countries is based on theoretically structured, thick descriptions, employing a shared theoretical framework. The studies accommodate the particular experiences of these countries that defined and shaped the significance of the role of the court in the different political contexts. Thus, we retain the richness of each country's experience, while enabling a systematic comparative analysis and a reassessment of central theories in the field. The country studies are based on many years of field-work in each of the ten Latin American and African countries, which include numerous interviews with key actors (judges, lawyers, activists, politicians, and academics) and extensive archival work.

A Roadmap for the Book

The next chapter (Chapter 2) presents the book's conceptual framework by integrating the most promising of the existing approaches seeking to explain variations in the accountability functions of courts. The framework serves the twin purpose of exploring the extent to which existing theories actually explain and "travel" across different empirical settings, and how they act as a basis for systematic exploration of combinations of factors that might provide a more robust multivariate explanation of judicial behavior with regard to holding political power to account.

The subsequent empirical chapters explore the various sets of variables identified in the framework and the interactions between them, in different country contexts. Chapter 3 examines three South American countries (Argentina, Chile, and Colombia) that exercised significantly different accountability functions despite the following common factors: these countries share a common history of colonization and independence; they employ related legal traditions; they have relatively analogous constitutions; and they have been similarly affected by changes in the international political and economic environment. Chapter 4 presents an in-depth study of Costa Rica's Constitutional Chamber of the Supreme Court and explores the factors that facilitated the development of a highly assertive court. Costa Rica, one of the region's oldest and best functioning democracies, created a new Constitutional Chamber of the Supreme Court in 1989 without a regime transition or any other major institutional disruption. As a result, a clear picture emerges as to the relevant factors that facilitated the Costa Rican court's exercise of an enhanced accountability function and its elevation as a guarantor of social rights.

Chapter 5 moves the book's focus to southern and eastern Africa. It compares and contrasts the accountability function of judiciaries in Malawi, South Africa, Tanzania, Uganda, and Zambia, all of which are former British colonies and share a common law heritage. After an extended period of authoritarian rule with strong executive presidents, all these countries made a shift in the 1990s toward a more democratic, and in most important respects, similar constitutional system, which vested strong powers in the judiciaries and broadened their jurisdiction. Despite the overall similarities, the judiciaries in the five countries have followed different trajectories. To further examine the relative impact of legal tradition, Chapter 6 focuses on Mozambique, which adheres to the civil law rather than the common law tradition.

To conclude, Chapter 7 draws lessons from the ten case studies across theoretical approaches and geographical regions. First, the book illustrates that the issues on which courts act in matters of accountability vary across regions. In Latin America, the provision of a check on executive power (abuse) has been a main concern, whereas electoral issues (clearing the channels of the democratic game) have played a larger role in African common law countries. This may have to do with the fact that electoral democracy is younger in Africa than in Latin America and also because of the huge social and economic importance of political careers in the African context. Second, the book proposes that single-factor explanations (dominant in the existing literatures) offer limited explanations for why some courts succeed in holding other power holders accountable when they overstep their powers whereas other courts fail to do so. Third, the chapter demonstrates that a combination of historical, legal-contextual, structural, and individual factors are useful in offering a more complete picture of the differences across countries and variations over time in courts' exercise of their accountability functions.

CHAPTER 2

Accountability Functions of Courts: A Framework for Inquiry

Many countries across the globe have in the past two decades undertaken substantial judicial and legal reforms to strengthen the democratic character of their governments. Yet, the ability and willingness of courts to restrain elected officials vary greatly. This book describes these experiences, analyzes the reasons for existing variations, and helps gain more secure knowledge about the conditions that favor the ability of courts to exercise an effective accountability function. The book describes the experiences of four Latin American and six African cases, and demonstrates the varying ability and willingness of courts to hold other state branches to account. We approach this task through a systematic comparison that is based on theoretically structured thick descriptions with each case focusing on the areas of law where, prima facie, accountability problems seem to be particularly important. Thus, we seek to retain the richness of each country's experience, while enabling a systematic comparative analysis and a reassessment of central theories in the field. This chapter provides the theoretical foundation for the descriptions in the following empirical case studies and the final chapter, which synthesizes the lessons drawn from the individual cases.

The accountability concept has been at the center of considerable scholarly debate since the early 1990s, engaging the literatures on democracy, democratization, the rule of law, judicial reform, and judicial activism (see, e.g., Mainwaring and Welna, 2003; Schedler, Diamond, and Plattner, 1999; on the accountability function of courts specifically, see Gloppen, Gargarella, and Skaar, 2004). Based on these literatures, we first develop a refined concept of the accountability functions of courts in modern democracies. This discussion also clarifies the concept of democracy for the purpose of our analysis. Taken together, vertical accountability and horizontal accountability represent the two classic pillars of democracy: namely, people's sovereignty through representation and the limitation of power through law and the separation of powers.

From the conceptual and theoretical level, we move on to describe the sociopolitical and institutional webs within which modern judiciaries operate and exercise their accountability functions. In the second part of this chapter, we offer a multivariate conceptual framework for exploring the behavior of courts, challenging monocausal explanations of judicial behavior. Drawing on existing theories, we construct a conceptual framework that integrates the most promising of the currently dominant approaches in order to better explain variations in the accountability function of courts across time, countries, and regions.

A satisfactory explanation needs to take account of the *opportunity structure* that to a greater or lesser extent enables judges to fill their accountability role, as well as the *motivation factors* that cause judges to act (or to refrain from acting) as accountability agents. Our framework combines three types of explanatory variables: (i) the social and political context (including the legal tradition; the political balance of power, the strength of civil society and the propensity to litigate); (ii) the legal and institutional framework (including the mandate and jurisdiction of the courts provided by the law; the structure of the legal system, the structural protection of judicial independence and provisions for access); and (iii) the actors involved (including the composition of the bench; the background, ideology, and capability of the judges; and the corporatist culture of the judiciary).

The framework serves as a basis for exploring combinations of factors across different empirical contexts, thus providing a more robust multivariate explanation of judicial behavior with regard to holding political power structures and individuals accountable. The proposed framework also allows us to assess how much existing theories explain, and how well they "travel" across different empirical settings. Before embarking on the conceptual framework, we want to specify and normatively address the underlying assumptions concerning the roles that courts and judges are, ideally, expected to play in a democratic society.

The Concept of Political Accountability

Since the 1990s, the concept of accountability has become increasingly central to debates on democratic theory and democratization (see, e.g.,

Austen-Smith and Banks, 1989; Goetz and Jenkins, 2005; Grant and Keohane, 2005; Mainwaring and Welna, 2003; Manin 1997; Maravall and Przeworski, 2003; Maskin and Tirole, 2004; O'Donnell 1998; Persson and Tabelini, 1996; Przeworski, Stokes, and Manin, 1999; Schedler, Diamond, and Plattner, 1999). Schmitter and Karl met with skepticism when in 1991 they suggested "the concept of accountability as the key to the broadest and most applicable definition of 'modern representative political democracy'" (Schmitter 2004: 47). But the accountability concept has provided a fruitful ground for thoughts around the challenges of institutionalizing democratic governance in contexts in which the problems of executive dominance and securing political representation and space for contestation of political power are predominant.

Political accountability entails a relationship between two sets of actors; citizens, who are the principals with whom legitimate political authority ultimately rests, and the rulers, who are their agents. The relationship involves an exchange of responsibilities and potential sanctions as the basis for legitimate rule. It is a relationship of power: the ruler, whom the citizens have entrusted with authority, is obliged to keep the citizens (or their representatives) informed and to offer explanations and justification for decisions made. If the ruler fails to do so, or the account is not satisfactory, the citizens (or their representatives) may impose predetermined sanctions (Goetz and Jenkins, 2005; Schmitter 2004). "It is thus a specific variety of power: the capacity to demand someone to engage in *reason-giving* to justify her behavior, and/or the capacity to impose a penalty for poor performance" (Goetz and Jenkins, 2005: 8).

Described in these terms, political accountability in a democratic context refers to a hierarchical relationship in which the people have the power to challenge, remove, and replace the ruler. This means reserving the accountability term for what the literature calls "vertical accountability" (or "democratic," "popular," or "external" controls), institutionalized principally though elections. Accountability in this sense is the main (procedural) mechanism of democracy. While there is disagreement on how best to secure vertical accountability, there is broad agreement on the need to pay close attention to these mechanisms.[1]

There has been more debate on what is referred to as "horizontal accountability" ("internal" or "intrastate" controls, and "checks and balances"), which deals with accountability relationships between different state institutions. In what O'Donnell (2003: 34) calls "the legal institutionalization of mistrust," bodies within the state are given a legal mandate to control other state institutions, which in turn are obliged to account for how they have exercised the powers with which they have been entrusted. In his well-known definition, horizontal accountability is "[t]he existence of state agencies that are legally enabled and empowered and factually willing and able, to take actions that span from routine oversight to criminal sanction or impeachment in relation to actions or omissions by other agents or agencies of the state that may be qualified as unlawful" (O'Donnell 1999: 38).

In horizontal accountability relations, the different agencies are institutionally independent. On some occasions, each of them has an independent mandate from the voters (as is the case with legislatures and executives in presidential systems with strict separation of powers). In other cases, the state institution acting as controller (courts, ombudspersons, human rights commissions, supreme audit institutions, and so on) is appointed and funded by one or more of the institutions that they are set to hold accountable (the executive and/or parliament).

There are debates as to whether these horizontal relationships in which the restraining body is not in a position to remove the other by withdrawing its trust, qualify as accountability or rather should be described as "intra-state controls" or as "veto-players."[2] O'Donnell (2003) argues, however, that it is a matter of accountability as long as the relationship is based in law with one party being under obligation to explain (answerability) and the other authorized to employ sanctions (controllability).

O'Donnell's definition has been criticized as being too narrow. Critics point to his limitation of the term "horizontal accountability" to relations that deal with legal transgressions and omissions—whether representatives comply with the constitution, the law, and the terms of their mandate. They want instead to include as accountability all activities that involve holding public officials accountable for their discharge of duties, not only where the relationship is formal and legally regulated (Mainwaring and Welna, 2003; Schedler, Diamond, and Plattner, 1999). Mainwaring (2003: 9), for instance, argues that the term accountability should also include political accounting, such as cabinet's accountability to the legislature in parliamentary systems. We believe that the latter, to the extent that it deals with political judgment (i.e., what is politically good to do), is more usefully seen as part of the vertical accountability relationship, which, in a parliamentary system, extends from the voters through parliament to cabinet, with parliament as an (intermediary) principal and the executive as agent. Vertical accountability can, however, coexist with predefined horizontal accountability relations between parliament and cabinet around issues of legality. We believe it is useful to distinguish horizontal accountability relations, in which the mandate is limited to holding power to law,[3] from vertical political accounting, which legitimately seeks to make representatives conform to a political program or view.

Furthermore, critics have voiced skepticism against placing too much emphasis on such intrastate relationships, which, in practice, tends to involve a narrow set of elites rather than keeping the focus on the vertical, popular controls on government (Goetz and Jenkins, 2005). While this is a valid and important concern,[4] we show how horizontal accountability—and principally that exercised by courts—can play a vital role in securing popular control.

The Accountability Structures of Modern Democracies

Modern representative democracies involve a range of accountability relationships, of which the courts form a central part. The main mechanism available to citizens for exercising vertical accountability is the election of representatives. Countries have put in place varied electoral structures to secure the accountability of national political bodies. Most parliamentary systems have elections only for the legislature, which then selects the executive—which, in turn (or together with the legislature), appoints the members of the judicial branch. Presidential systems usually have elections for the president in addition to the legislature.[5] Judiciaries are rarely directly elected.[6] The electoral channel may also facilitate popular control through referenda and recall of representatives. Elections are a formal, legally regulated accountability relation of high significance compared to other mechanisms for popular control.

The media and public debate (including mobilization through social protests, demonstrations, civil society movements, petitions and so on) are other important spaces for political deliberation, contestation of power, and the exercise of public control. These are not legally specified accountability relationships, but nevertheless are premised in legal rights—freedom of the press, speech, and assembly—that are central to the functioning of a democratic system and that the courts are central to protecting.

Courts may also serve as a mechanism for popular control or societal accountability by enabling individuals and groups to use litigation to protect and advance their rights and interests (Peruzzotti and Smulovitz, 2006). Similar to the electoral channel, this is a vertical accountability relationship that is legally specified. The relative importance of legal mobilization as a channel for vertical accountability varies and depends, among other things, on how well other channels for popular control function. But given the casuistic, and generally resource demanding and unrepresentative nature of litigation, it has limitations as a prime mechanism for democratic control.

This is, however, only one aspect of the accountability functions of courts. As mentioned, courts are crucial to the system of horizontal accountability between state institutions, and they hold other state actors to the law and the constitution. To the extent that they protect the law—the outcome of the political process—they serve a democratically highly relevant function. By acting on their responsibility to protect the law and the constitution,[7] they also serve to protect the channels for vertical, popular control of government (the electoral channel, media, and civil society activism) against self-seeking attempts by incumbents to evade accountability or block the channels of political change.

In this role, courts in modern democracies are assisted and comple- mented by other state agencies that exercise more specialized horizontal accountability functions. The division of labor between courts and other bodies with an accountability mandate, such as human rights commis- sions, ombudspersons, election tribunals and commissions, supreme audit institutions, and anti-corruption bodies, vary from country to country. The specialized accountability institutions fall into three categories, and each category carries out accountability functions similar or complementary to those of the courts.

The first category of institutions is aimed at protecting basic rights and includes, most centrally, ombudspersons and human rights commissions. Their operation and relationship to the courts vary between countries, but generally they serve a complementary role and do not take over protection of human rights or constitutional rights from the judiciary. There are varia- tions, however, regarding the extent to which the general judiciary concerns itself with constitutional and human rights cases. Many countries have a special constitutional court to hear constitutional cases, which is often sep- arate from the rest of the legal system.

The second group of special accountability institutions is principally concerned with economic accountability and includes supreme auditing institutions and anticorruption bodies. This category also includes indepen- dent central banks, which do not have a court-like accountability function, but rather serve to depoliticize important monetary decisions and remove them from political control. Economic accountability, nevertheless, remains a central aspect of the accountability function of courts, and these other bodies generally complement, rather than compete with, courts by investi- gating matters that may come before the courts at a later stage. In countries where courts have an investigative role, it is often the courts or specialized tribunals that perform this function.

The third category of accountability institutions aims to fortify the basic accountability structure already described. It includes independent electoral commissions that are established to strengthen the integrity of elections by placing responsibility for electoral management in an independent body to prevent (accusations of) incumbent manipulation of the process. It further includes commissions to strengthen the integrity of the civil service and boards to regulate and protect the media. This does not mean that courts no longer have a role to play with respect to elections or freedom of the media. Although these other institutions may take over some functions that would otherwise have rested in the courts, such as adjudication of certain types of electoral complaints, courts in most cases have an appeal function. Some countries also have special electoral tribunals, in which case the ordinary courts do not hear electoral cases, or only rarely. Hence, while election cases in some jurisdictions are the most crucial cases for higher courts to exercise an accountability function vis-à-vis political powers, such cases are virtually absent from the highest courts in other jurisdictions, due to a different institutional division of labor. This is important to remember when operationalizing the accountability function of courts in the latter part of this chapter.

The "protection of integrity category" also includes judicial councils and judicial service commissions, which are established to strengthen the integrity of the judiciary itself by playing a role in judicial appointments, in the administration of the judiciary, and/or in the disciplining of judges. The special challenge that these bodies are established to ease is that of "guarding the guardians" (holding the judiciary itself accountable to other state institutions) without compromising their independence.

The latter can be even more of a problem with regard to the specialized accountability institutions. The structural protection for their independence tends to be weaker than for the judiciary. Norms for professional conduct are also often weaker. Special accountability institutions may play a useful role, but from the perspective of an accountable government, it is not always the case that a higher number of such institutions is beneficial. To multiply accountability, institutions may serve as window dressing. It may also lead to forum shopping on the part of the government and marginalize the "bothersome" institutions. And these institutions themselves may become self-serving and corrupt in their competition for funding and recognition.

Our concentration on the accountability function performed by courts is thus informed by theoretical as well as practical, policy considerations. A growing web of institutions to hold government accountable does not eliminate the need for a strong, independent judicial branch (Carothers 2006; Domingo 1999; Linz and Stepan, 1996; Sieder 1996). Not only do core accountability functions remain with the courts, but they are also central to the functioning of the other accountability institutions, especially when the plethora of institutions with similar accountability functions give rise to jurisdictional conflicts. Hence, a better understanding of how and under which conditions courts develop a significant accountability function is important both from the perspective of democratic theory and for judicial reform policy. The accountability functions of courts in a democratic state constitute our dependent variable. We now provide a detailed discussion of what this entails, and how it can be assessed.

Courts' Accountability Functions—the Dependent Variable

The question of how to assess the accountability performance of courts cannot be separated from normative views on democracy. Although we aspire to be unbiased in our assessment of the performance of courts, there is inevitably a normative standard implicit in our (and in every) theoretical framework. This is of particular importance in the explication of the dependent variable (i.e., the accountability functions of courts). When we assess the performance of courts based on their accountability functions, the standard is based on a set of assumptions about what the courts are able and fit to do, combined with an understanding of what is required to uphold a well-functioning democracy. The following factors are in our view among the most central concerns that democratic judiciaries must strive to uphold and contribute toward: *genuine competition for positions of political power; equal opportunities for political participation; political space for deliberation and contestation of political decisions; and protection of basic rights.* These concerns, and the role of courts in protecting them, are not undisputed, as shown by the century-long—and ongoing—debate on the relationship between constitutionalism and democracy.[8] Still, the position adopted here is relatively weak in the sense that it is formulated to be compatible with different notions of democracy. Proponents of deliberative democracy and representative liberal democracy share the understanding of these factors as central concerns. They consider that credible institutions capable of holding political bodies and officeholders accountable for illegality, abuse of power, and neglect of responsibilities, are key to a stable well-functioning democracy.[9] There is also broad agreement that courts are central to this endeavor, although views may differ regarding what the priorities of courts should be.

What should the main focus be when assessing the accountability performance of courts? The short answer is: "To what extent have they contributed toward securing the democratic process?" However, we cannot prescribe how courts should proceed in their pursuit, and what their priorities should be. This depends, among other factors, on the political context and democratic challenges in the particular society. Furthermore, as the outline of the accountability structure of the already described modern democracies shows, the specific actions that courts should (and have the opportunity to) take depend on the institutional context and their position within the total structure of accountability institutions. The assessment of the accountability functions of courts requires us not only to examine the concrete behavior and decisions of the courts, but also take into consideration whether they actually can do what we normatively expect them to do.

When empirically comparing the accountability performance of different courts, we cannot rely only on direct comparison of court behavior in relevant areas of law since what is most salient from an accountability perspective will vary between countries and over time. Still, there are some key concerns that courts should attend to in a democratic society. We will outline these concerns in some detail later.

Courts, we presuppose, should have a democracy-enhancing role. We assume that in a democratic system the most crucial democracy-enhancing role of the courts is to clear the channels of political change and protect basic rights, particularly the rights of disadvantaged minorities, who are vulnerable to being marginalized in the political process.[10] In his influential book *Democracy and Distrust,* John Ely (1980) sees the constitutional role of the judges as defined by what he calls a "representative-reinforcing approach" (Ely 1980: 1).[11] Judges, in his opinion, should try to ensure the proper functioning of the constitution. Malfunctions occur in the following situations: " the ins [elected representatives] are choking off the channels of political change to ensure that they will stay in and the outs will stay out; or though no one is actually denied a voice or a vote, representatives beholden to an effective majority are systematically disadvantaging some minority out of simple hostility or a prejudiced refusal to recognize commonalities of interest, and thereby denying the minority the protection afforded other groups by a representative system" (Ely 1980:103). According to this view, courts are obliged to prevent attempts to acquire power and hold on to it by illegitimate means (for example, gerrymandering, censorship, discrimination, restriction of political rights, and also the alteration of election laws). Judges are the referees in the democratic game and are "to intervene only when one team is gaining unfair advantage, not because the 'wrong' team has scored" (Ely 1980: 103).

Given that periodic elections are the only institutionalized mechanism for control of political power-holders "by the people" in most modern democracies, it is particularly crucial to secure that this channel is "cleared" and functions properly and fairly. Courts have an important role to play in securing the integrity and trustworthiness of the electoral process. In assessing their accountability function, a relevant place to look at is their performance in relation to various aspects and stages of the electoral process. Courts may "clear" the electoral channel and contribute to a level electoral playing field in a number of ways: by assessing the constitutionality of the legal framework and institutional setup for the elections; by demanding compliance with the rules of the game and sanctioning illegality throughout the electoral process (e.g., in the registration and education of voters and also the compilation of the voters roll; in the campaign; in the polling and the counting processes); and by ruling on election petitions challenging the outcome (see Gloppen and Kanyongolo, 2006a; Gloppen, Kasimbazi, and Kibandama, 2008). As already noted, countries vary as to how much jurisdiction constitutional and supreme courts have in electoral matters relative to other institutions, such as special election tribunals, but normally they will have some form of appellate jurisdiction.

A more general set of cases important for the assessment of the accountability functions of courts are those that seek to enable popular contestation and control over political power by protecting space for political deliberation and social mobilization (among other cases regarding freedom of speech and assembly and also the freedom of the press), and those that seek to ensure that no groups, and particularly not disadvantaged minorities, are directly or indirectly discriminated or marginalized from the decision-making process.[12] As already noted, courts may serve as an independent channel for societal accountability through legal mobilization (Peruzzotti and Smulovitz, 2006). Individuals and groups may gain political voice through litigation aimed, for example, at advancing concerns related to social justice and protection of social rights. To the extent that the highest courts enable such societal accountability directly or through securing the conditions for such litigation, this forms a significant part of their accountability role.

In addition, the accountability functions of courts should be assessed on the basis of their willingness and ability to sanction abuse of political power and violations of rights. This is an important part of the legitimate and necessary democratic function of the highest courts in all the cases examined in this book. Given that modern democracies rely heavily on horizontal accountability mechanisms to guard against tyranny and abuse of power, the whole institutional system is at risk if these controls fail. The accountability functions of courts here include their role in sanctioning (and/or preventing) unlawful actions (or omissions) of public officers, and also their role in obliging political power-holders to engage in justifying the way they exercise their powers and fulfill (or not) their mandates. Given the predominance of executive dominance in the cases under examination, the relationship to the executive is here of particular importance. In addition to the direct role of the highest courts in holding executives accountable, they may also have a role in protecting the integrity and powers of other institutions that are established to secure accountability, as discussed earlier. The ways in which courts exercise this accountability function is particularly salient in emerging and/or fragile democracies in which political institutions tend to be weakly embedded in the political culture; the boundaries between the branches of power are less respected, and the powers of the president formally and informally are larger than in more stable democracies. Most of the cases in this book fall in this category. In these regimes, it is crucial for democratic consolidation that the courts contribute toward preventing power-holders (and the executive in particular) from exceeding the limits of their democratic mandate—and, in particular, hinder that they, once in power, "draw up the ladder," by opportunistically changing the rules of the game.

While we regard effective checks on executive power by the courts to be necessary in order to maintain and consolidate a modern democracy, the question remains of how extensive these controls should be. In our view, this cannot be determined a priori. The normative standard must be informed by the historical trajectory of each society to clarify what the main political problems are that the courts need to address. The normative standard is hence to be developed with a view to the pressing and specific needs of the contexts in which courts are to exercise their accountability functions. What society and the legal profession see as the appropriate role for the judges is also significant. This is related to views regarding the basis on which courts (with their unrepresentative nature) can claim legitimacy for their decisions in a democracy.[13] How this is negotiated depends on the legal tradition, the domestic political culture as well as the impact of current international ideological trends. In addition, it is important when setting an "accountability target" to take into account that an extensive system of horizontal checks on power incurs *costs*, both financially, in terms of efficient decision-making—and for the courts, in terms of increased politicization of their role (Domingo 2004; Shapiro and Stone Sweet, 2004). Another question concerns "how to guard the guardians" and prevent misuse of the power by the judiciary itself.

These concerns should be kept in mind as we turn from this general discussion of our dependent variable to a more specific discussion of how the accountability function of courts can be assessed and compared over time and across cases.

Assessing and Measuring the Accountability Functions of Courts

When investigating the accountability function of courts we are looking at their ability and willingness to say "no" when rules are violated and the democratic process is threatened, and make the decision "stick." Having indicated several ways in which the courts may fill this role, we propose an assessment based on the following aspects:

- Instances where the highest courts *sanction (and/or prevent) self-serving alterations* of the legal and institutional framework, with particular emphasis on attempts by the executive to encroach on the powers of other organs, undermine their function, or thwart the electoral process.
- Instances in which the highest courts *protect the rights* of actors in political and civil society and *preserve political space* for them to perform a meaningful vertical accountability role, whether through the electoral process, through broader processes of public deliberation and democratic political participation, or through litigation.
- Instances, including the area of social rights, in which the highest courts *sanction unconstitutional laws and policies.*
- Instances where the highest courts manifest their accountability function by the *sanction of illegal actions or corrupt behavior* by public officials.

An important distinction in this context is that between the accountability function of courts and judicial activism. Not all forms of activism by the courts contribute toward making government more accountable. Conversely, courts do not need to be particularly active to have a strong accountability function.

This raises a fundamental problem in assessing the accountability function courts as indicated by manifestation through cases. It is arguably more effective when it operates as a latent constraint on power—that is, when other institutions and actors refrain from actions that they assume the courts will sanction. To address this situation, we pay particular attention to cases of *failed accountability.* This includes cases, brought to court, in which the judges have failed to sanction violations, as well as instances where blatant transgressions of law and constitutional principles were not brought before the courts. We also assess, through interviews, whether courts are perceived to have a latent effect in preventing unconstitutional and illegal acts.

Finally, we need to assess the *effects* of these rulings—their ability to "stick." To that end, we mainly analyze whether adverse rulings are complied with, and whether rulings opposed to the interests of those in power have caused retaliation against the judiciary.

Case Selection and Methodological Considerations

To select which cases are the (most) relevant ones, decide which judgments are the most significant, what constitutes important instances of failed accountability by the courts, and what the political consequences and implications of the judgments are requires intimate knowledge of the context and also involves political judgment. It is thus important to establish a sound process for selecting relevant (non)decisions and evaluating them. One strategy for collecting the necessary information is to interview a balanced set of key informants in the legal–political community. This is the main approach relied on in this book. In some cases, existing literature has been of help. In addition, the judicial process was monitored through archival research, newspaper reports, examination of the court's roll, and scrutiny of decisions. The latter is a useful source of information about which cases the judges see as important precedents, and the legal strategies they use to justify their decisions.

Explaining the Accountability Functions of Courts: A Conceptual Framework for Comparative Analysis

Each of the countries analyzed in this book experienced a critical juncture, or constitutional moment, that serves as the focal point of our analysis.[14] Before this democratic and/or judicial reform process occurred, most of the countries shared a similar experience of judicial inactivity. Thus, the thrust of this book is to understand why some courts have developed stronger accountability functions than others. The "mapping" of the accountability functions of courts offered in Chapter 1 (Table 1.1) illustrates this variation and thus serves as the basis for an investigation into *why the judiciary—more specifically the judges of the highest courts—holds state officials to account when they overstep their powers.*

The next section discusses the dominant answers provided by the literature before integrating insights from various approaches in a way that enhances our understanding of the dynamics at play.

Explanations from the Social, Legal, and Political Context

Differences in the accountability function of courts are sometimes ascribed to historical trajectories and the way these have formed the culture, and the socioeconomic and political structure of the different societies. These explanations are diverse but share a focus on factors outside the judiciary and the legal system itself: factors that tend to change slowly and are difficult to reform intentionally. At the most general level, this may take the form of a reference to the level of state formation, but a range of more specific aspects are considered decisive for the functioning of the courts.

The *legal culture* in society is often considered of great importance. This includes the extent to which a culture of legalism permeates society generally—the political community that leads citizens to bring cases to the court and authorities to respect their rulings. A related set of explanations focuses on the nature of the culture within the judiciary. An explanation of judicial behavior based on legal cultures sometimes refers to differences between broad legal traditions—common law versus civil law tradition—while in other cases it refers to a more localized culture developing in a particular society. The literature has traditionally assumed that the civil law heritage is less conducive to a strong judicial accountability function than the common law (Merryman 1985; Rosenn 1987).[15] In principle, in civil law, systems codes and statutes passed by the legislative bodies represent the core of the law, while jurisprudence plays a secondary role. In common law systems, case law made by judges and developed over centuries constitutes the core of the system, while statutes only apply in certain areas of the law. In common law, precedents are binding, while earlier decisions usually do not have biding force in civil law systems. These differences explain why common law judges are assumed to play a more central role in the creation and not merely in the interpretation of the law. Our initial assessment of the countries under investigation does not, however, seem to sustain this hypothesis, and we will thus explore more systematically the influence of the civil versus common law tradition on the accountability function of courts in the concluding chapter.

The *political balance of powers* in society is another factor often presumed to be decisive for the ability of the courts to exercise an accountability function vis-à-vis the government. Where there is one dominant political party or coalition and alternation in power is unlikely in the foreseeable future, actions by the courts to hold political power accountable are more likely to prompt attempts by the government to reign in the judiciary and limit their independence. Awareness of their vulnerability may lead judges to exercise self-censorship. On the other hand, if the space for opposition in the political arena is limited, political actors may turn to the courts, which in turn may increase their case load and thus enhance their opportunity to decide cases that make the courts politically relevant. The lack of alternative means to influence political power or a weak civil society may also instill a sense of duty and urgency in the judiciary (Uprimny 2004).

The extent to which courts are able to exercise their accountability functions in a "hostile" political environment depends on the extent to which they have *protective constituencies* that make it costly for the government to encroach on their independence (Widner 1999, 2001). Protective constituencies may be a function of the judiciary's general legitimacy in society, but they may also be based on the support from more limited but politically significant groups, such as business or international donors or an active and vocal civil society.

The structural factors that characterize the broader society not only define the parameters within which legal institutions and judicial actors operate. Processes of institutionalization also shape the nature of these actors and institutions themselves. It is easy to agree that at some level such factors have an impact on the accountability functions of courts. But, taken in isolation, they become too deterministic and fail to account for differences between countries with a similar history and sociopolitical conditions, or sudden changes in the accountability performance of specific courts.

Explanations from Institutional Design

The literature focused on institutional design, which forms the dominant basis for the study of judicial reform policies, assumes that variations in the accountability function of courts stem from differences in the judicial institutions. This literature focuses primarily on the structural protection of judicial independence as a necessary condition for the accountability function of courts (Domingo 1999; Rosenn 1987; Skaar 2002).[16] This approach to the study of judicial independence is reflected in legal–political documents,[17] various judicial reform policies, and a variety of frameworks for assessment of judicial governance.[18]

Institutional design-centered approaches vary somewhat in their assumptions about the effects and importance of particular institutional features, but basically all rely on the same list of institutional factors. The factors highlighted in this literature fall into four categories.

The more theoretically informed institutional design literature focuses predominantly on arrangements to provide the judiciary with *structural independence* from the political branches. Emphasis lies primarily on appointment procedures but also on the procedures for promoting, disciplining and removing judges, the judges' protection for tenure, the adequacy of and security for remuneration (salaries and perks), and the judiciary's autonomy over their budgets. A second set of institutional variables are those affecting the *jurisdiction and powers* of courts. This includes the formal constitutional mandate given to the courts and the adequacy of the legal framework on the basis of which the courts are to develop their accountability functions. Included here is also the control of courts over their case load. A third set of factors regard the provision of *resources* available to the courts (infrastructure, staff, running costs, training, and legal material), which determines their ability to effectively process cases and deliver judgments. Not only the volume of resources, but also the security and sources of funding are central here. The last set of factors addresses institutions that affect the *professional competence* of the judiciary, the personal, and also the professional qualities of the judges on the bench. These are related to recruitment patterns, education, and training, as well as to professional forums that establish professional standards and make professional reputations matter.

A problem with much of the institutional design literature is that it seems to assume that the institutional structure operates in a vacuum. It lacks appreciation for how the design of legal-political institutions is influenced (although not determined) by the sociopolitical context. Whether the formal judicial institutions emerge "organically" over centuries or are "chosen anew" as part of a reform process, they are shaped by the social and political context in which they operate. Second, institutions cannot by themselves perform an accountability function. The assumption, underlying the institutional design approach, is that institutions constrain and enable actors by providing incentives and opportunities. But these actor-assumptions—what motivates the actors (judges) and how they act in relation to their motivations—are rarely made explicit and critically discussed in this literature (Carothers 2006).

Actor-Based Explanations

A prolific strand of court studies, especially in the United States, seeks to explain judicial behavior through focusing on the individual qualities of judges. Actor-centered approaches come in different varieties:

Attitudinal approaches assume that what is important for how judges act is who they are, which in turn determines the values and preferences they hold.[19] To understand the decisions of the court, the ideology of the judges matters. Justices—as assumed by this view—behave non-strategically. They do not engage in logrolling, and neither do they care about how other institutions react to their judgments. Since judicial decisions are understood to directly reflect the policy preferences of judges, the focus is on their ideology, moral and political orientation, and also other factors assumed to be relevant to their identity. The most relevant identity markers vary between contexts and may include class background, ethnicity, religion, or region. The attitudinal model has an antecedent in the work of Dahl (1957), who challenged the traditional view of the so-called countermajoritarian difficulty.[20] Using empirical evidence, he demonstrated that for the most part, "the Supreme

Court is inevitably a part of the dominant national alliance" (Dahl 1957: 293) Rather than serving as a countermajoritarian power, the court tended to be a promajoritarian institution. At the same time, Dahl's argument that judicial decisions resulted from the political preferences of judges gave foundation to the attitudinal model. While judges tended to reinforce "the major policies of the [dominant] alliance" by voting according to their sincere preferences, this alignment of preferences also explained why politicians had selected them in the first place (Epstein, Knight, and Martin, 2001: 587; see also 2003: 783).

Rational choice approaches, on the other hand, focus on the strategic self-interest of judges, given their incentive structures. The incentive structure or opportunity situation is usually defined by a selection of the institutional and context variables discussed earlier. An example is the *strategic defection* thesis discussed in some detail later (Helmke 2005). Here, the political balance of power and the *predictability* of the political context (who will be in power after the next elections) are seen as the crucial determinants of the question of whether judges find it in their interest to act on their accountability functions vis-à-vis the executive. Similarly, opportunities for a career in politics, or international recognition, may be seen to create incentive structures that motivate judges to exercise an accountability function. To the extent that actors are assumed to react identically when faced with the same incentive structure, rational choice approaches can be seen as the dynamic element of the institutional and/or social context-focused approaches already discussed.

Varieties of both attitudinal and rational choice approaches assume that judges are motivated by "higher order" values or preferences (such as a desire to preserve democracy or their institution). This may, in critical cases, motivate them to act strategically, sacrificing short-term "true" preferences (for example, for holding the executive accountable in the particular case) to safeguard this higher-order interest, or in other words they engage in *nested games*, which should be taken into account to understand their accountability performance.[21]

Critics of the attitudinal model have maintained that justices are not myopic, "single-minded seekers of legal policy," always voting according to sincere preferences (George and Epstein, 1992: 323). Rather, since they care about the promotion of their favored policies—and know that this does not simply depend on their own preferences and actions, but also on those of other actors and institutions—justices pay attention to how other relevant actors behave in relation to the decisions of the court. Sometimes, then, justices will vote in ways that do not exactly reflect their sincere and most favored preferences, but rather in ways that ensure their second best options, given existing political constrains (see, for example, Ferejohn and Weingast, 1992:12; see also Eskridge and Ferejohn, 1992; Knight 1992: 190).

There are different views on who the "relevant others" are. Some authors have studied how members of multimember courts interact and find that the voting patterns of judges change according to the composition of the court and that "a judge's likely vote is influenced by the other [judges] assigned to the same panel" (Sunstein, Schkade, and Ellman, 2004: 301; see also Miles and Sunstein, 2007; Sunstein et al. 2006).

Other authors claim that courts try to attend to the policy moods of the public to ensure compliance with their decisions and keep their public legitimacy. According to this view, the public has different ways of influencing courts, from exercising pressure indirectly through the political branches, to directly suffocating the tribunals with demands or organizing demonstrations against them or some of their members (see, for example, Smulovitz and Peruzzotti, 2000). Empirical studies show a significant correlation between public opinion and the decisions of courts as a result of such pressures. According to Mishler and Sheehan, court decisions "not only reflect changes in public opinion but also serve to reinforce and legitimize opinion change in an iterative process" (Mishler and Sheehan, 1993: 96; see also Flemming and Wood, 1997; Mishler and Sheehan, 1996).

Most typically, however, the strategic model has focused on how other branches of power influence the decisions of the justices (also known as the *separation of powers* model) (Epstein and Walker, 1995: 343). Advocates of this model argue that justices write their opinions with an eye on the other branches. Justices know that the political branches may change the composition of the court by appointing judges of a different ideology, change the size of the court, or—in extreme cases—impeach all or some of the judges. Or, less radically, they may combat their rulings and try to overcome them, fail to implement orders, modify the jurisdiction of courts, advance constitutional amendments, reform the system of judicial review, change the salaries and benefits of judges, or slash the court's budget (see also Rosenberg 1992). Therefore, Epstein, Knight, and Martin (2001: 592) maintain that justices "cannot, as the attitudinalists and Dahl suggest, simply vote their own ideological preferences as if they are operating in a vacuum; they must instead be attentive to the preferences of the other institutions and the actions they expect them to take if they want to generate enduring policy." This explains why justices sometimes avoid adopting decisions that manifestly defy what Congress and the president regard as acceptable; even when this runs against their sincerely held preferences.

Some authors have tried to extend the force of this separation-of-powers argument to more unstable and judicially politicized environments (Helmke

2002, 2003, 2005; Iaryczower, Spiller, and Tomassi, 2002; Scribner 2003).[22] They argue that while in more stable contexts courts tend to adjust their opinions to those of the current governments, in unstable and irregular environments, courts tend to begin interacting with the government's successors for fear of being punished by the coming authorities. Helmke (2005: 14) coined the concept of *strategic defection* to capture the phenomenon that "institutionally unstable settings generate a reverse legal-political cycle in which judges rule against the current government once it begins to lose power." This defection approach pays particular attention to the rulings *against* the government, which "increased significantly whenever judges began to sense that the current government was losing power and decreased when the incumbents grew strong" (ibid., 125).

While each of these approaches provides important insights, none of them offers satisfactory explanations for variation and shifts in the accountability functions of courts. Part of the problem rests with the predominantly monocausal nature of these approaches to explaining judicial behavior, whether they focus on the sociopolitical context or the structures within which judges operate (the institutional literature), or on the judges and their mindset (attitudinal and strategic models).[23] In this book, we want to take the debate a step further by suggesting that a more complete understanding of different legal outcomes requires us to look at a combination of different types of factors. We outline an alternative analytical framework that searches more widely for explanatory factors and considers the following: the legal texts in which the courts base their decisions; the legal traditions and cultures to which the judges belong; the social culture and the political circumstances within which each court makes its decisions; and also the composition of the courts in terms of the background, training and dominant ideology of judges, and the procedures and practice concerning judicial appointments and tenure that determines the career incentives of judges and, hence, the strategic games they engage in with other relevant political actors.

An Alternative to Monocausal Explanations of Judicial Behavior

Considered in isolation, existing explanations of judicial behavior are simultaneously overambitious and incomplete. The overambitiousness stems from a desire to explain judicial behavior by the use of one main—usually extra-legal—variable. Alternative sources of judicial motivation to act (such as principled conduct, an overriding concern for ensuring the consolidation of democracy, and so on) thus become invisible or improperly subsumed to the strategic behavior explanation. More specifically, monocausal approaches fail to take seriously a central part of the object of description, namely the law, which simply disappears from the explanatory picture of most of these models. Even when we share the assumption that the interpretation of the law is mediated by ideology, passions, and interests, we do not assume that it is virtually meaningless or without any independent normative force. By contrast, we think that even in less democratically institutionalized countries, the law plays a very significant role, forcing many judges to decide in ways they would not decide had the law been different.

In addition, many of these explanations tend to become irrefutable as a consequence of an overexpansion of the main explanatory variable. Typically, if all judicial actions (from those aimed at avoiding sanctions to those directed at keeping professional reputation, gaining popular approval, and so on) are redefined as strategic moves,[24] the notion of strategic decisions becomes capable of explaining almost everything, but at the cost of becoming trivial.

Some of these analyses seem to exaggerate the powers of other groups and institutions for undermining judicial authority.[25] And it is rarely carefully examined to what extent "strategic acts" by the Court, sacrificing sincere policy preferences for long-term policy goals, are not rather mere acts of "surrender." Or whether, when judges defer from opposing what the political branches prefer in order to increase their institutional legitimacy, this does not rather imply a loss of credibility and thus, of legitimacy.

Against this background, part of our contribution is simply "negative." We maintain that it is not possible to explain variations in the accountability function of courts by using monocausal explanations in the way much of the literature proceeds. In the chapters that follow, we provide examples supporting this claim. Each of the chapters helps us to identify the contribution, but also the significant limitations of various monocausal explanatory models. Through the comparative analysis of African and Latin American countries we demonstrate the need for adopting a more complex explanatory schema for understanding the accountability function of courts. This is the "positive" contribution of our book: a framework capable of providing a more comprehensive understanding of judicial behavior. Table 2.1 outlines the analytical schema that we propose as more adequate to guide investigations of the accountability functions of courts.

The analytical framework outlined in Table 2.1 combines elements from the approaches already discussed and highlights the interactions between these, and it also provides for a more nuanced understanding of what causes the variations we observe in the accountability function of judiciaries between countries and over time.

Table 2.1 Analytical framework for studying courts' accountability functions

Demand-side Factors		*Supply-side Factors*	
Litigants' opportunity structure. • Access to court (standing, support structures). • Alternative avenues to hold power to account (political mobilization, court-like institutions); legitimacy of the judiciary. • Civil society strength and legal resources.	Case load.	Judges' opportunity structure.	Sociopolitical context: political balance of power; supportive constituencies; legal tradition (judicial culture); career opportunities. Institutions: Structural protection of judicial independence; enabling legal framework (jurisdiction, powers); protection of resources; skills-enhancement.
		Motivation to act.	Actors: Judges' ideology and background, norms, rational self-interests (personal and institutional).

The table combines three sets of variables to explain why some judiciaries develop stronger accountability functions than others: (i) the social and political context (the legal-political culture and history of the country; the political balance of power and the strength of civil society); (ii) institutional variables (structure of the judicial institutions, the powers, competences, and independence of courts); and (iii) the actors (ideological, social, and professional characteristics of judges). The first two sets of factors, sociopolitical context and institutional structure, along with the case load of courts, combine to form the *opportunity structures* within which the judges operate and the incentives they face, while the third set of factors (actor variables) influences the *motivation to act*. The interaction between these factors—and in particular how judges respond to their opportunity structure—determines whether they, in fact, perform an accountability function.

Drawing on the institutional design literature, we assume a range of institutional factors impact the ability of judiciaries to establish and maintain a capacity to act as accountability agents. Most importantly, we assume that the *formal constitutional mandate and legal framework* secure sufficient jurisdiction and powers, and that there are arrangements in place to secure *structural independence* from the political branches and a degree of individual independence within the judicial hierarchy, particularly with regard to appointments and security of tenure (procedures for promoting, disciplining, and removing judges). Furthermore, it is assumed to matter that the courts have sufficient *resources* (infrastructure, administrative and research staff, and also legal material) to effectively process cases and deliver judgments, and that there are institutions established to enhance the *professional competence* of the judiciary (through recruitment criteria, education, training, and professional forums in which professional standards are developed and professional reputations matter).

The contextual factors assumed to be particularly important for the ability of courts to develop and maintain accountability functions vis-à-vis political authorities include the *legal culture* (exploring, for example, the impact of civil law versus common law and characteristics of the dominant culture of the judiciary), the *political balance of powers* (exploring differences between competitive political systems and the presence of a dominant party or coalition), the extent to which the courts have *protective constituencies,* and the *case load,* which reflects to what extent the courts are called on to hold political actors accountable (i.e., demand-side pressure).

The case load, or demand-side factors, merit particular attention. It is through deciding cases that courts exercise their accountability functions, and the cases that reach the courts are thus their raw material. The amount and type of cases, how they are framed in relation to the law, and the quality of the legal argument are important for the accountability function of the court everywhere and particular in countries where the courts do not have the power to investigate cases on their own initiative. The column on the left of Table 2.1 shows factors influencing the demand on courts to exercise an accountability function, which then is reflected in the case load. Our assumption is that this is a product of (potential) *litigant's opportunity structure,* which in turn is also defined by the following factors: *sociopolitical context* (in particular the existence of alternative avenues to voice their concerns, and the strength and resources of civil society); the legal *institutional structure* (in particular how easy or difficult it is to access the courts); and *actor variables* (the legitimacy of the judiciary). Demand for the services of courts are assumed to be greater where there are few alternative (more promising or easily accessible) avenues open for social actors to oppose political decisions and where actors who want to use the court have easy access (including to the necessary legal and organizational resources that enables them to lodge cases that express their demands in a legally sound way). Demands on the courts are also assumed to increase in places where relevant social actors trust the courts and expect to be given a fair (or favorable) hearing.

Turning again to the question of what motivates judges to take up an accountability function vis-à-vis political actors, we need to explore in depth how this is influenced by context and "design." How strongly does the institutional setting influence the decisions that judges make? How influential are the various aspects of the institutional structure? And how important is this relative to the social and political context? Drawing on the literature regarding judicial behavior (expanded on above), our assumption is that the motivation for judges to establish and maintain their independence depends predominantly on two sets of variables—*personal and professional interests*, or in other words, what the judges individually and the judiciary as an institution stand to gain or lose from challenging or supporting the government, and *the ethical standards and norms of appropriateness*, that is, the norms of professionalism in the legal community and the perception of judges of their own role.

When analyzing the differences between courts in the following chapters we seek to assess the explanatory power of each of the different sets of factors, asking how much of the observed variance can be explained by institutional factors, context, and actor variables respectively. At the same time, the framework aids a systematic exploration of the interaction between the different variables.

The emphasis on the dynamics between various sets of variables is central to our approach. Sociopolitical and institutional structures combine to provide incentives to which actors' responses vary. The individual and collective behavior of judges is formed by the institutional structure in which they operate, but the result is not predetermined. Courts whose structural independence is safeguarded may turn out to be timid and with little or no accountability functions vis-à-vis political power-holders. Similarly, sociopolitical factors (such as executive dominance and weak political opposition) form an important part of the opportunity structure of the judges, creating incentives that are central to understand judges' behavior regarding their accountability functions—but they do not determine judicial behavior. Furthermore, the sociopolitical and institutional variables interact. The sociopolitical context strongly influences the institutional structure of legal systems. On the other hand, comparable contexts produce different "designs" (more or less conducive to a strong judicial accountability function), depending on the cumulative choices that formed these institutions. Decisions made by domestic and international actors, historical and contemporary, determine the nature of legal institutions, as well as the balance of power in society, institutional capacity, and political will. By systematically investigating these various aspects across countries and over time, we hope to gain a better understanding of the accountability function of courts.

Conclusion

The rest of this book systematically applies the theoretical framework developed in this chapter to a selection of new or fragile democracies in Latin America and southern and east Africa. Through a combination of comparative chapters and single case studies, we explore in breadth and in depth the effects of and interactions between the variables listed above on the exercise of judicial accountability. The countries covered in the analysis are Argentina, Chile, Colombia, Costa Rica, Malawi, South Africa, Tanzania, Uganda, Zambia, and Mozambique. All ten countries experienced a critical juncture or constitutional moment where significant changes have occurred in the country's constitutional and legal framework. This has enabled us to study the effects of changing constitutional context on the behavior of courts.

Despite very different historical trajectories, different legal traditions, and varying levels of economic and institutional development, we find patterns of commonality and difference across the countries in Latin America and Africa, which may help explain varying degrees of judicial accountability. Factors that seem particularly important in limiting the exercise of judicial accountability include a deferential judicial culture, short renewable terms for judges, a political context with a dominant party/excessively strong president, and a lack of protective constituencies for the courts.

By contrast, factors that seem particularly favorable to the emergence of courts with strong accountability functions include a liberal rights-based constitution with strong review powers; appointment procedures and terms of tenure that in effect limit the influence of the executive over judges (given the political balance of powers), broad professional competence in the higher courts (including judges from academic backgrounds), and wide access to the courts. Reforms facilitating access to higher courts through provisions for direct access, broadened legal standing, or reductions in legal formalities have proved to have an exceptional potential for inducing changes in judicial behavior across very different contexts.

CHAPTER 3

The Accountability Functions of Latin American Courts

This chapter examines the accountability function of superior courts in three Latin American countries—Argentina, Chile, and Colombia—in the last two decades.[1] This comparison appears promising because the respective courts have assumed very dissimilar roles in countries that share a common colonial and independence history, similar legal traditions, and relatively parallel histories regarding the effects of the international economic environment. How, then, can we explain the different legal outcomes in these countries? More specifically, what explains the fact that some of the superior courts have exercised an active accountability function whereas others have been rather deferential to the executive?

Our answer builds on an understanding of the organization of courts and their actions. First, we describe the political context within which the courts have acted; we then discuss the way in which the courts are organized (appointment procedures and the scope of their powers). Finally, we review their main decisions. We conclude by comparing the functioning of the three courts and exploring different explanations for their actions, including a multicausal approach.

The Legal and Political Context

The Supreme Courts of Argentina and Chile and the Constitutional Court in Colombia have acted in similar contexts. All three countries have presidential systems that have been strengthened over time, developing "hyper-presidentialism" (Mainwaring and Shugart, 1997; Nino 1996, 1992). These hyper-presidentialist systems have arguably "unbalanced" the model of "checks and balances" established in their constitutions and opened space for potential abuses by the executive, which, in Argentina, was translated into extreme political and judicial instability. It is particularly in Argentina and Colombia that repeated abuses by the executives have called for judicial remedial interventions.

The three countries have also experienced massive human rights violations; in Argentina and Chile, these violations were related to long and recent periods of military rule. In all three cases, this created extremely difficult political situations after the transitions to democratic rule and also confronted their fragile elected governments with fundamental questions, such as how to deal with issues of transitional justice; what to do when thousands of people—including military officers—are identified with human rights atrocities; or whether a decent and rational society should adopt retributivist or consequentialist responses to such crimes. On all these questions, courts have been called into action. In addition, the three countries feature growing, but unstable, economies that coexist with high levels of poverty and also substantial levels of inequality. This potentially socially explosive situation has also necessitated increasing judicial interventions, particularly in Colombia.

By contrast, the three countries differ significantly regarding their levels of civic organization and social mobilization, which, one might argue, represent a crucial element for explaining the actions of courts. However, a society with a higher level of mobilization seems compatible with judicial activism, given the people's eagerness to defend their rights through all possible means, but also with judicial inactivity, given the people's seeming preference for political, direct actions.[2]

Although the countries share similar constitutional structures, they have developed in different directions. The Colombian Constitution of 1991 is presently the one most committed to social rights. Argentina's Constitution was substantially reformed in 1994 and granted constitutional status to ten international human rights treaties. Meanwhile, the Chilean Constitution appears to be the least protective of social rights. Perhaps the legal differences between the three countries are unrelated to the "thickness" of their respective Bill of Rights. Instead, maybe the differences that really matter are those related to the procedural aspects of their constitutional organization. Our cases suggest that the appointment procedures and the internal organization of each judicial system greatly favor the development of certain judicial practices. For instance, the highly hierarchical organization of the Chilean judiciary likely favors the development of disciplined and subordinate attitudes among Chile's lower judges. These judges have strong incentives to apply—and never defy—previous decisions and even to comply with the expectations of superior tribunals.

Existing rules of standing and, in general, the rules that organize access to the courts, are also of significance. Colombians, for example, created open rules and numerous resources to facilitate individuals' access to the courts. Again, a correlation between the existence of these open rules and the presence of more assertive courts is apparent, which theoretically is not difficult to explain: Courts under systematic popular pressure tend to be more responsive to popular demands than courts that are more isolated from those demands. The next sections explore these similarities and differences in some more detail.

Argentina: Context and Procedures

Argentina has experienced three recent and substantial changes in the composition of the court, which are consistent with a long history of political intervention regarding the Supreme Court. In fact, virtually every new government since 1947 (appointed in 1955, 1958, 1966, 1973, 1983, 1990, and 2004), whether democratically elected or not, changed either the entire court or the majority of its judges.

In 1983, newly democratically elected President Raul Alfonsín had the opportunity to appoint an entire new court to replace the court that had served during the 1976–83 dictatorship. The newly appointed court became one of the most liberal in Argentina's history and included among its members some distinguished academics. This court, after almost a decade of brutal dictatorship, had to confront and decide many fundamental questions regarding basic civil, political, and human rights. President Carlos Menem, Alfonsín's successor, gained control over the court through the enactment of law 23.774, which, while invoking the need to make the tribunal more efficient, increased the number of its members from five to nine judges, thus allowing the president to "pack" the court. The new court worked in a period marked by the closure of the trials against the military *junta* as well as a very intense privatization process that coincided with a concentration of power in the executive and repeated accusations of political corruption. This legal period was characterized by the reversal of many of the most important liberal decisions of the Alfonsín court.

In 2003, Néstor Kirchner was elected president. The incoming government confronted a very difficult political situation, because in 2001, after the resignation of Menem's successor President De la Rúa, Argentina faced one of its most serious (if not *the* most serious) political and economic crisis in history. The crisis reached its peak with the succession of five different presidents in less than one month. Kirchner took advantage of this situation and launched a profound reform of the widely distrusted Supreme Court. The president then had the opportunity to appoint the new majority of the court, following the resignation of three and the impeachment of two of its former members.

Argentina's 1994 Constitution refers to the jurisdiction of the court in article 116, which, following the U.S. example, grants the court ample freedom to act. In addition, article 117 defines the cases in which the Supreme Court has appellate and original jurisdiction. As far as the appointment procedures for judges are concerned, the new constitution departs from the rules of the old one, which had specified that the president was in charge of appointing all judges, including Supreme Court judges, with the agreement of the Senate (article 86.5). All these judges enjoyed life tenure. Congressional sessions for the appointments of judges became secret sessions. This practice undoubtedly distorted the entire selection process and allowed the selection of many poorly qualified judges. These abuses became particularly prominent during Menem's administration, when the government selected some judges who lacked professional experience. Constitutional delegates responded to these abuses by proposing major changes in the appointment process for judges in the 1994 Constitution that included mandating public sessions for the appointment of Supreme Court judges and the use of a Council of Magistracy that would present a binding proposal of three candidates to the president prior to the appointment of all lower federal judges.

Despite these important changes, many people continued to distrust the judiciary. This shared perception, together with a strong and growing dissatisfaction with the existent court, forced President Kirchner to introduce still more institutional changes. Thus, in one of his first and most celebrated decisions, he signed decree 222/03, which provided for a new designation process that was more transparent, equilibrated, and open to the public.

The 1994 Constitution also revised procedural resources for ensuring the protection of constitutional rights. First, it included the traditional *amparo* that was judicially created and then normatively recognized through law 16.986, and habeas corpus resources, also the product of a judicial creation. In addition, the constitution for the first time made reference to *amparos colectivos* again through the same article (n. 43). This new procedural tool allows those persons, whose basic rights are impinged on, and also the ombudsperson and nongovernmental organizations, to protest any form of discrimination, and claim environmental, consumer, and all other collective rights. There is still a considerable amount of controversy regarding who can demand what, and how the tribunals can react to those demands.

Chile: Context and Procedures

Chile features gradual changes in its legal history. We first discuss the period of ex-dictator Pinochet following the military coup against Salvador Allende (1973–1990);[3] second, the democratic period following the end of the Pinochet era; and finally, the period following Pinochet's arrest in Great Britain in 1998. Additional changes are expected following the latest 2005 reform of the 1980 Constitution (Couso and Hilbink, 2009). For example, the reformed constitution strengthens the authority of the *Tribunal Constitutional* vis-à-vis the Supreme Court, transferring part of the controlling powers of the latter to the former so that now the *Tribunal Constitutional* rather than the Supreme Court is in charge of declaring a statute inapplicable as a consequence of its tension with the constitution.

After the military coup, the Supreme Court remained basically blind toward General Pinochet's reform process, which carried with it gross and massive violations of human rights. Notably, the court did not accept more than ten of the 5,400 writs of *habeas corpus* filed by a religious human rights group, the Vicariate of Solidarity, during the years of military rule (Hilbink 1999a: 9). The court justified its behavior stating: "Courts are strict and loyal law enforcers, law that continues to be for them the written reason. According to such law, the judges ought to decide the cases...and they are not authorized to disdain and deviate from this rule and look for general principles of morality or law which could produce their decisions...The judges are aware that they must be strict appliers of the law" (quoted in Correa Sutil 1993: 93).

After the end of Pinochet's regime, the legal context experienced small changes. The new democratic administrations aimed at moderately reforming or correcting the dark legacy of the previous dictatorship. These efforts were also directed at improving the living conditions of the very poor, which Pinochet's regime had ignored or marginalized. Meanwhile, other important governmental decisions addressed Pinochet's grave record of human rights violations. President Patricio Aylwin, an active human rights lawyer during the dictatorship, was particularly concerned with these reforms. The creation of the National Commission of Truth and Reconciliation, the ratification of various international human rights treaties and conventions, and the pursuing of human rights cases that were not covered by the Amnesty Law approved by Pinochet's forces in 1978, are illustrative examples of this new attitude. The new democratic governments (and, again, Aylwin's administration in particular) sought to restructure the functioning of the legal apparatus, and primarily the judicial system, which was considered to be outdated (Galleguillos 1997: 15).

The initiatives for judicial reform were many. Aylwin made a first attempt to pack the Supreme Court, which, however, failed. He then promoted a constitutional reform to create a National Council of Justice, which also failed. In 1992, the new government promoted an impeachment process against three justices for violation of their legal duties, resulting in the removal of one of them. The outcome was quite spectacular, particularly considering that Congress had never managed to remove a Supreme Court justice, or that, since 1868, Congress had not attempted to impeach a member of the Supreme Court (Couso 2004: 76). Partly encouraged by this success, but mainly as a consequence of grave corruption scandals that involved some of the superior judges, new impeachment processes were promoted, on one occasion against the president of the court. The chief justice eventually resigned, even though he was not condemned by the Senate. At the same time, the growing discontent with the court also affected the traditional links between the members of the court and the political right, which feared that the country's economy could be adversely affected by this growing lack of confidence in the court. As a result of this new political alignment, Congress again discussed increasing the number of members of the court and, in 1998 under President Eduardo Frei, Congress finally succeeded in increasing the members of the court from 17 to 21.

Additional changes followed when the well-known Spanish judge Baltasar Garzón issued an order to detain Pinochet, who was in the United Kingdom for a medical analysis.[4] Garzón's decision demonstrated to many Chileans that Pinochet and many of his policies were unanimously condemned by international legal authorities—not only in Spain and the United Kingdom, but also in the many other countries, where similar protests and legal processes against Pinochet took place. It was in this context that President Lagos (1998–2004) assembled diverse social groups, including representatives of the army, with the purpose of forging agreements regarding past violations of human rights. On November 28, 2004, President Lagos appeared on state television to present the report written by the *Comisión Nacional sobre Prisión Política y Tortura* (or *Comisión Valech*) after hearing more than 35,000 people. Among its significant conclusions, the report maintained that torture had been a systematic practice during the dictatorship. However, in spite of facing more than 300 charges of gross human rights violations in Chilean courts, Pinochet died in jail before any of the cases were concluded.

The Chilean Constitution, reformed in 2003 and again in 2005, defines the powers and jurisdiction of the Supreme Court and grants it ample powers, but it leaves the functions of the tribunal to be regulated by federal law. Although the formal powers of the courts in Chile and Argentina are quite similar, some contextual differences between the two countries are worth mentioning. Most significantly, Chile's judicial history is much more stable than that of Argentina. According to Scribner (2003: 14), between 1933 and 2000 "Chilean justices have an average tenure of 10 years; and of these 75 justices, 72% either retired or died in office—none were removed by a coup." This contrasts starkly with Argentina, where justices "have an average tenure of 5.77 years; and of the 58 justices on the bench over the time period studied (1946–2000), only 10% died in office or retired; the greater majority (53%) resigned or were removed in coups (29%)" (Scribner 2003: 14).

However, the appointment procedures established in Chile's Constitution are responsible for "endogamic" conducts. Even though in most cases it is the president who finally selects the judges, the Supreme Court's participation is decisive in the entire process of appointing the judges of both the lower courts and the Supreme Court. For example, according to article 32.12 of the 1980 Constitution, the president appoints all judges on the appeal courts, but has to select the appointees from a list of candidates submitted by the Supreme Court. Also, article 78 specifies that the president appoints Supreme Court judges, in agreement with the Senate, by selecting them from a slate of five individuals proposed by the court itself.

This mechanism further enhances the authority of the court and strengthens the rigid hierarchy of the system. The system's internal discipline is reinforced by the Supreme Court's annual evaluation of inferior judges, which obviously influence their careers. These appointment procedures contain some explanatory potential. In particular, the Supreme Court's decisive role in the appointment of future Supreme Court justices helps us understand the Court's homogeneous character and its peculiar relationship with politics.

Judicial review was introduced very early in Chile through the Constitution of 1925. The 1980 Constitution maintained this power of the court and also empowered the main tribunal to exercise it upon its own initiative (article 80). The court, however, used this capacity only rarely (Friedler 2000: 342). The *Tribunal Constitucional*, created in 1970, also participates in the mission of controlling the validity of the laws (although its function is closer to that of a "negative legislator," article 93).

Finally, Chile's 1980 Constitution established two main routes for the protection of constitutional rights: the *recurso de inaplicabilidad de la ley* or writ of nonapplicability of laws and the *amparo* and the *recurso de protección* or writ of protection. The first instrument has rarely been used (Gómez 1986). It allows citizens to demand the nonapplicability of a certain norm that is considered to violate the constitution and also permits the court to do so on its own initiative (since the 2005 reform, however, the *Tribunal*

Constitucional has been the institution in charge of this power). The *writ of protection,* which was introduced by the 2005 constitution, has become more popular as it requires few formalities and establishes celerity of procedures. This provision allows individuals to demand relief from a court of appeals when their main constitutional rights are at risk or are violated by an act or omission of the state or another individual.

Colombia: Context and Procedures

Colombia's recent legal history is marked by the adoption of a new Constitution in 1991. In many ways, this new Constitution has been highly influential. It replaced the 1886 Constitution, one of the oldest and most stable constitutions in Latin America, which was widely considered to be extremely conservative in a heterogeneous, pluralistic, and complex society such as contemporary Colombia.[5]

A constitutional reform appeared promising when Colombia was experiencing one of its deepest crises, manifested in the lack of representativeness of the main political parties and extraordinary levels of political and urban violence. Within this context, the 1991 Constitution was considered an opportunity to introduce changes at all levels of society. This is, at least, what surveys at the time demonstrated, and is also indicated by the fact that almost 90 percent of the voters approved of the convocation of the Constituent Assembly.[6] Over a period of six months, the Constitution was written by a large and heterogeneous group of individuals, including members of the political and social forces traditionally excluded from politics—among them "representatives of demobilized guerrilla groups, indigenous and religious minorities" (García-Villegas 2001: 14). This peculiar composition of the constitutional convention, according to García-Villegas (2001: 14), explains some of the distinguishing features of the new text, such as "the broadening of participation mechanisms, the imposition of social justice and equality duties upon the state, and the incorporation of a Constitution that is rich in rights and new judicial mechanisms for their protection." Since its creation, the court has decided many significant issues of enormous public impact.[7]

The Colombian Constitutional Court was created by the constitution of 1991, which defines its functions in article 241. Article 239 establishes that the court be composed of an uneven number of members determined by law, with judges belonging to the different specialties of the law. Constitutional Court judges are appointed for nonrenewable eight-year terms. They are elected by the Senate from lists compiled by the President of the Republic, the Supreme Court of Justice, and the Council of State—a procedure that may be considered too politicized given the recent history of Colombian high courts. In effect, similar to Chile, Colombian highest judges have historically enjoyed an important level of independence and stability (see Uprimny, Rodríguez, and García-Villegas, 2002: 9).

Regarding access to the court, the Constitutional Convention introduced many innovations, which accompany the main existing procedural instrument for acceding to the tribunals, namely the *acción de inconstitucionalidad* (*actio popularis*). This action allows plaintiffs to challenge decrees, laws, and even the procedure of a constitutional reform and can be presented by anyone, with few formalities and without the assistance of a lawyer. Also, plaintiffs can present an *actio popularis* without demonstrating a specific interest in the issue at stake (Cepeda 2004: 555). In addition, since 1991, new procedural instruments have been available to the public and includes the following: the *acción de cumplimiento,* which is used to force public officers to fulfill their duties in particular cases; the *acción popular,* which protects collective interests, such as those related to environmental law; the *acción de grupo,* which is similar to the U.S. *class action*, and the *acción de tutela.* The *tutela* is the main procedural instrument for the protection of individual rights. It can be presented by any citizen, with few formal requirements, without a lawyer, before any judge, and in response to any violation or threat of violation of a fundamental right. Judges have just ten days to decide a case; the cases are automatically appealed to the Constitutional Court, which can pick which appeals it wants to decide, by taking into account the importance of the cases at stake.

Since its creation, the Colombian Constitutional Court has become a hyperactive court that, contrary to the courts in most of the countries of the region, managed to gain and maintain broad popular respect. Colombia has a legalistic tradition rooted in the early nineteenth century, which partly explains the influence gained by the court and the fact that the political powers tended to accept its rulings. However, it should be noted that Colombia is and historically has been a politically violent country, which has at times included the assassination of magistrates, social activists, and political figures.

Most Salient Judicial Decisions

Here, we examine recent significant judicial decisions in Argentina, Chile, and Colombia. We discover three models for the three courts: (i) a court that has exercised its accountability function quite strongly (the Colombian Court); (ii) a court that has been quite deferential to the actions of the political power (the Chilean Court); and (iii) a court that has not been as active as the Colombian Court, but also not as passive as the Chilean one (the Argentinean Court). However, several issues need to be clarified given that the trajectories of the countries have been neither linear nor static.

In Argentina, we can distinguish at least three very different patterns in the court's behavior, which basically coincide with the three most important changes of government since the early 1980s. During Raúl Alfonsín's presidency after 1983, the court was very much concerned with ensuring respect for basic liberal rights while it was respectful, but not wholly deferential, to the political branches. This court was succeeded by a new majority in President Menem's packed court, and undermined rather than strengthened liberal rights while being explicitly supportive of the executive's will. Since the beginning of the new century, yet another majority rules within the court that seems to readopt part of its former liberalism and displays a stronger concern for social rights and the interests of disadvantaged groups. This new court is also making efforts to rebuild its reputation as an independent tribunal.

Even though the accountability function of the Chilean courts has been subject to gradual modifications, the court's behavior has not been changing as radically and dramatically as in Argentina. During Pinochet's rule, it was a crucial ally of the dictator, continuing a long history of strong deference toward the executive. Since the return of democracy, however, this pattern has slowly changed. Some of these innovations were due to changes in the composition of the court, which resulted both from new appointments and also from unprecedented impeachment processes triggered after the detection of corruption scandals within the court. In addition, Chilean judges began to be subjected to external pressures, particularly after the detention and trial against Pinochet by international tribunals and also from intense internal demands in the wake of Pinochet's international trial. Finally, and partly as a consequence of its political history, the new democratic governments began to introduce structural changes in the organization of the judiciary, significantly through the 2005 constitutional reform. Notably, the reform shifted part of the powers of the Supreme Court to a *Tribunal Constitucional*.

Colombia's Constitutional Court, the newest of the three courts,[8] has assumed a strong role in controlling political power since its first decisions and immediately became a crucial player. The behavior of the tribunal was unexpected. The country had a tradition of rather independent and respected tribunals, but the existing Supreme Court had never appeared as a strong democratic actor. The new tribunal, instead, made significant accountability decisions in the protection of individual and social rights, in defense of the most disadvantaged groups, and against the ambitions of a still growing executive power. Successive changes in its composition (members of the court are appointed for eight-year terms rather than for life) are paving way for the gradual creation of a less assertive court. We analyze the activity of the Constitutional Court since its creation, paying particular attention to its decisions concerning the scope and limits of the executive's power and its decisions in the area of social and economic rights, which have severely limited the freedom of decision of the political branches.

Argentina

To analyze the evolution of Argentina's Supreme Court's jurisprudence, we organize its recent decisions under three headings: individual and social rights, human rights, and control over the executive's public policy initiatives (in particular, economic decisions). Clearly, these three areas are closely interrelated, that is, decisions on basic human rights are also decisions on fundamental constitutional rights. However, this classification is still helpful to examine the most salient decisions in these areas.

Individual and Social Rights
Regarding basic constitutional rights, the Court's views have been changing substantively during the last three decades. Not surprisingly, these substantive changes correspond to the changes in the court's composition, which followed the presidencies of Alfonsin, Menem, and Kirchner.

During Alfonsin's government, the court adopted a strongly liberal view, manifest in numerous cases. Thus, in *Sejean v. Zaks de Sejean—Sejean (Fallos* 308: 2268)— it recognized the right of divorce, confronting Congress' noted silence on the topic. The court also opposed the authority of Congress in *Bazterrica,* in which it considered that the constitutional right of privacy protected the personal consumption of narcotics. Through this decision, the court invalidated Law 20771, which established severe penalties for drug consumers.[9] Furthermore, in *Fiorentino (Fallos* 306:1752) the court defied the initiatives adopted by some hardliners against crime, maintaining that the evidence gathered in the home of an accused without judicial authorization was not valid. In *Ruíz (Fallos* 310: 1847) and *Francomano (Fallos* 310: 2384), the court opposed the use of evidence gathered after coerced confessions. Similarly, in *Portillo*, the court advanced another important piece of liberal doctrine by recognizing the rights of conscientious objectors (CSJN 1989: 18/4; ED 133–372). These decisions were clearly in line with the liberal agenda of the government, which was trying to leave behind the authoritarian legacy of the military dictatorship.[10]

After President Menem packed the court, the tribunal's decisions clearly contradicted its previous liberal record. By moving toward a strong conservative position, the court followed the ideological orientation of the government and its main supporters, which included some of the most reactionary sectors of the Catholic Church, such as the *Opus Dei*.[11] The numerous decisions that reflected this orientation include cases such as *Montalvo* (*Fallos* 313: 1033) in which the court reversed *Bazterrica* and authorized the criminalization of the personal consumption of drugs; *Fernández* (*Fallos* 400: 22) in which the court reversed *Fiorentino* and admitted the validity of evidence found through an unauthorized police search; or *Bramajo* (*Fallos* 319: 1840) in which the court quoted the most protective human rights clauses of the American Convention of Human Rights in order to limit, rather than expand, the rights of the accused.[12] Another important conservative decision appeared in the *C.H.A.* case (*Fallos* 314: 1531), in which the court validated an administrative decision that denied homosexuals their right to obtain authorization for constituting a legal association.

The new court at the beginning of President Nestor Kirchner's government seemed much more in line with its liberal predecessor than with the "Menemista" court. In fact, the new court promptly reversed or undermined some of the most polemic decisions adopted by the latter. In *Alitt,* decided in November 2006, it recognized the rights of legal association of a transsexuals' organization, which denied the previous *C.H.A.* decision most of its legal authority. In addition, the court adopted an aggressively liberal position regarding procedural rights and the rights of prisoners. Decisions such as *Gramajo* (September 2006), *Podesta* (March 2006), or *Noriega* (August 2007) represent insightful illustrations of this new trend. Other decisions (including *Martín,* CSJN 8/6/2004, or *Gas Natural,* CSJN 2/3/2004), suggest that the new court is particularly concerned with protecting the interests of disadvantaged groups and also the rights of consumers—two objectives that, again, do not seem to contradict the "spirit" of the new government.

More notably, perhaps, the new court adopted few, but very significant, decisions in the area of social/collective rights, involving complex litigation cases. In one of these decisions, the famous case *Verbitsky* (CSJN 5/3/2005), the court ordered the judiciary to put an end to existing irregularities concerning police detention of suspects, and also ordered the state executive to adopt different measures aimed at improving the penitentiary situation in the Province of Buenos Aires. Meanwhile, in *Mendoza* (June 2006), the court ordered Kirchner's administration to halt the contamination of the Riachuelo river, which was creating serious harm to the population living nearby. These two cases are particularly important because they show the court assuming a new role, which implied neither replacing the political branches, nor assuming a passive role before them. Rather, the court assumed the role of a "facilitator" of solutions and promoter of public dialogue, by addressing public audiences, denouncing the existing violation of basic rights, demanding reports from both the state and public companies, and urging the adoption of solutions in line with the constitution.

Human Rights

Human rights issues and human rights judicial decisions have been enormously important in Argentina's recent political and legal history. They have raised strong emotions among the population, involving the protests of victims and relatives of victims of the past dictatorship, the pressures of military groups, and the actions of national and international human rights organizations. On occasion, the tensions among all these groups threatened to jeopardize the stability of the new democracy.

During Alfonsin's government, the Supreme Court tended to back the president's courageous initiatives, which promoted the judgment of human rights violations committed by the previous military regime, at a time of high political turmoil. It supported both the president's decision to hold trials against the military *junta* and his initiatives for limiting the impact of the trials (most notably, in *Camps* (*Fallos* 310: 1163) the court backed the "Due Obedience" law that established an irrefutable presumption that inferior officers acted in due obedience to their superior when they committed human rights abuses).[13] This tendency in favor of forgiving the civil personal and military officers reached its peak when President Menem promoted their legal pardon through ten different decrees, enacted in late 1989.

A few years later, as a result of the tireless fight for justice by numerous human rights activists and also national and international organizations concerned with human rights, the policies in this area began to change radically, as did the decisions of the court. In effect, the new court appointed by President Kirchner appeared to follow Kirchner's views on human rights issues. The most remarkable decision made during this period appeared in the case *Simon*,[14] in which the court departed radically from its earlier positions. In *Simon*, in effect, the court considered unconstitutional the "Due Obedience" law, and also the "Full Stop" law,[15] which it had found valid in its recent decision in *Camps*. The court's sudden change is not easy to justify, although some important events in-between the two contradictory decisions may at least have partially contributed to the tribunal's new position—most significantly, Laws 24.952 and 25.779, which deprived the amnesty laws from all their legal effects by declaring them totally "null and void." Following this strong legislative trend, in *Simon*, the court ratified the validity of Law 25.779 and considered both norms (the "Due Obedience" and the "Full Stop" laws) incompatible with the constitution, thus reopening the possibility of prosecuting past violators of human rights.

The Court and Public Policy Initiatives

During Alfonsin's government, the court exhibited a mixed record with respect to public policy. At the times when the president most needed support, the court tended to render this support although it also "dared to say no" on significant occasions. For example, in *Rolón Zappa* (*Fallos* 308: 1855), the court opposed the executive's refusal to comply with a pension law, allegedly due to lack of resources. However, it then demonstrated its acquiescence with the executive when the latter issued a decree declaring the pension system in a state of emergency. At that point, the court delayed its decision on the topic for two years when Congress reorganized the entire pension system. Consequently, Miller (2000: 384) describes the attitude of the court as a tactic of "deference through delay." In his view, the court reproduced the same attitude regarding the president's decree changing the national currency (when the court virtually refused to act until Congress finally ratified the president's decision) and in other minor cases, for example, *Klein* (*Fallos* 308: 1489).

The court's behavior was consistently and aggressively favorable to the president's will. However, during Menem's two presidencies, despite the existence of some minor decisions in which the court ruled against the government, "there is no question that many of the Supreme Court's post-packing decisions show a much higher level of partisanship and deference to the Executive than did the Alfonsín Court, and than did the Court during most other periods in Argentine history" (Miller 2000: 399).

Two of the most important executive-friendly decisions of the period were *Peralta* (*Fallos* 313: 1513) and *Cocchia* (*Fallos* 316: 2624), which legitimized the delegation of legislative functions to the executive and afforded the president broad discretion regarding how to handle the ongoing privatization process. These decisions allowed the president to carry out a substantial program of economic reforms by circumventing Congress. These reforms managed to radically change Argentina's traditional organization of the economy and involved large-scale privatizations. Therefore, severe controls over the process seemed necessary. However, and contrary to what could have been expected, the court decisively contributed to undermining these controls. Thus, the court often legitimized the president's attacks against the judiciary itself.[16]

By contrast, the court in place since the government of Néstor Kirchner has demonstrated that it is ready to "say no" to the president. The court is still in the process of reorganization, and it has not yet produced a significant amount of decisions that could clearly reveal the contours of the new jurisprudence. Nonetheless, since 2004, the court has produced some significant decisions, many of which seem clearly contrary to the interests of the government. For example, in 2004, the court suspended the demand for a constitutional convention made by the local government of Santiago del Estero—a demand that enjoyed the support of the new national government. In *Bustos* (CSJN, *Fallos,* 324: 2107), it contradicted earlier rulings in analogous cases, such as *Smith* (2002) and *San Luis* (2003), and validated some of the government's initiatives regarding the remnants of the dramatic banking sector crisis of 2001. Also, in *Badaro* (November 2007), the court clearly defied the interests of the government by requiring it to adjust pensions.

Chile

Although the court's behavior during Pinochet's government was one of acquiescence, if not explicit support, during the 1990s, it began to abandon what it itself described as an attitude of formalist adherence to the law (Atria 2003). Incrementally, the court began to examine cases that it previously would have discarded as "political cases." Here, we analyze the Chilean Court's accountability function in three areas of jurisprudence where the main court has adopted significant decisions.

Human Rights Cases

Prior to Pinochet's 1998 arrest in London, the court had displayed a clear hostility toward human rights activism. In 1990, for instance, the court unanimously recognized the validity of the 1978 amnesty decree (passed by the same military government that would benefit from it) and systematically blocked the cases initiated in lower courts. According to Human Rights Watch, the amnesty represented "the single most important legal obstacle to human rights trials in Chile" (*Human Rights Watch Report* 1999: 6).[17] Even worse, the court repeatedly used its disciplinary powers to reproach the behavior of lower court judges who challenged the court's passive attitude toward human rights abuses.[18]

Similarly, in a 1990 decision, the court maintained that it was not possible to limit the effects of the amnesty decree by invoking international humanitarian law, which was not in force during the time of Pinochet's government. The court wanted to block all possible investigations regarding the "disappearances" that occurred during the period covered by the amnesty.[19] Even though most members in the legal community seemed to share the court's main assumption (namely, that it was not possible to invalidate the self-amnesty decree), the decision was met with significant criticisms. President Aylwin himself was quite active in this respect, and after the publication of the Rettig report, he asked the court to participate in the quest to "find the disappeared."[20]

It is perhaps not surprising, then, that the amnesty decree began to slowly weaken, particularly as a consequence of the Supreme Court's new interpretation. The new doctrine emerged after the appointment of new members to the Supreme Court, but the court had already begun to change its view on these issues.[21] The peak of the argument came in the "Caravan of Death" case (a case that involved multiple executions across the country, committed by the same group, in a short period of time), in which the court unanimously maintained that the "disappearance" of people constituted an ongoing crime. Because of that, the crime was not covered by the amnesty, and the court confirmed the arrest of five army officers who had taken part in the criminal action.

In August 2004, the court also argued a decision by Santiago Appeals Courts that allowed the trial of Pinochet for the "disappearance" of 20 people as part of the "Operación Cóndor."[22] However, it is difficult to evaluate whether the court had significantly changed its previous attitude regarding human rights cases, and how international law was used.

The Supreme Court also ordered a stay of prosecution regarding Pinochet in a 2002 decision because, the court maintained, he suffered from an incurable moderate dementia. According to the University Diego Portales' Annual Report on Human Rights for 2002, the Supreme Court decision "evinced a willingness to afford Pinochet a special treatment, notably by significantly lowering the threshold for dismissal of charges on medical grounds and by letting stand principles of due process not normally applied to common crimes" (*Informe Anual sobre Derechos Humanos* 2003: 15). Since then, over 300 lawsuits were filed to prosecute Pinochet. Most notably, the court began to investigate the numerous charges of corruption presented against the dictator and his family. Regarding inferior military officers, however, the "dilution" of the amnesty decree's effects has created the opportunity to bring many of them before the tribunals. The Supreme Court has directly been involved in some of these processes, for instance, confirming the sentence in the *Tucapel Jiménez* case.

Freedom of Expression and Censorship
Hilbink (1999c: 442) refers to the resistance of Chilean judges to control the political branches so as to protect political and civil rights. Although Chile's main court always resisted to get involved in salient public issues, as though it is possible to establish a clear separation between law and politics, the dynamics that followed the end of the dictatorship forced the tribunal to abandon its "distant" political attitude. The most important case concerned freedom of expression.

Even though Chile abolished censorship in 2002, the right to freedom of expression continues to suffer restrictions, emanating in many cases from the same judiciary apparatus. According to the annual human rights report for 2003 elaborated by the University Diego Portales, Chilean tribunals consider that the prohibitions on different types of expression that they themselves have been enforcing do not represent acts of censorship (*Informe Anual sobre Derechos Humanos* 2004: 208). The *Auto Acordado* from 2003, through which the Supreme Court, in plenum, regulated the behavior of judges and their opinions before the press, represents another problematic act of the court's criteria in this area.

In fact, some of the most significant cases in the area involved journalists[23] and judges.[24] Other cases referred to political figures and high members of the former military regime.[25] In another important case, the *Prat* case, the court was confronted with an attempt to censor a play that partly derided a nineteenth-century Chilean military hero. The court challenged a decision by the Court of Appeal that defended the exhibition of the play, although it did so through arguments that evinced its restrictive view regarding freedom of expression (a right that it deemed subordinated to the due respect of the people's "good name").[26]

Furthermore, the Inter-American Commission of Human Rights (CIDH) had frequent opportunities to examine the initiatives and decisions adopted by the Chilean Supreme Court. At least three of them were related to cases of censorship, which were in different ways promoted by the Chilean Court. Two of these cases directly involved criticisms against public authorities, and one was completed in 2001 with the CIDH issuing a critical report against the Chilean state.[27]

One of the most important situations of CIDH intervention related to a case of judicial censorship against a book that attacked some members of the judiciary. In *El libro negro de la justicia chilena*, the journalist Alejandra Matus Acuña severely questioned the functioning of the judicial branch in Chile. The day the book was launched, the Supreme Court Justice Servando Jordán López required the Court of Appeals of Santiago to investigate whether the publication of the book constituted an infraction to Chile's law (article 16, Ley 12927). The book was then immediately withdrawn from circulation despite the lack of a definite sentence on the case.[28]

Disadvantaged Groups

An analysis of the way in which the court deals with disadvantaged groups provides crucial information concerning the extent to which the tribunal is deferring to or defying political authorities.

In 1989, presidential candidate Patricio Aylwin signed an agreement (the *Nueva Imperial* Agreement) with most indigenous groups, including the *Mapuches*. The pact committed Aylwin to promote the recognition of the social, economic, and cultural rights of the indigenous groups and send a bill to Congress to grant constitutional recognition to all indigenous people. After the election, a Special Commission was constituted to study the situation of the indigenous people, resulting in a new law on indigenous groups. Despite the new law, the indigenous people's basic rights (particularly regarding their rights to land) were still violated, and their claim for a constitutional recognition of those rights was still unsatisfied, which generated enormous social and political tensions including violent protests (Observatorio de Derechos de los Pueblos Indígenas, n.d.).

The most conflictive episodes in the relationship between the indigenous groups and the state came with the state's decision to use antiterrorist laws against the *Mapuches* who had resorted to violent means of protest. Chile's Supreme Court made at least two important and debatable decisions on these issues.

The first decision appeared after a trial court unanimously acquitted two aborigines who had been accused of threats and acts of terrorism by stating that the evidence presented by the prosecutor was unreliable. This 2002 decision was followed by political pressure that ended one year later with a Supreme Court decision ordering a retrial (Contesse 2004). The court argued that the trial court had not fairly evaluated the evidence presented by the prosecutors. As a consequence of the court's decision, a new trial against the *Mapuches* was held, the antiterrorist laws were applied, and the aborigines were the first Chilean citizens to be held in prison under their application.

A second Supreme Court decision in 2004 also involved a *Mapuche* accused of terrorist actions. The Supreme Court ruling followed the decision of a trial judge, who decided not to follow the prosecutor's accusations of terrorism, and the ruling of the Temuco Appeals Court, which upheld the previous decision. Again, after a period of political pressure, the Supreme Court ordered a retrial, asserting that the main tribunal had the right to "correct on its own account the faults and abuses that any judges or judicial officials commit in the course of their duties" (Human Rights Watch Report 2004: 36). The retrial resulted in sentencing five people to over ten years in prison and high fines.

In 2006, representatives of the *Mapuches* carried out a hunger strike lasting two months, but they failed to get the attention of the government. A legal initiative was then presented to prevent the group from being prosecuted under the terrorist law, but the Supreme Court declared that the project contravened the principle of equality before the law.

Colombia

Since its creation in 1991, the Colombian Constitutional Court has become a hyperactive court that gained and maintained wide popular respect.

Although the court's activism has varied over time depending on its composition (becoming less activist and less radical over the years), its accountability record is impressive. The court made a considerable effort to establish limits to the different branches of power, including limits on the judicial branch itself.[29] Still more telling are the court's decisions in relation to the scope and limits of the powers of the executive branch.

The Court and the Executive

As far as the president's authority is concerned, the court has upheld the constitutionality of many laws aimed at increasing executive power. However, it also managed to limit and curtail its authority on several occasions, and the president has usually accepted the Court's rulings[30] including those involving the president's capacity to declare a "state of siege" or a "state of exception" and rule in those circumstances. Historically, the main national court assumed a passive role before the executive (Uprimny 2004: 54). For decades, and at least until the beginning of the 1980s, the court justified that passivity through the use of the doctrine of "political questions," which basically maintained that certain substantive decisions, such as the declaration of a state of emergency, were purely political decisions outside of the purview of the courts. From the beginning of the 1980s and until the enactment of the new constitution, the court adopted a different role and scrutinized these declarations of emergency more strictly. On some occasions, for example, the court invalidated executive measures because they were not related to the facts that justified the emergency in the first place.

Since the creation of the Constitutional Court in 1991, the level of scrutiny of the president's acts in critical circumstances became even higher. Again, and as a general rule, the Constitutional Court recognized extensive powers of the president in emergency situations. For example, the court usually recognized the president's discretion to decide when to declare a state of exception and for how long, or what to do in those circumstances. The tribunal, though, established significant limits on what the president could or could not do in crisis situations. *Decision C-004, 1992*, was the first decision where a court controlled a declaration of a state of emergency. Furthermore, a 1994 decision invalidated President Gaviria's decree establishing a state of internal commotion, marking the first time in Colombia's history that a court disallowed presidential use of emergency powers. The court issued a similar decision one year later (see *Decision C- 300, 1994*, and *Decision C-466, 1995*). Also, in *Decision C-327, 2003*, the tribunal limited the president's authority to renew an ongoing state of internal commotion. The court also invalidated particular legislative provisions that enabled the president to grant general amnesties or individual pardons during a state of exception. The court also scrutinized the cases when the president could declare an emergency as well as the executive's goals in those situations.

The decisions of the Constitutional Court encountered considerable criticism from public authorities, but, at the same time, gained support from civil society. Initially, President Samper (1994–98) threatened to promote a constitutional reform that aimed at reducing the court's powers. However, Samper reviewed his initiative after a new decision by the court moderated its own previous judgment.[31] At least two more attempts to curtail the court's power of material control were made, one by President Samper, the other one by President Uribe (since 2002).

In 2005, the court's independence and its willingness to stand up to the executive was tested when it had to decide whether the constitutional reform promoted by President Uribe to allow the reelection of the president was constitutionally valid. In a split decision on October 19, 2005, the court maintained that: (i) Congress was competent to carry out such a reform; (ii) the process through which the reform was promoted was not vitiated, that is, against the law, in spite of the numerous failures pointed out by jurists and public figures; and (iii) Congress was not allowed to delegate its powers to an executive agency (the *Consejo de Estado*), if these powers include the capacity to write a *Ley de Garantías* (the law that would regulate the following elections and ensure that all candidates participated in equal terms). Summarizing, the court considered that it had no powers to invalidate a constitutional reform that was promoted by the president to expand the president's own powers.[32]

Socioeconomic Decisions

The court also interfered with the president's powers through several significant decisions concerning public policy. Gradually, the court developed a series of legal principles to examine these cases, including the *principio de conexidad* ("principle of connection"), which establishes that social and economic rights virtually acquire the character of fundamental rights and thus can be the object of judicial protection through *tutelas* when the violation or nonsatisfaction of those rights puts fundamental rights at risk. In addition, in its decision *T-533, 1992*, the court has established the right to a *social minimum* ("*mínimo vital*"), which defined the state's obligation to fulfill numerous social obligations, and which has had an enormous impact on the design and administration of the state's budget. The court also created the category of *estado de cosas inconstitucional* ("unconstitutional state of affairs") to approach cases that involved different groups and state agencies and required long-term and complex solutions.

Among numerous significant decisions with serious economic impact, the court ordered the provision of medicines to AIDS patients (*Decision T-484, 1992*); it forced the government to develop a vaccination plan to grant health rights to children (*Decision SU-225, 1998*) and it forced a public institution to provide particular individuals' expensive medical treatments (for example, *Decision T-516, 2000* or *Decision T-590, 1999*). Moreover, in 2000, the court declared that part of the national budget was unconstitutional because it did not contemplate an appropriate increase in public officials' wages, a decision that was partially revised one year later (*Decision C-1433, 2000*). Other cases include *Decisions T-153, 1998* and *Decision T-025, 2004,* in which the court declared the existence of an "unconstitutional state of affairs," forcing the government to take immediate steps to put an end to the existing violation of rights. One of the first decisions of this type referred to Colombia's problematic prison system; another important one addressed the situation of the forcedly displaced population, that is, the victims of armed conflict who are forced to abandon their homes and belongings. Finally, the Constitutional Court frequently reviewed the level of private and public salaries and checked whether the affected workers had received the required annual increases. According to the court, "annual salary readjustments should never be lower than the inflation rates of the previous year in order to maintain minimum wage increases" (Cepeda 2004: 645). Also, in July 2008, the court decided a prominent health-rights case (*T-760/08*), which clarified its strongly activist stance in the area; organized the restructuring of the benefits plans (including precise instructions regarding its implementation—that is, requiring the direct participation of the medical community and the users of the health system); and urging the government to progressively ensure universal coverage by 2010 (Yamin and Parra Vera, 2008).

Probably the most important and polemic ruling was the "UPAC" decision, which concerned the national system of loans, created under President Pastrana. Through this system, the government wanted to promote the construction of houses even though it was extremely difficult to obtain long-term bank credits. After a period of macroeconomic instability, the system became inefficient, and its credits enormously expensive, resulting in 200,000 families on the verge of losing their homes because they could not pay their mortgages. The court's rulings amounted to the virtual elimination of the UPAC and the creation of a new system, in which interest rates would be governed not by the market but by the Central Bank (Pérez Salazar 2003).[33]

Explaining the Cases

Social, Legal, and Political Context

The social, legal, and political context is offered as an explanation for whether or not judges take on an accountability function. Analyses of the Colombian Constitutional Court's activism and assertiveness have addressed the social and political context and also the legal culture within which the court acts that includes the following: the long tradition of judicial review; the fact that access to the court is easy and inexpensive; the progressive character of the constitution, and its vagueness and ambiguity. In addition, studies emphasize that the court has acted in a sociopolitical vacuum. More precisely, they state that the court's activism has been stimulated by an existing crisis of representation and the weakness of social movements and opposition parties (Arrieta 2003; García-Villegas 2001; Uprimny 2004; Uprimny and García Villegas, 2002; Uprimny, García-Villegas, and Rodríguez, 2002). These explanations are nuanced and complex but, as the same authors point out, listing these factors still remains unsatisfactory. As García-Villegas (2001: 13) puts it: "All of the above may explain the court's activism but an obvious question remains: why did the court take on a progressive role when it could have undertaken activism of another nature?" More fundamentally, the question of why the court became activist in the first place remains unanswered.

Additional factors introduce "the characteristics of the constitutional transition" (García-Villegas 2001: 13). Thus, the constitution had a very progressive content because of the peculiar circumstances of its creation. Also, the political forces that advanced the progressive agenda within the constitutional convention became extremely weak after the convention's end, while the government became increasingly more "neoliberal." According to García-Villegas (2001: 15), all these circumstances "meant that one of the few institutions that was capable of applying the 1991 Constitution's progressive content was the Constitutional Court." However, it is not clear how convincing this argument is—perhaps the opposite result may have been just as likely.

At the opposite end of the spectrum, the politically deferential behavior of Chilean judges has often been explained by reference to the professionalism/formalism/legalism of the legal culture (Correa Sutil 1993). These approaches seem to minimize improperly the influence of a conservative ideology (Novoa Monreal 1970) within the courts (Correa Sutil 1993: 99 addresses this point explicitly). On the other hand, approaches that emphasize the importance of the ideological conservatism and antidemocratic ethos of Chilean judges (Frühling 1984; Hilbink 1999a) seem to unduly overestimate the explanatory importance of ideology. This is particularly the case when, as Couso (2004: 87) notes, Supreme Court judges "have also been deferential in cases involving private property suggests the explanation lies not in political ideology but elsewhere." Instead, Couso (2004: 87) proposes to look at the "historical background of the relationships between the judiciary and the other branches of government in Chile." For him, courts have been "deliberately passive" (ibid., 89), because they recognized that they could "acquire high levels of institutional autonomy by deliberately avoiding challenges to the 'political branches' of government, even at the cost of retreating from their constitutional powers of review of administrative and legislative acts" (ibid., 87). This "backward-looking" explanation of judicial deference in Chile exhibits problems in explaining some more recent decisions of the court, in which judges abandoned their traditional deferential attitude. Moreover, this view may not easily accommodate data that suggest they are also "forward-looking" judges, who try to act strategically regarding incoming authorities (Scribner 2003).

While a focus on the legal culture can contribute to an understanding of the weak accountability function of the Chilean judiciary, it alone cannot provide a convincing and complete explanation. In fact, the different explanations partially refute each other.

Institutional Design

The accountability function of courts in Argentina, Chile, and Colombia can also be explained, at least in part, with reference to the particularities of their institutional design. These include differences in the procedural rules regulating access, the types of cases, and the required formalities, which all appear influential in the "construction" of tribunals.

For example, the conservative character of the Chilean judiciary appears correlated with its severely hierarchical judicial organization. The disciplinary power of the Chilean Supreme Court is so strong that inferior judges are expected to exercise their powers timidly. However, this explanation of judicial behavior leaves several questions unanswered. For example, the conservatism of Chilean judges existed prior to and independently from the rules of judicial organization—going back to a history that taught judges not to challenge the authority of the other branches (Couso 2004). In addition, this explanation cannot account for why the Supreme Court became conservative in the first place, which many explain with the peculiarities of Chile's legal culture (ibid.).

Meanwhile, the case of Argentina illustrates the importance of the way in which judicial behavior is or may be influenced by those in control of the appointment procedures. In effect, since the beginning of the twentieth century, Argentina's presidents were able to make or made significant efforts to create their "own" courts, which provides some explanatory power for judicial developments. These radical changes in the composition of the court are clearly correlated with the jurisprudence developed in each period. Overall, it appears that the court that worked during the *Proceso* was quite deferential toward the military junta, particularly regarding the most "burning" issue of human rights violations. Also, the rather liberal government of Alfonsín, after appointing a new set of judges, enjoyed the presence of a very liberal court. Similarly, Menem found a friendly and safe ally in the court that was ready to please all the existing "corporate" powers, just as Menem was. Finally, Kirchner's quite progressive rhetoric was mirrored by a court that, judging from its early decisions, seems to be particularly sensitive to progressive causes.

The record of the Colombian Court has also been explained as a consequence of "the way in which the higher courts are organized and the manner in which the magistrates are chosen," which implies that magistrates "have very much the same incentives as politicians," and thus are "prone to render short term, populist decisions" (Kugler and Rosenthal, 2000: 14; Kalmanovitz 2000). The factors that would move judges to become "populists" include the fact that magistrates "are selected by peers and by the executive for relatively short periods of eight years and without the possibility of re-election"; the fact that members of the Court are "self-recruited from within the judiciary"; the "short span of career of a high court judge," who "cannot be reappointed" but can hold public office after one year, together with the multiple promises contained in the 1991 Constitution (Pérez Salazar 2003: 89). This analysis seems partially supported by empirical evidence (Pérez Salazar 2003: 89). However, one might still argue that this analysis is based on an incomplete (if not biased) picture of Colombia's institutional life. In fact, additional elements could produce the opposite conclusion. Thus, for example, one might argue that Colombian judges have the strongest incentives for not becoming populists given the long tradition of criminal political violence against those identified with the country's left (Gutiérrez Sanín and Stoller, 2001; Martz 1992). At the same time, the choice of joining or assisting the most powerful political and economic groups seems to be highly rewarded. These explanations, then, seem to be incomplete in their premises and counterintuitive in their conclusions.

One of our most interesting findings regarding the accountability function of Latin American courts relates to the remarkable influence of other procedural tools, namely those that refer to individuals' standing before the courts and their capacity to challenge existing legal norms. It seems evident that these procedures present a key element in explaining the variation in performance of different courts in different countries. Thus, for example, it seems quite obvious that in those countries where access to justice is more difficult and the rules of standing more restrictive—Chile may be quite an extreme case in this respect—the citizenry faces more hurdles to challenge those in power, and the tribunal has fewer incentives and opportunities to check the power holders. The opposite appears to happen in those countries where procedural rules facilitate individuals' access to the tribunals, as in Colombia. In this case, we find generous rules of standing, and broad instruments allowing individuals to challenge public authorities, such as the *acción popular* and the *tutela*. Both procedural resources can be used by any citizen, with few formal requirements, and even without the help of a lawyer. This legal scenario has likely changed the opportunity structure of those seeking to hold the government to account, built legitimacy and also a supportive constituency for the courts in broader sections of the population, thus helping to create the conditions for the emergence of a court as strong, activist, and progressive as the Colombian Constitutional Court. Without overemphasizing the importance of procedural tools, their amplitude or restrictive character appears to matter for explaining the accountability performance of the courts.

Actor-based Explanations

The last set of explanations focuses on the nature and background of the members of the courts. Explanations that rest on the biographies of particular judges are valuable for understanding the judicial behavior. Judges who spent most of their careers on courts are likely to identify with their peers, and slowly become part of the so-called *familia judicial,* which—like most families—has its internal rules and codes of mutual respect. Alternatively, judges who come from the legal academia might be more open to new arguments and less subordinate to judicial traditions. On the one hand, Chile represents a rather extreme case of an endogenous judiciary, disciplined, tradition-oriented, conservative, and rather hostile to the introduction of legal novelties. On the other hand, in Colombia, the Constitutional Court appears to be quite radical in its decisions, innovative in the legal criteria that it employs, and ready to challenge public officials. The Colombian Court's radicalism has decreased in recent years—a fact that seems closely correlated to the composition of the court: the Constitutional tribunal was more radical when its members (for example, Ciro Angarita, Gaviria, Cifuentes) were less attached to the *familia judicial* and more connected to the legal academia. Similarly in Argentina, the biographies and ideology of particular judges seem to have a strong explanatory power for their decisions. Liberal lawyers/judges, such as Petracchi, Bacqué, or Carrió, produced liberal decisions, while conservative lawyers/judges, such as Boggiano, tended to decide in a conservative way.

However, the explanatory capacity of these actor-based approaches also faces limitations. Our case studies provide numerous examples of judges who came from the "judicial family" and developed quite radical and independent views, such as Carmen Argibay in Argentina, and also examples of judges with strong links to the academia, who behaved quite conservatively as Supreme Court judges, such as Elena Highton from Argentina.

One of the explanations derived from rational choice analysis has proven to be particularly successful for understanding courts' decisions in Latin America, especially Argentina. Some recent analyses of Argentina's courts arrived at the conclusion that "judges rule against the rulers not because judges enjoy independence in a conventional sense but because they fear being punished by the government's successors" (Helmke 2005: 20; see also Iaryczower, Spiller, and Tommasi, 2002). This is the essence of the *strategic defection* phenomenon, which is the "logical ... judicial response to a particular institutional setting, namely one in which judges lack institutional security and the main threat to their security stems from incoming political actors rather than incumbents" (Helmke 2005: 20). Helmke's careful empirical analysis challenges part of the "conventional wisdom" on the topic, which maintains that courts "rarely challenge the government of the day," and rather assert that "judges under dictatorship and democracy alike defect from the government once it begins to lose power" (Helmke 2005: 126). This defection seems particularly evident in the last two years of the military dictatorship, Alfonsín's government, and Menem's second mandate. The evidence is powerful and signals at minimum that traditional analyses have dismissed or simply not considered the way in which judges behave strategically.

However, this approach cannot easily explain why the court at the end of Alfonsín's government acted in ways that seem to contradict her theory's predictions. Helmke finds it surprising that in "cases where the government clearly had an interest in appealing a negative lower court decision, the percentage of anti-government decisions ... declined to its lowest level in 1988," that is, one year after the end of Alfonsín's government (Helmke 2005: 107). According to the "strategic defection" argument, the court should have done exactly the contrary to what it did in those cases when it tried to approximate the views of the opposition. The court, however, stayed quite "close" to Alfonsín regarding many significant decisions. If we consider other motivational sources, such as those mentioned above, it appears less surprising that the court acted this way as it was, arguably, very concerned with ensuring other goals, such as the preservation of democracy.[34] Particularly in Chile the "strategic defection" approach holds little explanatory value. Helmke (2005: 164) recognizes this explicitly and concludes the existence of "some support for the view that Chile's judges strategically supported the government but no evidence of strategic defection."

Conclusion

These approaches for the accountability behavior of courts in the Southern Cone have some explanatory power but also suffer from serious weaknesses. To explain the trajectory of a specific court, such as the Colombian Constitutional Court, it seems indispensable to consider the openness of the judicial system and the existing procedural rules. However, we also know that even the more open and liberal judicial system may be compatible with courts having a poor record regarding their accountability function. These observations point toward the importance of the "personal" factors in explaining actions of courts. Typically, when a government manages to appoint mostly "amicable" judges, decisions will tend to strengthen, rather than undermine, the authority of the executive power. This, it could be argued, was the case in Argentina. However, we have also seen that judges tend to act strategically and are willing to "abandon" their loyalty to a particular government when they anticipate a regime change. The *strategic defection* argument provides some explanatory power in Argentina at key moments, but not in other cases.

Our provisional conclusion is that judicial accountability is a complex phenomenon that requires a complex explanation including multiple variables. We thus strive to understand the contributions from several explanations to account for the multifaceted picture we face. Explanations from institutional design, explanations from the social and political context, and explanations based on differences in the mindset of judges together contribute to an understanding of the behavior of judges. Taken together, they explain judicial accountability better than in isolation.

CHAPTER 4

Explaining the Rise of Accountability Functions of Costa Rica's Constitutional Court

The previous chapter contrasted the rise of Colombia's "hyperactive" Constitutional Court with the mixed record of the Argentine Supreme Court and the unquestionable reluctance of Chile's highest court to routinely exercise its accountability function. Of these three countries, Colombia's Constitutional Court was clearly the most extreme case of judicial assertiveness. In this chapter, we focus on Costa Rica's similarly hyperactive Constitutional Chamber of its Supreme Court—the *Sala IV*—to assess whether the explanation developed for the Colombian Court's transformation also holds in other cases of highly active courts. All the three cases analyzed in Chapter 3 experienced legal reforms simultaneously with other major institutional changes, such as the promulgation of a new constitution (Colombia), and/or transitions to democratic governance (Chile and Argentina). These simultaneous institutional changes can fog our view of the impact of legal reforms on court behavior. In Costa Rica, on the other hand, the only significant institutional reform was a minor constitutional amendment that created a new chamber within the Supreme Court; all other institutions remained constant. This *ceteris paribus* situation grants us a very clear picture of court behavior before and after the reforms, allowing us to demonstrate the possible effects of the reforms on the court's exercise of its accountability functions.

In 1989, a constitutional amendment created a Constitutional Chamber of the Costa Rican Supreme Court, which transformed the judicial branch (*Poder Judicial*) from being a political cipher that routinely failed to exercise its accountability function into a highly active, assertive court that was willing and able to challenge and rule against the popularly elected branches of government and their agencies. And, as noted by Fernando Cruz (2007: 559), a sitting magistrate of the *Sala IV*, the Constitution was transformed from being a "document of formal reference having little consequence . . . into a living body of law with actual application to all levels of Costa Rican society." Because the Supreme Court had enjoyed political and financial independence for over 30 years before it began to exercise an accountability function, we argue that judicial independence is perhaps a necessary precondition for increased accountability by high courts, but it is not a sufficient condition (this is also reflected in the Chilean case discussed in Chapter 3). Consequently, we examine institutional rules such as the court's internal operational rules, the rules of judicial appointment, the effectiveness of political parties in government, as well as the constitutional contents as keys to explaining the court's accountability function.

The first section describes Costa Rica's legal–political context over the last 20 years. A second section briefly outlines the constitutional reform that created the new Constitutional Chamber of the Supreme Court and examines the new court's operational rules and its powers. We then focus on the court's exercise of its accountability functions with examples of key cases in which actions of the executive and legislative bodies were effectively overturned or severely limited in their application. The subsequent section explains the continued hyperactivity of the Costa Rican Court in contrast to the recently diminished accountability functions of the Colombian Constitutional Court. Finally, the chapter explains the Costa Rican Court's accountability function in the context of the approaches that frame the book.

Political Context

Costa Rica is a small, middle-income developing country with over 50 years of continuous democratic governance and uninterrupted, free, democratic elections every four years since 1953 (Wilson 2007a). Modern Costa Rican politics are generally viewed to have begun with the end of the 1948 Civil War and the promulgation of a new constitution in 1949, which established the rules of the country's political life and deliberately created one of the weakest presidencies in Latin America (Mainwaring and Shugart, 1997: 432; Wilson 1998: 51–54). Political power was dispersed widely across the executive and legislature branches, a Supreme Court, many state-owned, autonomous agencies, and a quasi-fourth branch of government: the Supreme Elections Tribunal (TSE), which has complete responsibility for all issues related to elections.[1] The existence of the highly regarded TSE explains, in part, why the Supreme Court historically dealt with few electoral questions. According to the 1949 Constitution, "The government of the Republic is popular, representative, alternative and responsible. It is exercised by three distinct and independent branches: legislative, executive, and judicial. None of these branches can delegate the exercise of their own functions" (article 9). In reality, though, the judicial branch quickly resumed its prewar judicial inactivity and allowed the Legislative Assembly to pass laws as if its "power to legislate was absolute" (Urcuyo Fournier 1995: 44) and with scant respect for "the Constitution and fundamental rights" (Murillo 1994: 34–37).

The pattern of politics after the civil war until the early 1990s was marked by competition between two catch-all political parties, the social democratic *Partido Liberación Nacional* (National Liberation Party, PLN) and a conglomerate of Christian Democratic and conservative parties that eventually coalesced as a single party in 1982 as the *Partido Unidad Social Cristiana* (Social Christian Union Party, PUSC). These two parties agreed on a broad development strategy that included a commitment to state-led economic development and an extensive social welfare state. From the late 1970s until the mid-1980s, Costa Rica experienced its worst economic crisis since the Great Depression, which brought into question the country's longtime commitment to a state-led economic development model. Starting with the landslide election of 1982, in which the PLN won the presidency and a comfortable majority in the Legislative Assembly, the state-centered economic policies were gradually reformed and supplemented by free market-oriented policies, the fostering of a nontraditional export sector, and a diminished role for the state in the economy and provision of social services (Wilson 1998). These reforms were encouraged by international financial institutions (IFI) including the World Bank and the International Monetary Fund (IMF), but they were facilitated and implemented by domestic political and economic interests operating within the two major parties (Wilson 1994; Wilson, Rodríguez Cordero, and Handberg, 2004). The gradual nature of the implementation of the reforms stood in stark contrast to the "shock-therapy" implemented in some other Latin American countries such as Peru and prevented any sudden economic and/or political displacement. The neoliberal reforms, though, brought into stark relief the competing factions within the leading parties, ultimately resulting in the creation of a third major party in 2001, the *Partido Acción Cuidadana* (Citizens' Action Party, PAC) by former PLN leaders.

In 2006, Costa Rica experienced its fourteenth consecutive presidential and congressional elections since the 1948 Civil War. The election marked the end of the two-party system and the advent of a "new and fragile system" (Vargas 2007: 113). The 2006 election was the narrowest margin of victory in recent Costa Rican history; less than one percent separated the two lead-ing presidential candidates from the PAC and PLN. An automatic, manual recount by the TSE took almost a month to complete before it declared former president Oscar Arias Sánchez (PLN) the winner (Wilson 2007a, 2007b). The election was perhaps the most difficult in recent history for the TSE with the PAC presidential candidate alleging voter fraud and other irregularities. But once the TSE announced the final result, all relevant parties accepted the outcome.[2] These presidential elections were different from previous elections as it was the first time since 1969, when a constitu-tional amendment that prohibited presidential reelection had been adopted and a former president sought to be reelected. The election also marked the implosion of the PUSC, the rise of PAC as the second major party in the Legislative Assembly (and the presidential election), and the increased repre-sentation of minor parties in the assembly, which denied the new president's party a majority in the Congress (Wilson 2007a, 2007b).

Like most Latin American countries, historically Costa Rica used a civil law legal tradition that fostered a high level of deference by Supreme Court magistrates toward elected executives and legislators (Merryman 1985). The 1949 Constitution granted the Supreme Court equal standing with the executive and legislature and guaranteed it political autonomy. A 1957 constitutional amendment (article 177) guaranteed the court financial au-tonomy; six percent of the state's ordinary budget was assigned to the judicial branch.[3] Apart from the accountability function mandated on the Supreme Court (discussed later), the constitution also contains two chapters (*Título IV* and *V*), delineating over 50 articles, which guarantee a broad range of social and individual rights. A number of other constitutional articles protect free-doms, including education (*Título 7*), religion (*Título 6*), and voting rights (*Título 8*). Yet, even with these new powers and increased independence, the court quickly returned to its pre–civil war passivity, unwilling, or perhaps unable, to carry out its constitutionally mandated accountability functions.

In part, the court's continued inaction was a result of the internal insti-tutional rules under which the court operated (Murillo 1994; Wilson 2005). For example, the pre-reformed Supreme Court consisted of 17 magistrates, each serving on one of three chambers. To render a law or decree unconsti-tutional, it required all 17 magistrates sitting *en banc* to vote by a two-thirds supermajority (Cruz 2007: 557).[4] This requirement was a major obstacle to the court's ability to declare laws and decrees unconstitutional and was compounded by the adherence to a civil law tradition, excessive legal for-mality, slow pace of cases, and limited standing afforded to plaintiffs. It is not surprising that few individuals or groups saw the court as a likely arena to file a challenge to the constitutionality of governmental actions, laws, or

decrees. Consequently, few cases were filed, and even fewer were successful. It took a judicial reform creating the Constitutional Chamber of the
Supreme Court to mark the start of the regular application of the court's
accountability functions.

Judicial Reform and the Constitutional Chamber of the Supreme Court

The low-key parliamentary debate concerning the creation of the
Constitutional Chamber of the Supreme Court (*Sala IV*) reveals deputies'
expectations that the new court would act in a similar manner to the existing
Supreme Court and continue to show considerable deference to the popular
branches of government. Indeed, one of the arguments against the creation of
the *Sala IV*, offered by some sitting members of the Supreme Court, was the
clear lack of demand for such a court. It was noted that in 1980 the Supreme
Court addressed only one case of constitutionality and just 11 *amparo*[5] cases,
which, the magistrates argued, did not warrant the creation of a separate
court (Rodríguez Cordero 2002: 43). The empirical evidence appears to support this argument: In the 50 years from 1939 to 1989, the Supreme Court
received only 155 constitutionality cases (against laws, regulations, or public
institutions' actions) (PEN 2000: 290).

In 1989, during the final parliamentary debate on the constitutional
amendment (Law 7,128), deputies voted by a margin of 43 to 6 in favor of
creating the new court (Murrillo 1994: 40).[6] The puzzle of deputies voting
to create an institution that would diminish their own policy-making sovereignty seems, on the surface, to be confusing. However, interviews with
leading actors in the debate over the new court reveal that many deputies
failed to grasp the potential significance of the court they were creating.[7]
Furthermore, deputies of the 1986–1990 Congress who voted to create the
new court knew they would very likely not return to Congress once the
court was in operation. Sitting legislators would not cede their own political
power, but only surrender the policy-making sovereignty of future parliaments and presidents, in which they likely would not serve.[8]

With the passage of the constitutional amendment, the new Supreme
Court was expanded by five magistrates and reconfigured to include a
fourth chamber (*Sala Constitucional*, commonly referred to as the *Sala IV*).
In the newly expanded Supreme Court, the original three chambers were
assigned five members and the new Constitutional Chamber (*Sala IV*)
comprised seven members. Magistrates of the original three chambers are
elected by simple majority of the members of Congress to eight-year, renewable terms. The *Sala IV* magistrates serve similar terms, but are required

to garner supermajority support (two-thirds) from the deputies of the 57-member Legislative Assembly. Their terms are automatically renewed for a subsequent eight years, unless two-thirds of the deputies vote against the renewal of their terms (article 158). Neither the president nor the Legislative Assembly has the power to remove a magistrate; magistrates can only be removed by a secret two-thirds vote of the full Supreme Court (article 165). Since the *Sala IV's* inception, no magistrate has been removed or denied reappointment by the Legislative Assembly; *Sala IV* magistrates effectively enjoy life tenure. The magistrates have no "debt" to the executive branch (the president has no role in their appointment) and the Legislative Assembly has shown little willingness or ability to hold them to account (Wilson 2009).

The new chamber of the Supreme Court quickly broke with the pre-reformed Supreme Court's traditional inaction and deference to become a highly active court, protecting individual rights and holding other branches of government accountable. An indication of this rapid transition is the exponential growth of the *Sala IV's* caseload. In the court's first full year of operation (1990), it received less than 2,000 cases. By 1996, its caseload jumped to over 6,000 cases, 13,000 by 2002, and over 17,000 cases in 2008 (*Sala IV* 2009).

From the first year of operation, the overwhelming majority of the case-load was comprised of *amparo* cases. Over the period 1989–1995, on average 73 percent of the *Sala IV's* caseload was *amparo* cases. In recent years, this has increased to over 85 percent, and in 2008 it topped 90 percent (*La Nación* June 26, 2006; *Sala IV* 2009; Wilson 2005, 51). The *Sala IV* also resolved cases expeditiously and could rule a government decision, law, or decree unconstitutional with a simple majority of just four of the seven magistrates; previously, it had taken a two-thirds supermajority of the full court (12 of 17). The *Sala IV's* relatively rapid resolution of cases helped to send a signal that the Constitutional Chamber was a logical and effective arena to resolve various issues. In its first 19 years of operation, the *Sala IV* received almost 200,000 cases (*Sala IV* 2009). This growth in the number of cases filed and decided is impressive and speaks to a judicialization of Costa Rican politics; however, what is key is the significance of the cases decided rather than the volume of cases. This is particularly true for evaluating the exercise of the *Sala IV's* accountability function.

While the hyperactivity of the *Sala IV* might be attributable to a more activist mindset of the new magistrates, the initial composition of the *Sala IV* appeared no different from the pre-reformed Supreme Court. Indeed, two sitting Supreme Court magistrates were transferred to the new Constitutional Chamber and were joined by the sitting justice minister. Although currently no in-depth study of the magistrates exists, generally,

Sala IV magistrates are drawn from the same pool of candidates as those in the original Supreme Court and have similar legal training, career trajectories, and socioeconomic backgrounds to the magistrates of the pre-reformed court. Originally, there was an agreement between the two dominant parties (PLN and PUSC) to alternate nominees to the *Sala IV* to prevent either party from remaking the court in their party's image.[9] Also, since it takes a two-thirds majority of the whole Legislative Assembly to elect magistrates, no single party was in a position to load the new court with activist judges. This has become particularly true with the collapse of the PUSC, the failure of any party to secure majority control, and the rise of smaller parties in the Congress.

Furthermore, while just one excellent, but limited, study of magistrates' voting patterns exists, it reveals high levels of unanimity on the bench. The pioneering study of *Sala IV* magistrates' votes in mandatory consultations for constitutional amendments in the period 1989–2002 (Rodríguez Cordero 2003: 24) reveals that 96 percent of the magistrates' votes are unanimous. This suggests the explanation for the *Sala IV*'s hyperactivity might not be due to changes in the characteristics of the magistrates, but rather in some other area.

Perhaps a more useful location to search for the source of the increased activity might be found in the institutional rules under which the new chamber operated. The chamber's modified modus operandi coupled with its increased powers granted by the constitutional amendment is more likely to have facilitated its actions. First, the rules of the old Supreme Court, as noted below, effectively made it very difficult to employ its accountability function regardless of the inclination of the court's magistrates.

The *Sala IV* is mandated to "[g]uarantee the supremacy of the norms and constitutional principles, international law and community law in force in the republic, their uniform interpretation and application like fundamental rights and freedoms consecrated in the constitution or in international instruments in force in Costa Rica" (article 1 of the *Ley de la Jurisdicción Constitucional*). The court's decisions cannot be appealed and are binding on all other courts (except itself), government branches, state autonomous institutions, and private individuals.

According to Navia and Ríos-Figueroa (2005), the *Sala IV* enjoys among the most comprehensive powers of any Latin American Supreme Court. These include the power to

1. adjudicate conflicts of competency between government branches,
2. engage in judicial review: a priori (constitutional consultations) and a posteriori (unconstitutionality),

3. engage in concrete (based on a case) and abstract (general interest) judicial review,
4. make their rulings broadly effective: *inter partes* for cases of habeas corpus, and *amparo* and *erga omnes* for all judicial review and jurisprudence.

The *Sala IV*'s abandonment of strict procedural formalism and the use of simple majority votes to declare laws unconstitutional were coupled with greater access to the court for individuals, politicians, and groups. First, a broad definition of standing was introduced, allowing virtually anyone to file a case.[10] The expansive definition of standing is reflected in the volume of cases filed with the *Sala IV* as well as the cross-section of individuals who have taken their complaints to the court.

Second, in most instances, individuals can file a complaint directly with the *Sala IV* at any time of the day or night, without the need for legal representation, without incurring any fees, and without the need to understand which legal argument they are making. Claims can be submitted by anyone in Costa Rica, regardless of age, sex, or nationality and can be written on anything, in any language. According to one magistrate, cases have been filed with the *Sala IV* via "telegram, fax, and paper from a loaf of bread" (Jinesta 2005). The court has been approached by virtually every group in society, including the weakest groups such as prisoners, pensioners, women, and children. Indeed, one of the more persistent individuals to approach the court began his litigation "career" as a ten-year old from a poor neighborhood in San José seeking legal redress for a tardy school bus. Although he lost that particular case, in the following eight years, he filed over 140 more cases, winning a significant number of them. This child had no legal training or resources for legal representation, but was able to easily make use of a legal opportunity that allowed him (and other marginalized individuals) to bypass the traditional political brokers and instead seek a solution directly from the court, which is required to act on the case (Mora 2000; Wilson and Handberg, 1999; Wilson and Rodríguez, 2006). This requirement for the court to act, even if it is just to dismiss the case as being without merit, pushes all manners of cases before the magistrates for an opinion. This process emphasizes the importance of institutional rules of the *Sala IV*.

The Sala IV's Accountability Functions

In the analysis of presidential systems, the relevant measure of accountability is generally the ability or willingness of courts to challenge the actions of the executive branch. This, as we saw in the last chapter, is particularly true in Latin America, where hyper-presidentialism is pervasive. In Costa Rica, though, as noted earlier, the executive branch has, since the promulgation of the 1949 Constitution, been one of the weakest in the Americas (Mainwaring and Shugart, 1997). Most law-making power resides with the 57-member Legislative Assembly over which the president has little control, even when the president's own party controls a majority of the seats. Similarly, the president's veto powers are weak and decree powers limited; the president has little influence over the congressional agenda.[11]

Further weakening the president's power is the existence of a large number of autonomous institutions, many of which have constitutionally guaranteed budgets.[12] Thus, an understanding of the scope and willingness of the Costa Rican Supreme Court to exercise its accountability function is necessarily broader than just a measure of its holding the executive branch to account. Instead, the next section details the *Sala IV's* actions against both elected branches of the state as well and those of the state's semiautonomous agencies.

Here, we argue that the ability of the court to make its decisions stick is reflected in how policy-making and policy implementation have been affected by *Sala IV* rulings. First, a brief examination of limitations placed on executive actions (including the actions of some autonomous institutions such as the *Instituto Costarricense de Electricidad*, ICE, the power and phone state monopoly). The subsequent section details the curtailment of the Legislative Assembly's assumed policy-making sovereignty by the *Sala IV*, which is perhaps an even more significant use of the chamber's accountability functions.

Accountability and the Executive

The level of independence of the *Sala IV* from the executive is virtually absolute; the president cannot appoint, nominate, or remove *Sala IV* magistrates. Furthermore, the executive branch is unable to affect the judicial branch budget or intervene in any aspect of the operation of the court. The judicial branch is constitutionally guaranteed six percent of the national ordinary budget (article 177) and controlled exclusively by the Supreme Court magistrates. These magistrates appoint all other judges in the country, which affords them some control over their career paths. The lack of political and financial influence or control over the *Sala IV* is coupled with very limited constitutional powers granted to the president. In a practical sense, the president's political influence (soft power) is further weakened as the president is a lame duck immediately after taking office. Since the president is unable to further the political careers of sitting deputies, they tend to pay more attention to aspiring presidential candidates rather than the incumbent chief executive (Carey 1996; Taylor 1992; Wilson 1998).

The impact of *Sala IV* rulings on the president's already weak decree-making power is evidenced by the declining number of presidential decrees. During the 1980s, the presidents proclaimed over 10,000 decrees, but once the *Sala IV* was created in 1989, this number declined to 6,200 in the following decade (PEN 2001: 134): a drop of almost 40 percent. More specifically, three recent examples illustrate the willingness of the *Sala IV* to employ its accountability functions and the willingness of sitting presidents to accept the rulings.

First, in March 2003, President Abel Pacheco (PUSC) unilaterally declared Costa Rica's support for the U.S. invasion of Iraq. In many ways, it was an inexpensive political maneuver by the president to curry favor with the U.S. government; no financial or military aid was committed. The constitutionality of the president's action, though, was challenged by a private citizen and also separately by the Costa Rican Bar Association (*Colegio de Abogados*) and the Ombudsperson's Office (*Defensoría de los Habitantes*), all of whom filed cases with the *Sala IV.* In September 2004, the *Sala IV* unanimously ruled that the "Executive Branch had acted against the constitution, international law accepted by Costa Rica, and the international system of the United Nations" (*Sala IV* 2004). The *Sala IV* ordered the president to contact the U.S. government and to get Costa Rica's name removed from the "alliance of the willing." Foreign Secretary Roberto Tovar accepted the chamber's decision and immediately contacted the U.S. embassy to have Costa Rica's name removed from the list (Vizcaíno 2004). In a similar vein, in 2006 the *Sala IV* ruled against the executive and the Ministry of Public Security, noting that the executive was to refrain from sending delegates to participate in military parades because it implied that Costa Rica had an army, which is against the constitution's proscription on the existence of a standing army (Exp. 15245–06).[13]

A more profound policy rebuke for the executive branch is illustrated by a 2003 case concerning the Pacheco (PUSC 2002–2006) government's decision to reduce education expenditures by reducing the school year by 27 days for primary and secondary school children. The *Sala IV* declared the administration's decision unconstitutional and argued that the executive did not have the power to reduce the school year because the government was bound by an international agreement signed by a previous Costa Rican government, the *Convenio Centroamericano sobre la Unificación de la Educación Básica* (Central American Convention on Unifying Basic Education), which mandates a 200-day minimum academic year for elementary school pupils (Resolution No. 11515–02). Consequently, the government was forced to fund a 200-day school year and find budgetary savings elsewhere.

A third illustrative example lies in the area of health care priority setting and expenditure. With the start of the AIDS crisis in the early to mid-1980s, the state-owned and state-funded health care system *Caja Costarricense de Seguro Social* (Costa Rican Social Security Agency, CCSS), had to address the issue of how to deal with the medical treatment for people living with AIDS (PLWA). The initial response was to allow doctors to refuse patients treatment, laboratory work, and deny access to state-financed anti-AIDS medications.

By 1992 a group of PLWA filed a case with the *Sala IV* demanding access to state-funded antiretroviral drugs. The director of the CCSS argued that the drugs were too expensive and ineffectual. The *Sala IV* ruled against the AIDS patients (Resolution No. 280–292). Five years later, a similar case was filed by three seriously ill AIDS patients. Once again they demanded the state pay for and give them access to the latest anti-AIDS medications, which had been shown in U.S. studies to improve life quality and longevity. This time, the *Sala IV* sided with the patients and concluded, "What good are the rest of the rights and guarantees...the advantages and benefits of our system of liberties, if a person cannot count on the right to life and health assured?" (Resolution No. 5934–1997). The *Sala IV's* decision was a landmark case that forced the state agency to fund all similar AIDS patients' medical treatment. In subsequent years, other individuals and groups have used this articulated "constitutional right to medical treatment" to force the government to fund the treatment of other chronic diseases (Wilson and Rodríguez Cordero, 2006). Thus, the government's ability to engage in priority setting in health care has become severely curtailed by the *Sala IV* rulings that require the state to expend effort and money to cover treatments that its advisors had concluded should not be covered. These rulings against the government in divergent cases ranging from foreign policy to education and health care illustrate the ability and willingness of the *Sala IV* to hold even the executive branch accountable.

Accountability and the Legislative Assembly

Deputies' notion of having law-making sovereignty is perhaps derived from their reading of article 105 of the constitution that states "The power to legislate resides in the people, who delegate this power, by suffrage, to the Legislative Assembly. This power may not be waived or subject to limitations by any agreement or contract, either directly or indirectly, except in the case of treaties, in accordance with the principles of International Law." But since the creation of the *Sala IV* this assumed that policy-making sovereignty has been checked by the court in three broad ways. First, any constitutional amendment, convention, or international treaty discussed by the Legislative Assembly must be sent to the *Sala IV* for a *consulta de constitucionalidad* (constitutional consult) after the first parliamentary debate. The *Sala IV's* consult is obligatory, although its decision concerning the bill is not binding (Ley de la Jurisdicción Constitucional 1989). If the deputies choose to proceed with the bill without correcting it in line with the *Sala IV's* recommendation, its constitutionality is likely to be challenged shortly after it is promulgated.

A second major accountability function relating to the Legislative Assembly is the *consulta facultativa previa*. This consult can be initiated by as few as ten deputies and requires any bill being considered in the Legislative Assembly to be sent to the *Sala IV* for a ruling on its constitutionality. This is not limited to the constitutional content of the bill, but also the constitutionality of the parliamentary procedure used to usher the bill through Congress. In recent years, the *Sala IV* has become increasingly concerned with proper legislative procedure for passing bills into laws and has become increasingly willing to declare a law unconstitutional due to a procedural error (PEN 2006: 151). Due to the small number of deputies required to send the bill to the *Sala IV*, this type of consult has become a favorite tactic of minority party deputies in the Legislative Assembly to block, delay, or amend bills they disagree with. This pattern appears to have been exacerbated by the collapse of the two-party system and the rise of multiple small parties in Congress.

The debate over an Emergency Response Law in 2005 serves as an illustrative example. The bill was designed to allow the *Comisión Nacional de Emergencias* to respond to small natural disasters without a presidential decree and to establish a separate fund for such actions. The bill sailed through the first legislative debate with a positive vote of 40 against only two negative votes. Despite this overwhelming congressional support, an independent deputy, José Miguel Corrales (along with nine other deputies), sent the bill to the *Sala IV* for a *consulta facultativa*. The chamber ruled that part of the bill would be, if passed into law, unconstitutional. Corrales notes that this was not a mandatory ruling, but that the assembly necessarily had to take the chamber's ruling into account before the bill became law (Alvarado 2005). The bill finally became law in January 2006, after having been amended to meet the criticism of the *Sala IV*.

A brief example of an important item of legislation that was tripped up by the *Sala IV* due to procedural irregularities includes a major tax reform bill in 2006. This contentious bill had taken more than two years to be shaped into a form that would garner a majority of deputies' votes. In response to a constitutional consult, the *Sala IV* declared the bill unconstitutional on procedural grounds; the bill would need to be returned to the committee stage and the process restarted. Because this ruling came toward the end of the 2002–2006 congressional term, there was insufficient time to correct the errors and pass the revised bill into law. The bill, even though it had received majority support in Congress, was effectively killed as a result of the *Sala IV's* ruling.

Deputies quickly realized the utility of harnessing the *Sala IV's* accountability functions and regularly challenged bills they disagreed with and sent them to the chamber for a consultation. This is a particularly attractive strategy for minor parties. Indeed, the deputies of *Movimiento Libertario* (Libertarian Party) use this tactic frequently and with a significant success rate. The *Sala IV* has found constitutional defects in 43 percent of the bills sent to it for review (Echeverría Martín 2000: 216), which the Congress then needs to invest more time to rectify the errors. Even for the other 57 percent of the bills for which the *Sala IV* finds no error, the bills were successfully delayed.

A recent use of the *Sala IV* (and the TSE as an accountability agent) has been related to the question of Costa Rica joining the Central American Free Trade Agreement (CAFTA). Costa Rica's participation in the free trade agreement was one of the major issues of the 2006 presidential and legislative elections. The passage of the bill in Congress was delayed, at first by PAC deputies using various parliamentary procedures. José Miguel Corrales, a former presidential candidate and vocal opponent of the trade agreement, then filed a request with the TSE for a referendum (*consulta popular*) on the issue, which if successful would have required the collection of 100,000 voters' signatures. Corrales understood that the collection of signatures would be a very slow process and, once complete, would have required a nationwide vote on the agreement. The goal appeared to be to use the demand for a referendum to delay any congressional action by a further nine months.

President Oscar Arias recognized the intent behind the tactic and instead called for a referendum himself, which was quickly supported by the Legislative Assembly. The main opposition party in the assembly, PAC, that had used parliamentary procedures to delay action on the trade agreement, used its parliamentary position to question the constitutionality of the CAFTA agreement and requested a ruling from the *Sala IV*. This followed a separate *consultiva previa* filed with the *Sala IV* by *defensora* (Ombudswoman) Lisbeth Quesada on April 27, 2007, on the issue of potential human rights infringements that she believed might result from the implementation of the CAFTA agreement, arguing that this was a legitimate question for the *Defensoría* to raise before the *Sala IV*. She argued that a ruling from the *Sala IV* would "increase confidence in the referendum and its final outcome" and would guarantee that the treaty people would vote on in the referendum contained no unconstitutional aspects (Mora 2007). In this case, the *Sala IV* sided with the executive and declared the CAFTA agreement constitutional.

One final example of the willingness of the *Sala IV* to exercise its accountability functions with respect to the Legislative Assembly is perhaps the most restrictive ruling of the chamber. In 1969, a constitutional amendment (Law No. 4339) prohibited presidential reelection. Prior to the amendment, presidents could seek reelection after sitting out two four-year terms. In the late 1990s, former President Arias encouraged deputies to reverse the 1969 prohibition on reelection. Arias argued that the assembly had the constitutional power to reverse its earlier decision (Herrera 1999). The assembly, though, showed little enthusiasm for reversing the prohibition (as did most other former presidents) even though public opinion was in favor of it (Wilson 2005: 52–5).

The issue was then filed with the *Sala IV*, which rejected the case in a split decision (Expediente No. 7428–990). Subsequently, the assembly debated and rejected the bill by a vote of 32 to 13 (Venegas 2000). While this was the end of the discussion of the issue in the Legislative Assembly, the case was resubmitted to the *Sala IV* in 2003. This time, though, lawyers argued the discrimination and individual rights angle and also that the Legislative Assembly did not have the constitutional power to pass the amendment in the first place. The challenge to the power of the assembly was a new basis of the legal argument, but perhaps more important were the two new magistrates serving on the *Sala IV*. On April 4, 2003, the *Sala IV* came to another split decision, but this time five to two against the reelection prohibition amendment (Expediente No. 02–005494-007-CO; Resolution No. 2003–02771).

This ruling was a profound challenge to the assembly's assumed policy-making sovereignty. The vast majority of deputies had twice in the recent past voted not to overturn the 1969 amendment and allow presidential reelection; yet the *Sala IV's* decision effectively took away the assembly's power to amend key parts of the constitution. The court's explanation for its decision to declare Constitutional Amendment 132 (the presidential reelection prohibition) unconstitutional was because it restricted citizens' fundamental constitutional rights to seek election and elect people. The *Sala IV* explained that Congress, "cannot reduce, amputate, or limit rights and fundamental guarantees, or political rights of the citizens or the essential aspects of the country's political organization" (Herrera 2003). It was not just that the *Sala IV* ruled an action of the Legislative Assembly unconstitutional, but it was that deputies were officially and explicitly given notice that they had no constitutional right to legislate significant areas of policy and that their perception of their own policy and law-making sovereignty was mistaken.

A final limitation on the once presumed law-making sovereignty of Congress comes from the *Sala IV's* ability to also rule on the constitutionality of a bill once it becomes a law. This is a widely used post hoc tool to overturn legislation passed by the Legislative Assembly. These three methods of challenging the legislative power of the Congress collectively produce a more subtle (and difficult to measure) impact on the policy-making. While historically, majority parties in the assembly could pass laws and pay little heed to the interests and demands of opposition parties, the existence of these three paths to challenge the constitutionality, all of which are readily available to minor parties, has altered the content of laws.

The Possibility of a Backlash?

As noted in the last chapter, the hyperactivity of the Colombian court spawned a significant backlash against the court from various sectors of society, particularly economic interests, such as bankers (Clavijo 2001) who accused the court of "legal despotism" and advocated constitutional reforms to limit its actions (Palacios 2001: 12). The *Sala IV's* vigorous exercise of its accountability functions has similarly elicited visceral criticism from some sectors. Deputies from the dominant political parties, for example, quickly realized early that their ability to write and pass laws was increasingly limited and made progressively more difficult by the *Sala IV's* actions. Complaints by dominant party deputies and executive members about these accountability actions are mounting. Procurator General (solicitor general) Román Solís, for example, publicly voiced his fears and frustration over the growing role of the *Sala IV*, accusing it of usurping the powers of other state organs by hearing and ruling on cases that should have been dealt with in other fora and "effectively leaving the Executive and legislative Assembly with little power" (Méndez Garita 2000). He noted that this pattern of usurpation was reflected in the *Sala IV* hearing the case of the constitutionality of presidential reelection; he argued the chamber lacked a constitutional right to hear the case (Méndez Garita 2000).

When the court agreed to rule on the presidential reelection for a second time in 2003, the criticism grew louder (Díaz 2003). This ruling produced a vitriolic backlash from deputies in both major parties in the Congress, with some labeling the *Sala IV* a "super power" (Bermúdez 2003). Ex-deputy Alberto Cañas, for example, classified the *Sala IV's* reelection ruling as a "*golpe de estado*," as did former president Luis Alberto Monge (PLN). Another PLN militant claimed the court's ruling was a "judicial barbarity," while Jorge Eduardo Sánchez, the PUSC Secretary General, claimed that the *Sala IV* had usurped powers and had become a "co-administrator and co-legislator" (Díaz 2003).

Beyond voicing criticism of specific *Sala IV* actions and its perceived overreach, little has been done to reign in the court and the exercise of its accountability function. Apart from a very contentious reconfirmation hearing in 2005 for the chief justice of the Supreme Court (who is also a magistrate of the *Sala IV*) and one of his colleagues from the *Sala IV*, few actions have attempted to systematically reduce the power of the chamber.[14] This situation stands in contrast to the Colombian case, in which rules of appointment for Supreme Court magistrates and the single eight-year term rule allowed the executive and legislature to replace activist magistrates once their terms expired with more restrained ones. Also, in Colombia, it is relatively easy to change the constitution: thus, it is possible to amend the parts of the constitution that the court cited when declaring laws unconstitutional. In Costa Rica, on the other hand, constitutional amendments are difficult to achieve and are the product of a deliberately slow process. Thus, Costa Rican lawmakers do not possess this legislative tool to limit the actions of the court. Indeed, in Costa Rica, the Congress and executive have very limited legislative tools at their disposal to influence either the composition of the court or the content of the constitution.

The lack of successful proposals to limit the powers of the *Sala IV* is not due to a lack of desire on the part of the popularly elected branches or the court itself. Rather, for the Assembly, it is a difficult technical hurdle to cross as it would require a supermajority (38 out of 57 deputies) to successfully change the law to limit the powers of the court. The current governing party (PLN) has only 25 members in the Legislative Assembly, and the weakness of parties makes it unlikely that they could muster all those votes, never mind convincing 13 more deputies from other parties to support a judicial reform project to limit the powers of the court. This is particularly true since some of the smaller parties have found that the *Sala IV's* existence and actions have increased their political power in the Congress. This is especially true for the *Movimiento Libertario* (ML), which is one of the most frequent users of the *Sala IV* to block, delay or amend government-sponsored bills (Echeverría 2000).

Explaining the Accountability Functions of
Costa Rican Courts

Although by 1957, Costa Rica's Superior Court enjoyed sole judicial review powers and political and financial independence, it remained politically insignificant. This changed rapidly with the creation of the Constitutional Chamber of the Supreme Court in 1989. Which specific approach—legal–political context, institutional design, or actor-based—can best account for the metamorphosis of the Supreme Court?

Social, Legal, and Political Context

Prior to 1989, the long-standing constitutional mandate for Superior Court independence and the separation of powers effectively protected the court from political interference. Yet, in spite of the court's constitutionally granted powers of judicial review and enumeration of many individual and collective rights, it was effectively moribund and politically insignificant. The court remained highly deferential to the political branches of government, a behavior reinforced by its adherence to the civil law legal tradition restrictions that afforded a minimal role to superior courts. This deference and inaction removed any need for the political parties to attempt to pack the court, as was common in many other Latin American countries. While the legal–political context can readily account for the inaction of the court, it is unable to offer any insight into the actions of the reformed court after its creation in 1989.

The civil law legal tradition, the constitutional document, and the political system remained constant in the two time periods. Yet, the reformed court behaved very differently and harnessed and employed its constitutionally mandated powers to hold the other branches of government to the account. The court's previous view of the constitution as "a dead letter" was replaced by an understanding of the document as the fundamental law, "a vital set of enforceable rights of the highest importance" (Calzado 2008). Perhaps, then, the changing in institutional design can account for the behavior of Costa Rica's Constitutional Court.

Institutional Design

Institutional design potentially provides the most promising explanation for the *Sala IV's* aggressive exercise of its accountability function because the only significant change between the period of superior court inaction and aggressive application of its accountability function was the creation of the new chamber of the court itself and the institutional rules that guide its behavior. The institutional design of the pre-reformed court, strict legal formality, narrow definition of standing, and supermajority votes for unconstitutionality, encouraged, if not demanded, an inactive deferential superior court. The institutional design of the reformed court, on the other hand, facilitated the reversal of the most restrictive of these rules. The *Sala IV* is very informal, uses a broad definition of standing, is granted increased constitutional powers to referee disputes between branches of government, can adjudicate the constitutionality of laws before and after promulgation, and has opened its doors to allow the widest possible access to bring cases to the court with few legal requirements or costs.

The new institutional rules for appointing magistrates to the *Sala IV* guarantees that no political party can pack the court. The supermajority vote of the deputies in the assembly required to deny a subsequent term on the court to a magistrate is very difficult to achieve and has not happened in almost 20 years of the court's existence. These institutional rules removed the many constraints that limited pre-reform superior court magistrates' behavior. Open access to the general citizenry to file cases and easy application of legislative consults pushed the court to consider a wide range of cases that would not have appeared on the pre-reformed court's docket. At the same time, however, it is not impossible that changes in actors might also have contributed to the differences in the court's accountability function.

Actor-based Explanations

Recently, the President of the *Sala IV* argued that the creation of the Constitutional Court "implied a substantial change in attitude, in the sense that Constitutional law must take immediate and direct effect on society" (Calzada 2008). As shown in this chapter, the reformed court has engaged its accountability function to the fullest extent with very little dissent among the magistrates, even as retiring magistrates are replaced by new ones. The behavior of the reformed court, then, might logically be attributed to a new type of magistrate with a different attitude about the proper function of a superior court. Although no systematic study of the magistrates exists, generally, *Sala IV* magistrates are drawn from the same pool of candidates as those in the original Supreme Court; they have similar legal training, career trajectories, and socioeconomic backgrounds to the magistrates of the pre-reformed court. Indeed, two of the magistrates appointed to the new court were already sitting members of the pre-reformed court.

The required two-thirds supermajority vote of the Legislative Assembly to confirm magistrates to the *Sala IV* has precluded any single party from packing the court with its supporters. Selection of magistrates is necessarily a compromise between the parties that limits the ability of successful candidates for the court to be very different from the center.[15] In cases in which the court is divided, it is clear that the individuals on the court can make a difference, but these are relatively rare situations.

The vast majority of the rulings from the *Sala IV* are unanimous; thus changing the composition of the court would not readily change the nature of the court's decisions. On some issues, the composition of the court has been pivotal. The two presidential reelection votes already discussed demonstrate this clearly, but these types of votes are relatively rare and are not determined by judicial philosophy. It might be concluded that neither the legal tradition, political context, nor the magistrates themselves changed in an appreciable manner that would account for the willingness and ability of the court to employ a strong accountability function after the reforms.

Conclusion

The court's accountability function was broadly and vigorously applied to all governmental branches only after the creation of the Constitutional Chamber of the Supreme Court in 1989. Before 1989, even though the constitution granted the Supreme Court judicial review powers and considerable levels of political and financial (operational) independence, the court was unable or unwilling to fulfill its accountability functions. The nature of the magistrates (training, class, and so on) was insignificantly different from magistrates who served on the pre-reformed Supreme Court.

The *Sala IV's* operational rules mandated it take a key role in the policy-making process through constitutional consults. The changing nature of Costa Rican party politics increased the representation of smaller parties in the Legislative Assembly. These deputies from minor political parties have harnessed the *Sala IV's* institutional rules to delay, amend, and/or block bills with which they disagree. So, on the one hand, the court's internal operational rules made it easier for it to activate its accountability functions and, on the other hand, changes in the composition of the national assembly (more representatives of smaller parties and no single-party majority) made it more likely that deputies would request the court to exercise that function. That deputies from minor parties routinely use the *Sala IV* in this manner may also protect the *Sala IV* from legislative efforts to weaken its accountability functions as it is unlikely that these deputies would vote to amend the *Sala IV's* rules of operation, as this would harm their own interests. Thus, in the case of Costa Rica, the newly invigorated accountability functions of the Supreme Court can be traced not to constitutional provisions, nor to changes in the mindset of the magistrates. Instead, institutional structures and operational rules of the *Sala IV*, combined with a fragmentation of the party system, appear to offer the most insight into the court's behavior since its inception in 1989.

CHAPTER 5

The Accountability Functions of African Courts

This chapter compares the accountability functions of courts in Zambia, Malawi, South Africa, Tanzania, and Uganda. These five countries share important characteristics that suggest a similar role for the courts; yet, the accountability functions of the higher courts differ significantly, both across countries and over time. How can this variation in similar cases be explained?

Historically, the political role of courts was limited in all five countries. Under British rule, there was no significant judicial restraint on the exercise of power. The colonial power established a dual legal system, with "traditional" courts for disputes that arose between local subjects and a formal, British-style legal system staffed by British (later non-European, but British-educated) lawyers. There was no separation of powers or institutional protection for judicial independence. "Traditional" courts were merged with executive power and formed part of the colonial administration. The formal judiciary was only provided proper security for their tenure on the eve of independence. The lack of constitutional authority to review administrative acts and decisions, combined with the judges' adherence to the formal conservatism of the British legal and judicial culture, ensured that the courts did not play a role in limiting executive authority in the colonial period (Pfeiffer 1978). At the time of independence, the judiciary was kept largely intact, and English common law continued to dominate the formal legal system.

Despite differences in their postcolonial experiences, the five countries share a history of executive dominance. In South Africa, British colonialism ended in 1910, but was followed by internal white minority rule. The *Apartheid* state (1948–1994) was characterized by strong rule by law, but weak judicial restraints on executive power. The other four countries were granted independence on terms that included a constitution combining a Westminster-style political system with a legally enforceable Bill of Rights, vesting strong powers in the judiciary. However, Tanzania's Independence Constitution (1961) only included the Bill of Rights in the preamble, not as part of the constitution itself. Consequently, the courts' review powers were weaker so as "not to invite conflict between the executive and the judiciary" (Pfeiffer 1978: 56). Zambia, Malawi, and Tanzania all developed into one-party states under the "imperial" presidencies of their respective liberation heroes—Kenneth Kaunda, Hastings Banda, and Julius Nyerere. Parliaments were reduced to rubber stamps, and the courts did little to check the abuse of power or otherwise challenge the ruling party. Uganda had a compara-tively assertive judiciary at the time of independence (1962), but this soon changed when the initial period of (deteriorating) multiparty democracy was followed by the dictatorship of Idi Amin (1971–1979), under which there was no rule of law. Political opponents were summarily executed. The suppression of the judiciary is epitomized by the 1972 incident in which Chief Justice Kiwanuka was taken from the High Court and killed. After highly disputed elections marking the return to civilian rule, a bloody civil war followed. Museveni took over power in 1986 and inaugurated a "no-party-democracy" or "movement system," in which individual candidates could contest political positions (including the presidency) on their own merit, but not as party representatives.

In the 1990s, pro-democracy movements forced constitutional changes in all the five countries that had opened up for competitive elections and strengthened the judicial powers and independence. Zambia, Malawi, and South Africa went through pacted transitions with pro-democracy move-ments becoming the new ruling party. In Tanzania and Uganda, a more gradual process of constitutional reforms controlled from above saw the former ruling parties open for multiparty politics, while continuing to win elections.

South Africa has a far stronger economy than the other African countries in this analysis (as Table 1.2 shows, it is more in line with the Latin American cases). The other African countries analyzed here are heavily dependent on foreign aid, and a political career often represents the main opportunity for economic and social advancement. South Africa also emerged from the tran-sition with stronger state institutions, including a more firmly institution-alized and professional judiciary. However, the judiciaries were politically weak in all five countries. They were controlled by the ruling party through appointments (Zambia, Uganda, and South Africa), or marginalized by keeping central policy areas outside of the domain of the court (Tanzania) or even creating a parallel structure of traditional courts to deal with political cases (Malawi). After new constitutions were enacted in the 1990s, thus strengthening the legal basis for the judiciary to hold the political branches accountable, the accountability performance of the upper courts have followed different trajectories.

In Zambia, the 1991 Constitution inaugurated a stronger accountability role for the judiciary, resulting in some very important judgments in the first years of the democratic dispensation. However, within half a decade, Zambia experienced a marked dent in the accountability functions of the courts, illustrating the vulnerability of these judiciaries.

In South Africa, a democratic Constitution (1994) and the establishment of a new Constitutional Court were followed by several judicial decisions demonstrating a significant accountability role vis-à-vis the political branches. But, after a strong start, the court's accountability function has leveled off. Significant judgments serve as a countervailing force in a political context that is marked by an increasingly centralized dominant party, but in other cases, caution is displayed.

In Malawi, the formerly marginal judiciary contributed significantly to the 1993–1994 democratic transition, and the courts have become increasingly central to the political process exercising substantial, although uneven, accountability functions. While the judicial institution is comparatively small and poorly resourced, it is a democratic stronghold in a context in which the quality of the country's political institutions has otherwise declined.

The most dramatic rise in the accountability functions of the judiciary has occurred in contemporary Uganda, where, since the early 2000s, parts of the judiciary have overtly clashed with the political branches. The Ugandan Constitution of 1995, with its bill of rights, review powers, and structural protection for judicial independence, provided for a stronger judicial accountability function, but induced no immediate change in judicial behavior. For half a decade, the courts remained cautious. The increased assertiveness of the courts coincide with the decline of the "no-party system," which was retained in the 1995 Constitution, affirmed in a subsequent referendum, and only formally abolished in a 2005 referendum that paved the way for multiparty elections, which were won by the incumbent president and ruling party.

In Tanzania, constitutional changes have also been gradual and from above, but here legal–political relations have been stable. The judiciary exerts significant authority in "routine cases," but notable judgments in which the courts have exercised a political accountability function are few, and in most politically charged cases, the highest court displays a deferential attitude.

What, then, explains these differences in legal outcomes? To understand why the judiciaries differ in their performance between countries and over time, this chapter examines the political context and institutional framework within which the judges operate in each of the five countries, as well as the nature of their main decisions, using the sequence of their *constitutional moments* as an organizing principle. Against this background, we explore possible explanations for the differences in observed judicial behavior.

Legal–Political Context

Zambia

Zambia's multiparty Constitution (1991) broadened the jurisdiction and review powers of the judiciary and provided constitutional safeguards to protect its independence. But other factors perpetuated political ties. Notably, when the chief justice resigned (under pressure), the newly elected president, Frederic Chiluba, replaced him with his own man.[1] In his first years in office, Chief Justice Ngulube wrote some noteworthy judgments that were commended by lawyers and human rights activists and strongly disliked by the government. However, later he—and the judiciary generally—were criticized for moving toward a pro-government stance, particularly after the judgment upholding the 1996 presidential election. In June 2002, Ngulube withdrew after it was revealed that he had secretly received money from a Chiluba-controlled trust since 1998. Public confidence suffered,[2] but the criticism eased with the appointment of a widely respected new chief justice rather than the sitting deputy, who was considered a political appointee.

In interviews, Zambian judges expressed caution concerning the separation of powers, and some complained over the extent to which political actors take their battles to court, stating that matters of politics should be fought out in other arenas (Gloppen 2004). Yet, the degree to which political and civil society actors take their concerns to court is lower than in neighboring Malawi, even though Zambian civil society is comparatively stronger and has mobilized effectively when judicial independence has been threatened (VonDoepp 2008).

While the Movement for Multiparty Democracy (MMD) has won all presidential elections since 2001, elections have been relatively close. The dominance of the MMD is to a large extent due to a fragmented opposition, with parliamentarians defecting to the government.

Malawi

Unlike in the Zambian one-party state, where the judiciary was "captured from within" and subjected through politically appointed chief justices, President Banda's marginalization of the Malawian judiciary from political cases ironically enabled the institution to emerge relatively untainted from the one-party regime.[3] This partly explains the judiciary's relative strength and integrity during and after the 1993/94 political transition. Surviving the transition largely intact and aided by the 1994 Constitution, the judiciary established itself as a relatively robust and politically significant institution in a context of dwindling trust in political institutions and processes.[4] Extensive use of injunctions to stop or delay government actions established the courts a source of "instant justice."[5] As one interviewee phrased it, "Democracy in Malawi is to have a judge on call."[6]

More than in any of the other countries analyzed here, elections in Malawi have been relatively open. The United Democratic Front won the first three elections, but did not have a majority and, following a split, has been in opposition since 2005. Still, parliament is weak and ineffective. A lack of alternative institutions capable of solving political disputes and a willingness on part of the judges to take on political cases help explain why the courts have become a key arena in Malawian politics.

While the judiciary stands out in a polity that struggles to achieve viable governing institutions and consolidate its democracy,[7] signs of democratic decline indicate that even if we find that Malawi's courts have exercised an accountability function as guardians of the constitution, this is at best a limited success. Looking narrowly at the judgments, the accountability record of courts in the post-1994 period is also mixed. Several rulings, particularly at the High Court level, hold the executive to account, but the courts are also successfully used by the government in political battles against its opponents. The judiciary is also increasingly contested. In 2001, three of the judges involved in politically significant adverse rulings were impeached; however, in the face of domestic and international pressure, the impeachments were never implemented. Adverse rulings are often strongly condemned and at times ignored. Rumors of undue contact and favors being bestowed on judges persist, and in 2007, the chief justice resigned citing undue political pressure. The subsequent appointment process broke with established principles of seniority that had helped depoliticize the judiciary.

Malawi does not have a strong civil society or well-functioning legal aid nongovernmental organizations (NGOs). Yet, a few active and competent organizations have actively used the courts, initiating what we may term "accountability-litigation."[8]

South Africa

Until 1994, the South African judiciary was institutionally strong, but politically marginal, with very limited review powers extending only to procedures. The government ruled through law and generally respected the courts' authority, but the judiciary rarely represented a political challenge. With the exception of a few independent-minded judges who used their entire scope of interpretation, the courts adopted a formalistic stance, faithfully applying repressive legislation.[9] Through appointments to the Supreme Courts and the appellate division, the state ensured that liberal interpretations were struck down (Corder 1989).

The first democratic elections in 1994 brought the African National Congress (ANC) to power, gaining almost two-thirds of the votes. It also brought constitutional supremacy with strong review powers. An extensive Bill of Rights, containing civil and political rights as well as justiciable social rights, antidiscrimination clauses, and affirmative action provisions, reflected the incoming government's concern for social transformation.[10] Concessions to the former regime included federal arrangements, property rights, and a proportional representation (PR) electoral system catering to minority representation. Still, the opposition remained weak while the ANC ruled as the dominant and increasingly centralized political force. Party cohesion and discipline was strengthened by the party-list PR system combined with a floor-crossing (also referred to as antidefection or party-switching) clause. Despite growing internal conflicts, the ANC did not experience a major split until late 2008, when Thabo Mbeki was recalled as president, and his supporters established a new party, the Congress of the People (COPE).[11]

The court structure and personnel remained unaltered in the 1994 transition except for the new Constitutional Court that was introduced at the apex of the legal system and shared appellate jurisdiction with the reconstituted Supreme Court of Appeal. An unreformed judiciary could not be trusted to interpret and institutionalize the new constitutional values; hence, a minority of the Constitutional Court was appointed from among sitting judges. The remainder was mainly composed of legal academics, several from within the antiapartheid movement and engaged in the constitution-making process (Gloppen 2001).

The immediate post-apartheid period was characterized by internal tension and subtle struggle for authority within the judiciary. The Constitutional Court strove to establish itself as a professional court, earn respect in the legal community, and vied with the Supreme Court of Appeal for authority over "the real law." Criticized at the time of appointment as an ANC bench, it sought to establish itself as politically impartial. While keeping with the ideological vision laid down in the constitution and generally endorsing the ANC's political project of social transformation, the judiciary handed down significant decisions against the government in the early years. Most notably, they refused to certify the first version of the 1996 "Final" constitution. President Mandela publicly acknowledged the judiciary's authority to rule against the government (Gloppen 2001: 247).

Thabo Mbeki's presidency (1999–2008) brought a more contentious relationship between the government and the judiciary and also a politicization of the courts. Shrinking space for contestation of government policy and fewer checks on malpractice in the parliamentary arena— and within the ANC itself—fuelled legal strategies. This resulted in several rulings against the government in politically important cases (including *Grootboom* on the right to housing and *Treatment Action Campaign,* challenging the government's HIV/AIDS policy), but also more politically cautious rulings (as in the classic accountability case on *floor-crossing*). The government's stated intention of transforming the judiciary, aligning it more closely with the government's political project, has influenced appointments to the bench. A series of "Justice Bills" proposing structural changes to the judicial system, perceived to limit the independence and autonomy of the judiciary, triggered heated public debates on judicial independence, which led the government to reconsider the legislation (Gordon and Bruce, 2007). However, in the aftermath of the April 2009 elections that brought Jacob Zuma to the presidency, these initiatives have reemerged, causing renewed concern for the independence of the judiciary. Adding to this are growing tensions within the judiciary and the process of replacing four of the eleven judges of the Constitutional Court, including the chief justice (Alcock 2009a, 2009b, 2009c).

Tanzania

Tanzania adopted a multiparty system in 1992, paving the way for country-wide elections in October 1995, an important step in a gradual process of constitutional change. The constitution had already been amended in 1985 to include a Bill of Rights, and President Nyerere, who had led the country since independence, voluntarily stepped down to facilitate elections on the mainland (Kituo Cha Katiba).

But while elections in principle became competitive, political contestation has remained very limited. Power has been handed over exclusively within the governing party (Chama Cha Mapinduzi, CCM), whose presidential candidates have won with very comfortable margins.[12] Unlike in Zambia, Malawi, and Uganda, Tanzanian presidents have made no attempt to extend their term in office.

During the one-party state, the judiciary was characterized as "independent from the executive and excluded from important areas of public policy" (Pfeiffer 1978: 56). It was marginalized through restrictions in the constitutional framework and failure by the government to underpin its policies with legislation—but also by the ideological orientation of the political and judicial leadership. The adoption of the Bill of Rights in 1988 ushered in a period of activism on the part of some High Court judges. However, this came to an end with the *Basic Rights and Duties Enforcement Act* (1994), which required cases involving constitutional rights to be heard by a constitutional panel (Ellet 2008). Generally, the Tanzanian judiciary has been reluctant to tread onto politically contested terrain (Peter and Kijo-Bisimba, 2007). There are few spectacular rulings against the government in the post-1995 era, but there are also few "high-politics" cases brought before the courts. While individuals within the opposition and in civil society bring cases to court, broad legal mobilization around politically significant cases does not occur. In cases in which the political stakes are lower, it is not unusual for the state to lose. The trend seems to indicate increased judicial independence and assertiveness despite some exceptions (Peter and Kijo-Bisimba, 2007).

What some observers characterize as an unduly deferential attitude among the judges is attributed mainly to the legal culture. Few suspected the existence of direct political pressure or corruption in individual cases in the higher courts (on the mainland)—unlike in the lower courts, where corruption is considered rampant.[13] Tanzanian judges claim that, at least under the multiparty system, they are free to decide matters on professional grounds.[14] But they acknowledge that political influence is a problem in the lower judiciary and the existence of "psychological constraints and fears ... The mental process of adjusting to the multiparty conditions is still ongoing" (Gloppen 2004: 115).

Uganda

Uganda shares with Tanzania the experience of a one-party/"no-party" system gradually opening for political competition and multiparty elections, but stopping short of a fully democratic system of free and fair competition. Furthermore, despite a considerably more vital opposition, the incumbent party has retained its dominant position and control over the levers of political power.

Unlike Tanzania, Uganda has experienced radical shifts in legal–political relations. Since colonial rule, periods of significant judicial activism and overt, even violent conflicts with the executive branch, have alternated with political deference. The historically more active role of the Ugandan judiciary can be understood in the context of the country's quasifederal structure, competing centers of political authority, and separate agreements between the colonial government and the various kingdoms (Pfeiffer 1978).

After the National Resistance Movement came to power in Uganda in 1986, it initiated a widely consultative constitution-making process (Moehler 2006; Odoki 2005). The 1995 Constitution restructured the judiciary, established it as an independent branch of government, and opened for a more active political role by granting the courts powers of judicial review, giving prominence to the protection and enforcement of fundamental rights and freedoms, and establishing a Constitutional Court to interpret the constitution.

Still, for quite some time, the courts continued to exercise judicial restraint. Over time, more assertive constitutional interpretations have been forthcoming, which, in turn, has made the courts more attractive as an arena for the political opposition to contest legislation and executive actions. The number of politically important cases increased at the time of the transition to a multiparty system, which took hold in 2003 and culminated with the February 2006 elections. Important judgments enforced constitutional rules regarding referenda, opened space for political parties to organize, and protected the freedom of the press, the independence of the electoral commission, and also the jurisdiction of the civil courts. This has, in turn, given the political opposition more hope and faith in the judiciary, perceived as an arena in which to challenge the government. However, decisions in which the courts assert a robust accountability function vis-à-vis the executive continue to coexist with politically deferential decisions and an active use of the courts by the Ugandan government to repress opposition (Ellet 2008; Gloppen, Kasimibazi, and Kimbandama, 2008).

The growing number of political cases has involved the courts in political struggles. An ongoing battle over the loyalty of the judiciary is visible in the recent pattern of split decisions on the Constitutional Court and Supreme Court, where judges who seek to hold the government to account for unconstitutional action lose out to the majority of more deferential judges.

Institutional Structure: Judicial Powers and Independence

The accountability functions of courts are assumed to depend in part on an institutional structure that insulates the judiciary from other political actors.[15] The constitutions under scrutiny all secure the independence of the judiciary in formal terms (Tanzania only since 2000) and have broadly similar institutional structures to safeguard judicial powers and independence.

Yet, differences exist, as illustrated by the following discussion of the aspects of the institutional structure that is assumed to matter for judiciaries' accountability functions.

Structure of the Court System

Which courts are most relevant in assessing accountability performance across countries depends on the court structure as well as the type(s) of cases carrying most political significance in each context—in Africa, often cases concerning political succession/elections. Differences in court structures may also influence judicial independence and accountability performance.

South Africa's higher judiciary consists of the High Court, the Court of Appeal, which is the highest authority in nonconstitutional matters, and the Constitutional Court (SACC), on which we focus here. The SAAC was established in 1994 as the highest authority on constitutional matters, and since 2001, it is the apex court, with the president of the court serving as the chief justice.[16] Courts at all levels can hear constitutional cases, and the Constitutional Court may hear appeals from any court as well as direct applications, but in practice, these are rarely allowed (Dugard 2006). This decentralized model means that litigants go through three levels before (maybe) reaching the Constitutional Court. While the right to appeal provides security for litigants, it also raises the barriers as costs and time increase.

Uganda has three tiers of higher courts: the High Court, the Court of Appeal, and the Supreme Court. A Constitutional Court was established in 1995, but this is not an apex court. It hears constitutional cases as a court of first instance and consists of a panel of five judges drawn from the Court of Appeal (rotating basis, varying in composition from case to case). Judgments can be appealed to the Supreme Court, our main focus. The Supreme Court is also the court of first and last instance for hearing presidential election petitions.

In Malawi, Tanzania, and Zambia, the higher judiciary consists of the High Court and the Supreme Court of Appeal.[17] Tanzania and Malawi have constitutional panels consisting of High Court judges (on a rotating basis).[18] In Malawi, panels are required to hear cases involving constitutional *interpretation*, whereas in Tanzania, panels are also required for cases involving the *application* of constitutional, human, and civil rights. As in Uganda, these "Constitutional Courts" are courts of first instance in constitutional matters with the possibility of an appeal to the Supreme Court. The most relevant comparison here is thus between the South African Constitutional Court and the other countries' Supreme Courts rather than their Constitutional Courts or panels.

Still, constitutional panels are significant in this context. They may strengthen judiciaries' accountability functions by rendering individual judges less vulnerable to political repercussions and by providing the opportunity for a more thorough treatment of constitutional cases before they go to a Supreme Court of general jurisdiction—while avoiding the drain on financial resources and legal expertise that a separate constitutional court would entail. This is of central importance in small judiciaries with limited resources. Panels may, however, also adversely affect the judiciary's accountability performance. In Tanzania, the introduction of the panel procedure witnessed a sharp decline in cases involving constitutional, human, and civil rights.[19] Partly, this is due to delays and increased costs (most High Court divisions only have one or two judges). The chief justice also gained increased control and was able to avoid judges with a record for activism, or team them with more conservative colleagues.

Neither of these countries have simple or court-aided direct application procedures of the kind we find in Latin American countries like Colombia and Costa Rica. All countries in practice operate a two-tier system (or more) for constitutional decisions, raising barriers and causing delays. Several of the countries do, however, have time limits or a fast track for urgent political cases and/or election disputes, which appear important for the accountability functions of courts.

Scope and Protection of Jurisdiction and Review Powers

The powers of courts depend on the constitution, law, and custom—and their interpretation. All the constitutions scrutinized here include a Bill of Rights and provide the judiciary with powers to review legislation, and executive and administrative actions for constitutionality. The courts also have substantial review powers under administrative law. Still, there are differences. On paper, South Africa's judiciary has the strongest review powers with the broad range of justiciable constitutional rights, including the "right to just administrative action."[20] The other countries also recognize comprehensive lists of socioeconomic rights in their constitutions, but as "fundamental principles of state policy" rather than justiciable rights.

As important as formal jurisdiction and powers is their protection against infringement. Uganda faces the problem of military courts, eroding the jurisdiction of the civil courts,[21] while Malawi's Constitution most explicitly protects against erosion of the courts' review powers and jurisdiction.[22] In all the countries, limitation clauses reduce the application of the rights. Tanzania and Zambia have extensive clawback and ouster clauses, limiting the courts' jurisdiction and review powers. Most significantly, in Tanzania, parts of the Election Act of 1984 are shielded from review. Once someone is declared president, it is "final and conclusive." Presidential petitions that are common in the region (Zambia, Malawi, and Uganda) are thus not admissible. In contrast to South Africa, the constitutionality of ouster clauses has not been challenged in Tanzania.

Appointment Procedures

Limitations in executive power over appointments (through legislative confirmation and/or an "apolitical" vetting and nomination process) are, together with security of tenure, considered crucial to judicial independence. In all these cases, the president appoints judges, but parliamentary approval is required in Uganda and Zambia and for the chief justice in Malawi. Everywhere, judicial service commissions (JSC) are involved in the nomination and vetting of candidates, but the JSCs' composition and mode of operation vary, as does the status of their recommendations. Importantly, this extends to the criteria for judgeship that determine the pool of eligible candidates. For most of the courts discussed here, requirements include a law degree and ten years of legal practice on the bench or the bar. Tanzania stands out, demanding only five years of practice, while, in Uganda, appointment to the Supreme Court requires 15 years of practice and an appointment as chief justice requires 20 years of practice. No law degree or legal practice is required to be a judge on the South African Constitutional Court, but four of the 11 justices must be appointed from among sitting judges, thereby securing legal qualifications on the bench.[23]

Ugandan judges are appointed by the president on the advice of the JSC and are subject to approval by parliament. This is, in theory, a strong check on the executive's appointing authority. However, given the president's control over parliament, approval becomes a formality. Restraints on presidential discretion thus hinges on the nomination process. The JSC is composed of legal professionals and lay people, the majority of whom are nominated and appointed by the president, subject to parliamentary approval. The president enjoys full discretion in choosing among the judicial nominees, and, according to JSC staff, also influences who is nominated.[24] The president has delayed the appointment of new commissioners, leaving the JSC dysfunctional for considerable periods of time, which, in turn, has led to vacancies on the bench. Most notably, in 2005, a lack of quorum on the Supreme Court rendered it unable to hear the appeal in a case brought by the political opposition challenging the July 2005 referendum (the *Okello-Okello* case, discussed later). A new justice was only appointed after the case was moot. The main barrier against court-packing in Uganda is arguably the long period of legal practice needed for judicial appointments, particularly to the highest positions.[25] This reduces the pool of candidates and secures that all are socialized into the legal culture and professional norms. Still, observers claim that more judges loyal to the government have been appointed in recent years—in line with President Museveni's stated intention to appoint "cadres to the bench."

Zambia resembles Uganda in that the president's appointment of the chief justice, Supreme, and High Court judges must be approved by a parliamentary majority. Again, though, the parliamentary approval process has been a mere formality. The JSC nominates the High Court judges, and while the president generally follows the commission's recommendation, no formal obligation exists to do so.

In Malawi, the president appoints the chief justice subject to confirmation by a two-thirds majority in parliament. Until recently, appointments have followed a natural cycle of retirement rather than a political cycle and have been in accordance with seniority, with nominees receiving broad support. Former Chief Justice Unyolo received a unanimous vote in parliament when he was appointed in 2005. In 2007, shortly before his term ended, he retired, citing unnecessary political interference. The president chose an alleged political ally, Lovemore Munlo, brought in from outside the judiciary as his replacement (Kufa 2007; VonDoepp 2009). The appointment came only days after a landmark Supreme Court judgment (Section 65), and the president reportedly motivated the selection by the need to "clean up and bring sanity to the Judicial Service" (Kufa 2007). Met with criticism from civil society and refusal by the opposition party leaders to confirm the appointment, the president backtracked and appointed an acting chief justice in accordance with seniority.[26] However, in May 2008, Munlo was approved as chief justice by parliament while it was sitting without a duly constituted quorum due to an opposition boycott (Jamali 2008). Other Malawian judges are appointed by the president "on the recommendation of the JSC," but since the list of nominees is not public, it is difficult to know what weight the president attaches to the commission's recommendations. Again, the president has a strong hand in the composition of the nominating body.[27] The president's potential control is (as elsewhere) strengthened by the absence of fixed terms for the commissioners, opening the possibility of replacing members if the commission proves "uncooperative."[28]

The South African president enjoys considerable discretion in judicial appointments and appoints the chief justice and the deputy chief justice (head of the Court of Appeal) "after consulting the JSC and the leaders of parties represented in the National Assembly" (§174). For other judicial positions, the choice is restricted to the—public—list of nominees prepared by the JSC after a process of open interviews (the president may require a supplementary list, but must provide reasons). The president and the ruling party also strongly influence the composition of the JSC, which comprises legal professionals and a majority of politicians.[29]

The Tanzanian president is most unencumbered, appointing the chief justice with full discretion, and Appeal Court judges (and until recently High Court judges) on the advice of the chief justice, and parliamentary confirmation is not required. High Court judges are appointed on the advice of the JSC, but unlike in South Africa, this is not an open process, and the status of the nominations is not formalized. This detracts from its accountability function, as do the more lenient criteria for judicial appointment that require only five years of practice.[30]

Malawi and South Africa advertise judicial positions, and qualified candidates apply. In Tanzania, Uganda, and Zambia, lack of transparency, regarding the initial stage of the nomination process, is a major concern. Particularly with a regime-loyal JSC, potentially bothersome candidates might not even be considered. Few, even within the judiciary, seem to have a clear understanding of the selection criteria and the practice followed and how seniority and merit is balanced against other factors such as gender, region, or loyalty.

Generally, a limited pool of candidates restrains the presidents' ability to appoint politically loyal judges. Not only is the number of lawyers with sufficient experience to meet the requirements for judgeship limited, many are also (often for economic reasons) reluctant to put themselves forward for nomination. Even in South Africa, where the pool of potential candidates is larger, appointment of good black lawyers to the bench is hampered by the lucrative conditions offered to them by the private sector. VonDoepp (2009) also illustrates for Zambia and Malawi that there are limits on government abilities to identify and insure the loyalties of those appointed to the bench. Acting judgeships are, however, common, presenting a concern from an accountability perspective. The president's choice is largely unrestrained in appointing acting judges, who also have limited protection for tenure. A widespread practice of acting judgeships serves to test prospective candidates for judicial office not only for their skill, but also potentially for their political loyalty.

To sum up, political appointments have been cited as a manifest problem in Uganda and Zambia and increasingly in Malawi. Complaints in South Africa are less about bias in those who are selected than about political considerations barring superior candidates. In Tanzania, the involvement of the president is primarily considered a problem for public confidence in the judges' independence. Few complaints concern the actual judicial appointments.

Tenure, Conditions of Service, and Financial Autonomy

In all five countries, judges are appointed for life, except for the South African Constitutional Court, where they are appointed for 12 years term. The retirement age for judges is in most cases 65 years (70 or 75 years in some of the superior courts), after which they can be asked to stay on as contract judges. Due to relatively poor pensions, judges usually depend on continued work, often with the government, and there are concerns that this may impact on their independence in the years prior to retirement. Otherwise, security for tenure is generally seen as adequate. In practice, judges have remained in office with changing administrations and through the transitions, although in Zambia and Uganda, more or less forced resignations have allowed presidents to appoint a new chief justice shortly after taking office. Impeachment of judges for (perceived) political reasons is rare. Malawi provides the only clear example when parliament voted in 2001 to impeach three judges (see Gloppen and Kanyongolo, 2006a, 2006b; International Commission of Jurists 2002; VonDoepp 2009).

In Malawi, impeachment requires both that parliament petitions the president to remove the judge, and that the JSC—after investigating the complaint—finds that the specified grounds for removal (gross incompetence or misconduct) exist.[31] Also, in South Africa, the JSC exercises disciplinary powers over judges.[32] Elsewhere, a Commission of Inquiry is appointed consisting of three judges, of which one is normally drawn from another commonwealth jurisdiction. If the committee has concluded that gross misconduct or gross incompetence is present, the president may dismiss the judge (Corder and Van de Vijver, 2006). Some concern regards the president's role in dismissals, particularly in Zambia, but more so transfers: "[A] judge who falls foul of the executive could easily find himself appointed to head an obscure Public Commission..." (Ng'andu and Chanda, 2002).

The executive's influence on the judges' service conditions is also noted as a problem, particularly in Zambia, where large salary increases have been granted at times when the government had very important cases before the court, most importantly when Chiluba's reelection was at stake (VonDoepp 2009).

The level of remuneration is generally a concern. Modest pay is considered to reduce the status of judges, hinder recruitment of good candidates, and make the (lower) judiciary susceptible to corruption. Resource shortages obstruct the efficient running, particularly, of the lower courts. With the partial exception of South Africa, poor infrastructure, and lack of access to legal material and research staff, hamper the speed and quality of judgments.

The budget of all the judiciaries discussed here depends on the Ministry of Justice. Yet, in formal terms, the financial and administrative autonomy of the courts is somewhat better protected in South Africa and Uganda (Corder and Van de Vijver, 2006).[33] The authority of courts to raise their own resources from fees and donor funding has increased over time, improving the resource situation and independence from the government, but draining administrative capacity and possibly leaving the courts more vulnerable to allegations of foreign influence.

Important Judicial Decisions

Here, we examine important decisions in which the five judiciaries have either exercised an accountability function vis-à-vis the executive, or failed to do so. These cases illustrate the potential—as well as the vulnerability and limitations—of African judiciaries in the face of political power. They fall into four categories: decisions regarding the democratic system (the "rules of the game" and protection of political space); decisions regarding political succession, including elections; politically charged criminal cases; and decisions regarding public policy. Some cases fall in several categories. The countries differ with regard to the relative importance of different types of cases, but generally the accountability function of courts is most crucial—and difficult—with regard to *political succession*, with presidential election petitions as an important and challenging subset. This can in part be ascribed to the crucial role of politics as the main vehicle for resource mobilization and social mobility in Africa.

Zambia

The performance of the Zambian judiciary in preventing unconstitutional laws and abuse of power has vacillated. Still, when analyzing High Court decisions in "political cases" between 1992 and 2003, VonDoepp (2006) finds that 46 percent went against the government.[34] His analysis indicates, however, that the stronger the interest of the government in the case, the less likely it is that the courts rule against it. He also finds that the Supreme Court has been significantly less willing to rule against the government than the High Court (VonDoepp 2009). Again, most antigovernment decisions are in unspectacular cases. While our focus is on cases in which the stakes for the government are high and are central to protect the democratic system, the pattern of routine cases nevertheless indicates a useful accountability function.

Democratic "Rules of the Game," Political Space
In Zambia, several significant judgments help to maintain political space. A prominent case protecting the space for public activism is *Christine Mulundika*, in which the Supreme Court struck down a legislation requiring a police permit to hold a public meeting or demonstration because it infringed upon the constitutional freedom of expression and assembly (1995 SCZ 25).

Another aspect of political space regards the freedom of the media. Despite a restrictive legal framework,[35] few court cases against journalists end in convictions. Landmark cases include the High Court's dismissal of a case against three journalists charged with receiving confidential documents in violation of the State Security Act (1996 HP 38). In 2002, while the *Second Presidential Petition* was in court (see later in the chapter), two journalists were charged with contempt of court following an article alleging that President Mwanawasa had increased the salaries of Supreme Court Judges "to soften the judiciary ahead of the Presidential petition hearing" (Amnesty International 2003).[36] The Supreme Court dismissed the application. The protection provided by the courts, and especially the High Court, has contributed toward maintaining a degree of pluralism in the press, at least in the print media, despite repeated harassment of journalists and newspapers. This space for criticism facilitates the existence of a relatively vocal civil society.

Political Succession
Cases concerning political succession have presented the greatest challenge for the Zambian judiciary, particularly the presidential election petitions of 1996 and 2001. Allegations of electoral misconduct also gave rise to large numbers of parliamentary election petitions, predominantly against the ruling party.

In the *First Presidential Petition*,[37] President Chiluba's reelection (1996) was challenged by the opposition. The Supreme Court upheld the election and was widely presumed to have bowed to executive pressure. The case is frequently cited as a failure by the Zambian judiciary to hold the executive to account. In the judgment—delivered almost two years after the election—the court acknowledged irregularities and instances of rigging, but not sufficiently grave and systematic to justify the election's invalidation. The court rejected the opposition's claim that Chiluba failed to satisfy the formal requirement (recently introduced by the government itself in what was perceived as a strategic move to disqualify opponents) that presidential candidates must be Zambian citizens born to parents who are Zambian by birth or descent. The opposition alleged that Chiluba's father was from Zaire and demanded a DNA test to prove this, but the Supreme Court declined. The 1998 Supreme Court decision fuelled the widespread criticism of the judiciary that was seen as bowing to the executive (Gloppen 2004).

But the Zambian courts still demonstrated instances of independence. In early 2001, the judiciary played an important role in defeating President Chiluba's bid to self-servingly amend the constitution to enable him to run for a third presidential term.[38] The opposition also won several of the parliamentary election petitions lodged after the 2001 elections (Ng'andu and Chanda, 2002), although some were later reversed (VanDoepp 2009). But the *Second Presidential Petition,* contesting the integrity of the 2001 presidential elections, became yet another source of criticism for political bias. The ruling party's candidate, Levy Mwanawasa, was elected president with a narrow margin and immediately after the results were announced, and before the new president took office, the opposition sought to have votes recounted. The Supreme Court judge who was to hear the case eventually declined and maintained that it lacked the discretion to delay the inauguration.[39] A full petition, challenging the elections on grounds of vote rigging and corruption, was subsequently lodged. In November 2005, more than three years into Mwanawasa's presidential term, the judgment was handed down. Again, the Supreme Court acknowledged that the ballot was flawed, but found that the irregularities had not affected the final result and upheld the election. The opposition and civil society criticized the material content of the judgment, as well as the time it took to decide, perceived as a strategy of deference by delay.

Prior to the 2006 election, the political opposition, backed by a coalition of civil society groups and churches (the Oasis Forum), had demanded a new constitution—drawn up by an inclusive Constituent Assembly and put to a referendum[40]—to form the basis for the elections. Although the vocal demands, backed by mass demonstrations, were rejected, the opposition decided to participate in the elections. And when Mwanawasa was reelected with 41 percent of the vote, the opposition refrained from challenging the election in court. Election management had improved,[41] but the two failed petitions, and a jurisprudential precedent, placing a tough onus on the petitioners to prove that the scale of misconduct is sufficient to affect the election outcome, had also created disenchantment with the courts. Prominent opposition politician Michael Sata was quoted as saying that "it would be a waste of time to petition the results in the court of law" (Simwanza 2006). However, when a new presidential election was held in 2008, after the death of President Mwanawasa, the opposition went to court to dispute the victory of Rupiah Banda, the ruling party candidate.

In presidential petitions, the courts are up against the powers of the state in an exceptionally stark way, and the Zambian experience points to two factors exacerbating the challenges. Petitions can only be brought after the new president is sworn into office. Hence, they inevitably become a matter of dislodging the incumbent, the consequences of which may seem direr than if the petition is decided before the swearing in (as is the case in Uganda). The absence of time limits (as the court has interpreted it) by which a decision has to be handed down detracts further from the likelihood of a decision nullifying the election. By delaying judgment, the courts may avoid excessive politicization (and may have a particular reason to do so where pay raises seem to occur when the executive has important cases *sub judice*).

Politically Significant Criminal Cases

Criminal cases against government officials, including corruption cases, may indicate a strong accountability function—or they may serve executive interests, particularly when they involve the former administration or intraparty rivals. An assessment of these cases requires in-depth contextual knowledge. President Mwanawasa's time in office witnessed several high profile corruption cases, most notably the prosecution of his predecessor and mentor, Frederic Chiluba.[42] While this is a politically important case, the courts, in convicting a former president, did not fulfill an accountability function vis-à-vis the sitting government, as is sometimes assumed. In contrast, to have the former president charged and convicted may serve the sitting administration well. In some cases, criminal charges are levied on political grounds to weaken political opponents and rivals. In *dismissing* (some) seemingly politically motivated charges against the opposition, such as in the *Chief Inyambo Yeta* treason case,[43] the Zambian courts have performed a significant accountability function.

Malawi

In Malawi, judges perform more active accountability functions and decide more "spectacular" cases against the government than their Zambian counterparts. Between 1994 and 2003, the share of antigovernment decisions was higher (54 percent compared to 46 percent in Zambia), and this appears to be equally high for cases in which the government has a strong interest (VonDoepp 2006, 2009). In Malawi, as in Zambia, accountability is best reflected in cases concerning political succession, "rules of the political game," and preservation of democratic space.

Democratic "Rules of the Game," Political Space

Already during Malawi's political transition, culminating with the 1993 referendum, the courts displayed an emerging willingness to constrain the abuse of power by state institutions and secure a democratic process: The High Court reversed a decision barring members of the army and police from voting,[44] and an order banning specific people from addressing public rallies[45] or performing in secondary schools.[46] These and other decisions enabled broader participation.[47] In the subsequent 1994 multiparty elections, the judiciary enforced the "rules of the game" in relation to nominations, polling, and counting of votes[48] (see Gloppen and Kanyongolo, 2006a; VonDoepp 2009).

Battles over "the rules of the game" are often played out in the context of elections. With reference to the 1999 elections, the Malawian judiciary ruled that presidential candidates were allowed to contest with a vice-presidential candidate from another party;[49] it ordered the Electoral Commission to register prisoners as voters,[50] instructed it to ensure that the elections were free and fair,[51] and ordered the date of polling to be set in accordance with the constitution, despite a provision to the contrary in the Parliamentary and Presidential Elections Act.[52] This enhanced voter participation and promoted constitutionalism.[53] A particularly significant case concerning political space was *Kafumba v. Electoral Commission and Malawi Broadcasting Corporation (MBC)*, in which the High Court ordered the MBC to give balanced coverage of campaign activities of both the ruling party and the opposition.[54] On paper, the judgment was a victory for the opposition, but the MBC continued to defy the principle laid down by the court (Gloppen and Kanyongolo, 2006a).

Regarding the 2004 elections, significant court cases also addressed the rules of the game and political space. Most significant from an accountability perspective was the Supreme Court's ruling ordering a postponement of election day to allow further inspection of the voters' roll.[55] It also underscored the Electoral Commission's obligation to prevent the use of state resources for partisan campaign purposes. Again, one case addressed bias in media coverage.[56] But instead of using the precedent from the 1999 *Kafumba* judgment on biased media coverage (see earlier text), the court dismissed the case on technical grounds (Gloppen and Kanyongolo, 2006a).

After Mutharika was elected president in 2004, the political opposition has increasingly turned to the courts to hold the executive to account in relation to appointments. The courts have blocked appointments, among others for the Electoral Commission and the Malawi Communications Regulatory Authority (MACRA), for breach of procedure (MISA 2007). The latter is important to preserve space for criticism and should be placed in the context of the government's attempt to limit the freedom of the press by requiring private radio stations to obtain permission from MACRA before conducting live broadcasts. This was also blocked by the courts (see CPJ 2007; MISA 2008).

Political Succession

Many of the cases cited earlier relate indirectly to battles over political succession. In Malawi, as elsewhere, these are cases in which the political stakes are the highest and the accountability function of the judiciary most thoroughly tested.

The first major succession case[57] occurred in the 1999 presidential election petition, in which the election result was challenged, alleging irregularities. The term "majority of the votes" was also disputed. The Electoral Commission interpreted this as a plurality of votes cast, while the petitioners held that it meant 50 percent plus one of those entitled to vote. Malawian courts are notable for deciding election cases swiftly, but took almost a year to decide the petition, and the judiciary faced criticism both for the delay and for upholding President Muluzi's reelection. When interviewed, several judges indicated that a decision to unseat the incumbent might have been easier immediately after the election (Gloppen and Kanyongolo, 2006a).

The judiciary was even more deeply involved in the battles over political succession related to the 2004 election. When President Muluzi sought to have the constitution changed to enable him to stand for a third term, the courts were instrumental in preventing him from achieving the required two-thirds parliamentary majority. When seven Muluzi-critical MPs were expelled from their seats for crossing the floor, the High Court issued an injunction against the Speaker and ordered their lawyers to file for judicial review (VonDoepp 2005).[58] A ban imposed on demonstrations related to the third term was found unconstitutional, which kept open space for contestation and added to the political momentum that eventually saw Muluzi bow down.

Reacting to this judicial activism, parliament, as noted earlier, passed a motion to impeach three judges on allegations of incompetence and misbehavior. This resulted in an outcry from civil society and fact-finding missions from international organizations including the International Commission. Donors reacted sharply, with the Danish government withdrawing aid, citing the deterioration of respect for rule of law. Eventually the president pardoned the judges (Gloppen and Kanyongolo, 2006a).

Muluzi concentrated on getting his handpicked successor, Bingu wa Mutharika, elected. The 2004 election process was poorly organized and gave rise to a number of court cases including a presidential petition, which, however, collapsed mainly for political reasons.[59]

Soon after his election, President Mutharika initiated an anticorruption campaign, affecting several prominent members of the previous government, including ex-president Muluzi himself. As a result, he fell out with the UDF, left the party in January 2005, and established his own Democratic

Peoples Party (DPP). When the UDF found itself in opposition despite its electoral victory, it joined forces with other opposition parties and initiated a parliamentary process to impeach the president. However, the High Court and, later, the constitutional panel (Constitutional Court) ordered parliament to stop the proceedings until the courts had tested the procedural rules for the impeachment process—with the slowness of the process working to the president's advantage. Hemorrhaging MPs to the president's new party, the opposition asked the Speaker to enforce Section 65 of the constitution, a "floor-crossing clause" that holds that parliamentary representatives elected on a party ticket will lose their seat if they voluntarily leave and join another party. They held that not only those who had formally resigned, but also MPs who had been elected for another party and who now consistently supported the president, should lose their seats. The president replied by asking for a constitutional review of Article 65, arguing that it violated MPs' freedom of association as secured by the constitution. In the meantime, the parliamentary session ended, and President Mutharika refused to call parliament for a new session for over half a year, by which time he had secured enough support to prevent the impeachment motion from succeeding.

Meanwhile, the floor-crossing (or Section 65) case went through the court system. First, the Constitutional Panel of the High Court, and then, on June 15, 2007, the Supreme Court ruled against the president.[60] This ruling authorized the Speaker of Parliament to declare as vacant the seats of an estimated 80 MPs who had shifted their allegiance from other parties to the DPP. MPs fearing for their seats sought—and obtained—court injunctions barring the Speaker from executing the order. This led to a standoff between the government and the opposition. The latter refused to pass the budget for the 2007–08 fiscal year unless Section 65 was enforced and the defecting MPs removed, while the government side refused to discuss the issue until the budget was passed. Eventually, when public opinion turned against the opposition, which was considered to jeopardize the welfare of the country for personal gain, the opposition gave in and passed the budget. The understanding was that Section 65 would subsequently be enacted, but the president reversed his stance and immediately prorogued parliament for the remaining of the session (Gloppen, Rakner, and Svåsand, 2007). Similar proroguements took place four times the following year, and by the May 19, 2009 elections, the judgment on Section 65 had still not been implemented.

From an accountability perspective, the Section 65 ruling marks both a high and a low point for the Malawi judiciary. Fully aware that their decision would be highly unpopular with the government, the judges sought to prevent an attempt by the president to bolster his position by unconstitutional means. However, while the judgment itself demonstrates the strength of the court and has potentially devastating consequences for the president, the effects were lacking. The process bought the president time, thus working to his advantage. The lengthy court process afforded the president a respite of more than two years. Section 65 also had implications for the judiciary itself as political pressure related to the case led to the early retirement of Chief Justice Unyolo in June 2007 and a more politicized appointment process for the next chief justice.

Politically Significant Criminal Cases

Soon after President Mutharika took office, corruption cases were set in motion against ex-president Muluzi and members of his government. As noted earlier, corruption cases against the previous administration are often politically opportune for the sitting government, in which case the courts do not serve an accountability function, as defined here. Even when its opponents are not convicted, the government may be well served by having cases matters *sub judice* for long periods. Politically motivated corruption charges are not necessarily unsubstantiated. In situations in which corruption is widespread and most politicians have some "dirty laundry," it is a matter of selective prosecution—or, as the Latin American saying implies, "for my friends everything, for my enemies, the law."[61]

Another corruption case that was initiated in 2005 found the sitting minister of education, Yusuf Mwawa, guilty of stealing US$1,360 to fund his wedding party. Despite the small amount of money involved, he lost his ministerial position prior to the conviction as well as his parliamentary seat, and he was denied bail and jailed.[62] Some commentators hailed the case as an indication of Mutharika's commitment to fight corruption, but again, on a closer reading, the case was quite convenient for the president. In the split that occurred in the UDF, Mwawa was considered to side with Muluzi and Vice President Chilumpha.

Vice President Chilumpha remained in the UDF after the split, and Mutharika's attempt to fire him was stopped by a court order. In April 2006, President Mutharika returned with a treason charge against his deputy and placed him under house arrest. Three years and an election later, the case is still not—and is unlikely to be—concluded, as the court case has served its purpose, and Chilumpha no longer represents a political problem for President Mutharika.[63] Again, the judiciary was conducive in putting a problem on hold. While the treason charges were taken up by the judicial system, attempts to remove Chilumpha as vice president and remove his vice-presidential prerogatives were blocked by the courts (Gloppen, Rakner, and Svåsand, 2007; VonDoepp 2009).

South Africa

In a political context in which one party enjoys close to a two-thirds majority in parliament, the need to keep open political space and protect the rules of the game against self-serving changes is particularly important and challenging.

Democratic "Rules of the Game," Political Space

One of the most spectacular decisions handed down by the SACC is the *First Certification Judgment*. The Constitutional Court held that the 1996 Constitution failed to meet the requirements of the 1994 constitutional principles and sent it back to the Constitutional Assembly. This was a victory for the opposition. Their bargaining position was weakened by the elections, which saw the ANC win close to the two-thirds majority in parliament that was required to single-handedly pass the new constitution. The court ratified a slightly modified second draft, and in material terms, the most important gain for the opposition was somewhat stronger federal provisions (Gloppen 2001). But while the changes were limited, the first certification judgment, along with a handful of other early cases, was important to the opposition's trust in the Constitutional Court. Another early case in which the Constitutional Court held the government accountable to "the rules of the game" was a 1996 ruling upholding prisoners' right to vote.[64]

In 2002, the constitution was amended to allow floor-crossing during specific "windows" during the legislative term, subject to a threshold: at least 10 percent of a party's MPs had to cross at the same time in order not to lose their seats.[65] With a two-thirds majority in the 400-member National Assembly, it is more difficult for ANC MPs to cross to other parties (the minimum is 30) than it is for MPs from smaller parties to cross over to the ANC—many of whom can cross on their own. Thus, the opposition reasonably feared that the relaxation would benefit the ANC. Not only would it be more likely to gain representatives, it would also retain the advantages of the antidefection clause, most importantly the disciplining effect vis-à-vis its own representatives.

The Constitutional Court upheld the High Court's decision against the amendment, but only on procedural grounds: It was adopted according to an expired interim provision in the constitution. Thus, while the ruling in part upheld the opposition's challenge, in practice, it set the stage for valid legislation to the same effect. It thus served at best a weak accountability function and potentially weakened the courts' accountability mandate for future cases.

Political Succession and Criminal Cases

Election petitions do not figure prominently in South Africa. This is partly a function of the proportional representation electoral system, which reduces the number of elections, and leaves "the big prize"—the presidential office—to be elected by parliament. In addition, electoral battles are rarely close due to the strong majority of the ruling ANC nationally and in most of the provinces. Still, some court cases relate to succession—or are at least perceived as such by at least one side. Most prominent are the well-publicized criminal cases involving then Vice President Jacob Zuma.[66] Ironically, the cases, which repeatedly threatened to derail Zuma's political future, led to the fall of President Thabo Mbeki, while Zuma emerged victorious in the April 2009 elections.

Zuma's legal battles were eventually discontinued when the prosecuting authority decided to drop the charges shortly before the elections and did not centrally involve the Constitutional Court. Still, the case is interesting as an example of how the South African judiciary exercises its accountability function in relation to top political officials, and how this may entangle them in intraparty political battles with huge political consequences.

In June 2005, Zuma was fired as vice president after being implicated in a corruption case related to an arms deal concluded shortly after 1994. In October 2005, the National Prosecuting Authority (NPA) charged him with corruption, tax evasion, money laundering, and racketeering, but the case failed. In December 2005, he was charged with rape, for which he was acquitted, but emerged politically damaged.[67] Nevertheless, he was elected ANC party president in December 2007 and the party's presidential candidate. This caused a fierce power struggle in the party, with Zuma's supporters viewing the criminal cases as a strategy to marginalize him politically (Harber, de Plessis, and Kupe, 2006; Mabuza 2009).

In December 2007, after court victories secured the gathering and admissibility of critical evidence, Zuma was again charged with racketeering, money laundering, corruption, and fraud.[68] Zuma alleged that his rights were infringed when he was not heard by the prosecuting authority (NPA) before he was charged the second time, and in September 2008, he won an important victory in the High Court.[69] The ruling was not only in Zuma's favor, but it also alleged political motives and meddling by President Mbeki, which led the ANC to force Mbeki's resignation six months prior to the end of his term. The judgment was appealed and in January 2009, the Supreme Court of Appeal pronounced its decision, slamming the judgment of the lower court on all counts. It found no basis for the conclusions regarding political influence. Charges were reinstated, but were later dropped by the NPA on technical grounds.

This case exemplifies how criminal cases often carry political implications. Furthermore, it shows how the courts' ability to avoid being turned into a political instrument of the government is an important aspect of their accountability function. Corruption cases are important from an accountability perspective, not least in contexts in which one party remains in power over an extended period of time. On the other hand, and particularly in situations in which corruption is widespread, it is challenging to distinguish "neutral" investigations from selective prosecution and political witch hunts. Regardless of the final verdict, ostensibly "nonpolitical" criminal cases inflict substantial damage, particularly in a campaign situation, whether in a national election or an intraparty context. The Zuma saga also illustrates how such cases may divide and politicize the judicial institutions themselves. In a related case, Judge President Hlophe of the Cape High Court allegedly sought to unduly influence two Constitutional Court judges to side with Zuma. This, in turn, led to exacerbating conflicts in the legal community and to impeachment proceedings against Hlophe, during which the Judicial Service Commission was accused of racism and bias (Alcock 2009a).

Public Policy
Unlike in the other countries analyzed here, cases regarding public policy initiatives lie at the core of the accountability functions of the South African courts. In the context of a dominant party state and an increasingly centralized ruling party (ANC), the judiciary and the Constitutional Court have been important as an arena in which public policy could be contested.

The *Grootboom* case[70] was the SACC's first major ruling regarding social rights, and stands as a telling example of how a creative court can decide social rights claims within the limits of its powers (Gargarella, Domingo, and Roux, 2006). In this case, a homeless community challenged its local municipality's refusal to provide them with temporary shelter. The Constitutional Court held that the state's failure to make provisions for people in desperate need violated its constitutional obligation to "take reasonable and other measures within its available resources" to fulfill the right to housing and to "devise a comprehensive and coordinated program progressively to realise the right of access to housing."[71] One remarkable aspect of this ruling is that the court ordered the state "...to achieve the progressive realisation of the right...within available resources" (*Grootboom* Section 38) but maintained that in doing so the state could choose between a range of measures.

Grootboom demonstrated that the judicial enforcement of rights was possible and not incompatible with the separation of powers doctrine. According to Cass Sunstein, "... for the first time in the history of the world, a constitutional court has initiated a process that might well succeed in the endeavor of ensuring that protection without placing courts in an unacceptable managerial role" (Sunstein 2001). The judgment was, however, only declaratory. The court did not set time limits or require the government to report back on progress, and implementation has been slow. In 2008, Ms Grootboom, the first claimant in the case, died, still without a house. The judgment has nevertheless been important, serving as a basis for further social rights cases (see, for example, Brand and Heyns, 2005; Gloppen 2005; Liebenberg 2005; Wickeri 2004).

In the *Treatment Action Campaign* case, the Treatment Action Campaign (TAC), a broad AIDS-activist movement, challenged the government's policy on HIV/AIDS.[72] The political stakes were high, as President Mbeki had invested much prestige in the government's antiretroviral stance, an AIDS policy that runs counter to scientific recommendations as well as prevailing positions in South African society, and also within the ANC itself. The TAC's litigation focused on the policy regarding the provision of Nevirapine, a drug proved effective in preventing the transmission of the virus from HIV-positive mothers to their babies at birth. The Constitutional Court ruled against the existing policy of providing medication only at certain trial sites and required a progressive expansion of the policy to cover all pregnant mothers. The government accepted the decision reluctantly and with harsh rhetoric, and implementation has been slow (Heywood 2005; Roux 2004).

According to Roux (2004: 93), the South African Constitutional Court has, through its social rights jurisprudence, "scripted a role for itself as legitimator of the post-apartheid social transformation project." This has allowed the court to build its legitimacy by endorsing the political branches' efforts. At the same time, the court has been able to give meaningful effect to the Bill of Rights, while remaining respectful of the political branches' prerogative to determine public policy (Roux 2004: 93). In sum, the SACC has exercised an important accountability role in several landmark cases, but there are also cases that are weak in this regard, most notably the *floor-crossing* judgment.

Tanzania

As in South Africa, Tanzania is a dominant party state where the ruling party (CCM) is supported by a very comfortable majority of the voters. Elections are less fiercely contested than in Zambia, Uganda, and Malawi, which explains why succession battles figure less prominently in the courts. And while attempts by incumbents to gain a third term have sparked court battles in these countries, the Tanzanian CCM has strong norms regulating intraparty succession, and no incumbents have attempted to obtain a third term. Parts of the Tanzanian Election Act of 1984 are also shielded from review, which precludes on formal grounds the presidential elections petitions that are common elsewhere. This does not, however, mean that cases related to elections do not go to court.

Democratic "Rules of the Game," Political Space

The case most frequently cited to illustrate the independence of the Tanzanian judiciary, characterized by one respondent as "the only important human-rights decision since 1994"—is known as the *5 mill. Shilling judgment*.[73] In this case, the Supreme Court found unconstitutional a law requiring a deposit of Tsh 5 million (then, approximately US$ 5,500) from anybody who wanted to lodge a petition in an election case. This, the court held, would effectively bar people from challenging flawed elections in court and thus violated the constitutional right to equality and access to justice. Parliament was found to have overstepped its constitutional powers in enacting the unconstitutional provision, which the court declared null and void. This caused considerable political conflict. The Speaker of the Bunge went public in a newspaper article strongly hinting that the Appeal Court did not observe the proper separation of powers, and that the judges, rather than parliament, had overstepped their constitutional powers by acting as legislators. A heated public debate followed in which prominent members of the legal community openly defended the court (Gloppen 2004). Of great significance is also the judgment ruling as unconstitutional the procedure for suing the government. Litigants were required to apply for permission from the government to sue them, which could often take two to three years. The court found this to be unconstitutional, and the offending clauses were amended by parliament.[74]

Another significant judgment in which the Tanzanian judiciary asserted its authority vis-à-vis the government was Judge Lugakingira's judgment in the *Mtikila* case (1993), which found unconstitutional the ban on independent candidates and legislation regulating political rallies.[75] Parliament did, however, reintroduce the clauses in a slightly modified form (Gloppen 2004).

The *Pumbun* case concerned the scope of the derogation clauses limiting the application of the basic rights in the constitution (Tanzanian Constitution, Article 30).[76] The Court of Appeal ruled that constitutional derogations or limitations of basic rights must be nonarbitrary and satisfy the principle of proportionality, or in other words, the limitation imposed must not be more than is reasonably necessary to achieve the legitimate object (Chanda 2000).

These politically significant cases, in which Tanzanian courts have ruled contrary to government interests, illustrate manifest judicial independence. In other cases, courts have lost important opportunities to exercise their accountability function and protect and enforce fundamental rights and freedoms. The death penalty is a case in point.[77] The Court of Appeal conceded that the death penalty amounted to torture, inhuman and degrading treatment, and punishment, but decided that it did not violate Article 14 of the Constitution of the United Republic of Tanzania on the right to life as it was saved by Article 30(2), regarding the public interest. A constitutional justification of the death penalty was thus given despite a global stance against this form of punishment (Peter and Kijo-Bisimba, 2007). Also in Tanzania, the High Court has generally been more assertive than the Court of Appeal, which, in several cases, has overturned antigovernment rulings, and also criticized lower court judges for actively exercising their accountability function.[78]

Uganda

Ugandan courts have strengthened their accountability functions significantly ever since the 1995 Constitution allowed a more active political role for the judiciary. Remarkable decisions have occurred, particularly since 2004. However, the government's strategic use of the judicial process to get at political opponents and critics is pronounced, especially in the context of elections.

Democratic "Rules of the Game," Political Space

The 1995 Constitution left some fundamental questions to be decided through referenda, including the future form of government. In 2000, parliament passed legislation approving the referendum, but the Constitutional Court struck it down on procedural grounds.[79] While the case was heard, parliament preemptively enacted another, in effect identical, referendum law.[80] It was passed into law within two hours and was made retrospective. The new law was also challenged, both on procedural grounds and on its retrospective character.[81] However, the petition was not heard until after the June 2000 referendum and was, eventually, dismissed (Gloppen, Kasimbazi, and Kibandama, 2008).

A related case argued that the constitutional provision for a referendum contravened fundamental constitutional rights and freedoms, but here the Constitutional Court held that it lacked jurisdiction to reconcile conflicting provisions in the constitution.[82]

Following the referendum, the Constitutional (Amendment) Act of 2000 was passed to retrospectively legalize the legislation under which the referendum was held. Three years later, in January 2004, the Supreme Court reversed the decision[83] and ruled the Constitutional (Amendment) Act unconstitutional for procedural reasons.[84] Consequently, the opposition challenged the legitimacy of President Museveni's government, which had been formed on the basis of the invalidated legislation. The Constitutional Court ruled unanimously that since the Referendum Act was invalid, so was the referendum, and hence the government was illegal. The government appealed to the Supreme Court, which overturned the Constitutional Court's ruling. Agreeing that the act, which had set up the vote, had been unconstitutional, it nevertheless upheld the referendum result as valid.[85]

The constitution required parliament to pass legislation regulating the activities of political parties, and in 2002, a new Political Parties Organization Act (PPOA) was enacted. Parties were prohibited from holding public meetings and could not open branches below national level or hold more than one national conference a year. The Constitutional Court found these sections incompatible with Article 75 of the constitution, which says that parliament shall have no power to enact a law establishing a one-party state.[86] This allowed political organizations to participate more freely in public life (Gloppen, Kasimbazi, and Kibandama, 2008).

In June 2004, the Ugandan government announced that it would relax restrictions on political party activity and hold a new referendum to decide whether the country should return to multiparty politics. The opposition considered this proposal as delay tactics and claimed that the referendum would be unconstitutional since it posed as a status quo alternative, an unconstitutional, "non-existent system."[87] A majority of the Constitutional Court judges dismissed the *Okello-Okello* application, and the appeal to the Supreme Court could not be heard due to lack of quorum. A retired judge was only replaced after the referendum, when the appeal was moot, despite timely submission of nominees by the JSC.[88] By keeping the Supreme Court nonoperational, the executive effectively denied the opposition justice.

The media constitute an important political space, and Uganda has seen several cases against journalists. In *Charles Onyango Obbo & Andrew Mwenda v. Attorney General,* two leading journalists, who were prosecuted for publication of false news, challenged the constitutionality of Section 50 of the Penal Code, which makes publication of false news a criminal offence.[89] In February 2004, the Supreme Court struck down the legislation as unconstitutional, emphasizing the importance of freedom of speech to the democratic process. This established a high threshold for limiting the freedom of the press, but legal action against journalists continued. In August 2005, Mwenda[90] was again arrested and charged with sedition and "promoting sectarianism," which was punishable by five years in jail. In December 2005, two other journalists were arrested on equally serious charges of inciting sectarianism after criticizing President Museveni.[91] Ugandan journalists are rarely convicted on such charges, but they serve to intimidate and hinder the press from developing their role in supporting democracy (Gloppen, Kasibazi, and Kibandama, 2008).

Another case concerning the rules of the game and political space, where the judiciary's performance is lackluster, is *Brigadier Henry Tumukunde v. Attorney General & The Electoral Commission.*[92] A quota of parliamentary seats is reserved for the army. An army MP, Brigadier Tumukunde, publicly criticized the government's position and was directed by the president to resign his parliamentary seat; he was arrested and charged with subordination in the military court. While incarcerated, he petitioned the court to restrain the Electoral Commission from holding a by-election to fill his seat. A divided Constitutional Court (3-to-2) dismissed the petition using "the political question doctrine," limiting the role of the courts in political processes.[93] Split rulings are increasingly common in political cases, both in the Constitutional Court and in the Supreme Court of Appeal (Ellet 2008; Gloppen, Kasibazi, and Kibandama, 2008).

Political Succession

The presidential elections of 2001 returned President Museveni with a comfortable margin. Kizza Besygie, the main opposition candidate, petitioned the result, alleging widespread electoral malpractice and violence.[94] The Supreme Court, with a 3-to-2 majority, dismissed the petition, holding there was no evidence that the irregularities had substantially affected the election outcome.[95] The same position was taken by the Zambian Supreme Court in Zambia's presidential petitions.

In February 2005, an "Omnibus" constitutional amendment bill was tabled before parliament, seeking to amend a large number of constitutional provisions at once, including lifting the two-term limit for the president. While the bill was still under consideration, a petition emerged challenging its constitutionality.[96] The Constitutional Court, again on a 3-to-2 majority, dismissed the petition because the bill was not yet enacted.

A large number of petitions arose after the 2006 elections, relating to parliamentary and local elections, but the most important was Kizza Besigye's second presidential election petition, filed in the Supreme Court ten days after Museveni's victory was announced.[97] Unlike the other cases discussed here, the Ugandan Constitution sets tight time frames for filing a challenge to the elections (ten days), disposal of the petition by court (30 days), and holding of another election.

President Museveni's margin was narrower than in the previous election, and based on the court's ground for upholding the 2001 election, the opposition sought to demonstrate that this time the *scale* of irregularities was sufficient to affect the outcome. The court agreed that the Electoral Commission had in effect disenfranchised voters by deleting their names from the voters' register or denying them the right to vote; that there were irregularities in the counting and tallying of results; and that bribery, intimidation, violence, multiple voting, and vote stuffing compromised the election in some areas of the country. Yet, a majority of four of the seven judges found that "it was not proved to the satisfaction of the Court, that the failure to comply with the provisions and principles...affected the results of the presidential election in a substantial manner."[98] Hence, the court set a very high threshold for overturning a presidential election (Gloppen, Kasibazi, and Kibandama, 2008).

Politically Significant Criminal Cases

In Uganda, the extent to which criminal cases became part of the 2006 election campaign is noteworthy. These were in particular directed at Kizza Besigye, Museveni's main opponent, and his party (FDC). In the previous presidential campaign (2001), Besigye was charged with "seditious intent." This resurfaced as treason and terrorism charges in the run-up to the February 2006 elections, resulting in Besigye's arrest and frustrating his presidential campaign. He was also charged with rape in a case that proved weak and had clear links to the president.

The arrests of Besigye and his coaccused fall into a pattern of arresting political opponents on "un-bailable" charges such as murder, treason, and terrorism by which they can be kept in pretrial remand for a prolonged period—particularly prior to elections (Gloppen, Kasimbazi, and Kibandama, 2006, 2008). It is thus highly significant that the High Court decided to release Besigye on bail, claiming this to be a constitutional right and overriding legislation classifying treason charges as unbailable for the first six months. The international diplomatic corps closely followed the Besigye case and were represented in the audience. While this may have strengthened the judge's resolve, it did not prevent the government from responding by posting paramilitaries in and around the High Court buildings. To keep Besigye and his coaccused in jail, they were recharged with terrorism in the military court system. The conflict was exacerbated by the open defiance displayed by the Court Martial against judicial authorities. Despite a history of harsh rhetoric after antigovernment rulings,[99] the militant intimidation of the judiciary, reminiscent of the time of Idi Amin, came as a shock. The threats against judicial independence released broad support for the judiciary and unprecedentedly strong reactions from the legal community[100] (Ellet 2008; Gloppen, Kasimbazi, and Kibandama, 2006).

By detaining Besigye, the government attempted to prevent his nomination as presidential candidate, but the Electoral Commission accepted Besigye's nomination *in absentia* while he was still arrested. When this was petitioned, the Constitutional Court upheld the nomination and underscored the independence of the Electoral Commission.[101] Besigye remained incarcerated until six weeks prior to the elections, when he was released on "interim bail." Even then, he was forced to divide his time between court hearings and campaigns, which affected his ability to campaign effectively throughout the country. It also caused a consistent negative portrayal in the news media (Gloppen, Kasimbazi, and Kibandama, 2008).

Overall Evaluation

In all our cases, the superior courts strengthened their accountability functions after new constitutions were enacted in the 1990s.[102] In each country, judges have ruled against the government in politically sensitive cases, but none of the judiciaries has used to the maximum their opportunities to check unconstitutionality, illegality, and abuse of power. Still, marked differences in accountability performance among the countries and over time exist. The cases divide into two distinct patterns:

In South Africa and Tanzania, the performance of the courts after the constitutional transition forms a relatively even trend, although at different levels of assertiveness. The South African Constitutional Court has a consistent accountability performance as it has made several strong decisions, and few cases are widely criticized as displaying undue executive deference. The strongest performance came in its early years. Over time, the court seems more cautious and aware of the risks of politicization. This is reflected in the cases it allows, and a tendency to decide potentially difficult cases on narrow, technical grounds. The Tanzanian Supreme Court generally displays a cautious approach vis-à-vis the government. It exercises an accountability function in few notable cases; however, blatant executive deference is present in only few clear cases (although the Supreme Court in some cases has overruled antigovernment decisions by lower courts).

Courts in Zambia, Malawi, and Uganda display a much more turbulent pattern, at times performing a very strong accountability function, at other times seemingly bowing to executive pressure. The Zambian Supreme Court exercised its strongest accountability function in the first years after the transition. Since the 1996 election, it has demonstrated a vacillating pattern, with some significant decisions alternating with judgments that are widely criticized for political deference. In Malawi, judgments that are strong from an accountability perspective also mix with weak decisions. But overall, the Malawi judiciary occupies a more central role in the political process than in any of the other countries discussed here (save in the last election period in Uganda). Its accountability function has increased in importance over time and is strong in the context of the country's otherwise weak political institutions. Ugandan courts have strengthened their accountability function significantly in the post-1995 period, particularly since 2004. At the same time, the government's strategic use of the judicial process to get at political opponents and critics is pronounced. Attempts from the judiciary to counter this has led to politicization of the judiciary, including appointment of party-loyal judges and a trend of split decisions in politically sensitive cases both in the Constitutional Court and the Supreme Court is apparent. The internal judicial hierarchy is used to restrain individual judges, among other through restrictions on the publishing of dissent.[103]

Uganda illustrates most clearly how a strengthening of the courts' accountability functions has led to confrontation and executive attempts undermine judicial independence. But all our cases have witnessed reactions to the increased political significance of the judiciary. In Tanzania, the panel procedure for constitutional cases was seemingly introduced to curb too independent-minded judges. In Zambia, the executive reacted to adverse rulings by undermining the chief justice through false criminal allegations, before apparently corrupting him. In South Africa, there have been attempts to limit the autonomy of the judiciary; the Judicial Service Commission has been politicized, and the executive has refrained from appointing independent-minded candidates to the bench. In Malawi, the successful use of courts to curb executive interests in 2001 led to impeachment proceedings against three judges. In 2007, the early retirement of Chief Justice Unyolo resulted in protest against political pressure, resulting in an unprecedented politicized process to appoint his successor. The growing prominence of the courts in the political arena is thus also a cause for concern. It reflects a lack of trust in political institutions and increases executive incentives to control the judicial branch (see also VonDoepp 2009; VonDoepp and Ellett, 2008).

Explaining the Accountability Function of Courts

Chapter 2 outlines three types of explanations for court behavior. To what extent can they explain the differences between these judiciaries and within countries over time? How important is the judges' *opportunity situation*—the incentives and constraints they face when deciding whether and how to hold political power to account? And is the opportunity situation determined mainly by (i) differences in the legal-political institutional structure; or (ii) differences in the social and political context? And to what extent do we need to take account of (iii) differences in the nature of the actors (higher court judges)?

Social, Legal, and Political Context

When judicial behavior is explained with reference to the broader social, legal, and political context, two types of arguments emerge: *external* explanations emphasize how social and political structures condition and constrain the operating space open to the courts, while *internal* explanations stress how contextual factors affect judges' incentives to act independently.

External explanations assume that courts are powerless institutions and only exercise an accountability function if the government is willing to accept their authority—and are unlikely to try unless they believe this to be the case. Governments are assumed to bow to judicial authority in social and political context in which this brings a benefit—or where undermining judicial independence carries a cost—that is equal to or greater than the burden of judicial accountability. Fear of losing power in the next election is a key incentive for political power holders to respect the independence and authority of courts (for a discussion and criticism of such "thin strategic models" applied to Africa, see VonDoepp 2009; VonDoepp and Ellett, 2008). This implies that courts have more opportunities to develop accountability functions in contexts of competitive elections. Elections are least competitive in Tanzania and South Africa, most competitive in Malawi and Zambia, and increasingly competitive in Uganda. This predicts well the weak accountability function of the Tanzanian judiciary compared to Malawi, and the increasing significance of the Ugandan courts, but cannot explain the relatively strong performance of the South African Constitutional Court.

Other external factors are more favorable in South Africa, illustrated by *protective constituencies*. For courts to develop accountability functions they need supporters—whether among political parties, the legal community, donors, business, or the general public—to make it opportune for the government to accede to judicial authority (Widner 1999, 2001). Government officials are more likely to submit to judicial authority where there is a *culture of legalism* and respect for the rule of law is central to the legitimacy of the regime. Similarly, where the legal community is strong, or where a strong business community requires a functioning legal system, it is more costly to ignore or overrule the courts (Widner 1999, 2001). As far as the the strength of the legal community and business is concerned, South Africa is unique in the region. The government's backtracking on proposed legal reforms in response to resistance from the legal community and other sectors indicate that such protective constituencies are important. The other countries discussed have weaker legal communities (albeit not insignificant) and generally weaker domestic protective constituencies. The NGO sector and, in Malawi, the churches, have at times served as protective constituencies. Donors and international organizations have also been important, for example when the courts in Malawi and Uganda were placed under pressure, international donors and organizations such as the International Commission of Jurists played a protective role.[104] The presence and strength of protective constituencies for the courts thus seem to carry some explanatory power in the African context.

Another aspect of the external contextual argument regards the *demand-side factors* that drive cases into court (the degree of legalization or judicialization of political issues). Central here is the existence of alternative, effective channels for political mobilization and for holding power holders accountable, such as competitive elections, quasijudicial institutions such as human rights commissions and ombudspersons, or societal accountability mechanisms. Where governments are unresponsive toward significant social and political interests, these are more likely to try to use the courts. This is to some extent the case in all our cases, albeit in different ways. In South Africa, Tanzania, and (partly due to a skewed electoral playing field) in Uganda, one centralized party clearly dominates the electoral channel. In Malawi, political competition is more extensive, but political accountability institutions are largely ineffectual. The courts are also likely to become central to the electoral process itself in the absence of trusted electoral management bodies and political structures.

In Malawi, a weak civil society and political party structures appear to drive political cases to the courts. Court action is easier than collective mobilization in which civil society is weak and provides a mechanism for conflict resolution when party structures and political bodies are incapable. In Uganda, the ability of political and civil society to mobilize remains closely circumscribed, and civil society is closely intertwined with "the Movement" (NRM). This helps explain the importance of courts as an important mobilization arena, but it cannot fully explain why court mobilization is more pronounced in Uganda and Malawi than in Tanzania (also lacking a strong civil society) or Zambia (where previously important trade unions are weakened.) On the other hand, in South Africa, where civil society is much stronger, we still see significant legal mobilization around political issues such as HIV/AIDS, housing and water rights, as well as on the rules of the political game. External explanations for the accountability functions of courts, stemming from differences in the social and political context, hold significant explanatory power, but still are incapable of fully accounting for the observed differences across and within these African countries.

How do these explanations hold up against the experience of our African cases? One factor distinguishing South Africa and Tanzania—where the courts show an even accountability trend (albeit at different levels)—from those cases with a fluctuating pattern is a dominant ruling party and limited electoral competition. In the countries where the accountability performance of courts oscillates, there is more electoral competition.

But other explanations can also account for this pattern and seem to capture better the dynamics at work in countries such as Malawi and Uganda. Competitive election processes increase the demand for the services of the courts and provide more opportunities for the courts to exercise their accountability function. To be called on when democracy is at stake may generate a sense of urgency and compel judges to do what they believe to be normatively right. Interviews indicate such a dynamic, particularly at historical moments when "all eyes" are on the judiciary—often the case at election time, when major court decisions are scrutinized nationally and internationally. This normative urgency better explains the sudden rise in the accountability performance of Ugandan courts before the 2006 elections. Few expected President Museveni to leave, but there was a strong sense that the democratic transition was in danger. Parts of the judiciary also seemed to act out of resentment against being used strategically to get rid of political opponents.[105]

The moral urgency explanation can be coupled with a broadened strategic defection argument. Judges may strategically defect from the government and strengthen their accountability function even when they do not anticipate a political shift if they position themselves for alternative career opportunities, whether in national politics or international organizations. This may effectively trigger a display of independence, particularly when dealing with cases receiving international attention, which appears to be a factor in all the countries.

Countries with a fluctuating accountability pattern witness more overt "battles over the bench" in reaction to adverse judgments (impeachments, criticism, and informal pressure in Malawi; more overt smear campaigns, bribes, and political appointments in Zambia; and in Uganda, everything ranging from harsh rhetoric and a display of physical force on court premises, to political appointments and attempts to undercut the powers and independence of courts though constitutional reform). This seems to polarize the judiciary—timorous souls become more deferent, others are emboldened. In Malawi, the 2001 impeachment incident appeared to strengthen the judiciary and demonstrated their protective constituency. The Ugandan government is less sensitive to external pressure, and donors are unstable as a protective constituency, "strategically defecting" once the elections are over, and the power holders for the next five years have been identified.[106]

In all the "vacillating countries," presidential election petitions provide the most spectacular accountability cases (in Zambia in 1996 and 2001; in Malawi in 1999 and 2004; and in Uganda in 2001 and 2006) and patterns are similar. Despite acknowledging gross irregularities, the courts eventually verify the elections. The reluctance to do so is clearest in Uganda, where both the presidential petition judgments contained severe criticism of the election process and ended with a split decision with the narrowest possible margin. While the Ugandan chief justice smiled when commenting that to nullify a presidential election would be suicidal,[107] to remove a sitting president from office, however justified and formally within their powers, seems in reality to be outside the realistic opportunity structure of these judiciaries.

To see the accountability performance of courts as a function of political space carries significant explanatory power. The concept of protective constituencies, combined with a broadened notion of strategic defection (see later), conveys that for courts to exercise a significant accountability function there must be cracks in the political power structure and counterforces to executive power that make it politically sensible to tolerate judicial authority. This, in turn, raises judges' interest to stand up to the government, or at least provides some confidence that this is not professional suicide. The specific constituencies that fill the protective role vary between countries and over time and extend to a significant political opposition that use the courts, the legal community, and also the national and international civil society, or external donor pressure.

Institutional Design

Explanations of judicial behavior from variations in institutional design take as their point of departure widely shared assumptions about how institutional mechanisms preserve the authority of the judiciary and insulate judges from government interference. A limited role for the executive in the selection and disciplining of judges, and also security of tenure and resources are expected to yield judiciaries that are better positioned to hold executives to account. The probability of a strong judicial accountability function is also assumed to increase with stronger formal powers and broad jurisdiction.

While our analysis finds broadly similar institutional structures in the five African legal systems, the question is whether the differences among them can account for observed variance in court behavior.

Political influence on *appointments* clearly affects the performance of courts, but it is less obvious how this links to formal procedures. Judicial appointments are most open to executive influence in Tanzania and best protected in Uganda and Zambia, where parliamentary approval is required for all judicial positions, and in Malawi, where appointment of a chief justice requires approval by two-thirds of parliament. While the high threshold for appointment of the chief justice in Malawi is consistent with the relative integrity of the institution, the countries where the formal procedures for judicial appointments are strongest (Uganda and Zambia), are where political influence is perceived to be most of a problem. Parliamentary approval is rendered ineffective due to a weak political opposition. The accountability provided by South Africa's more transparent nomination process, with public interviews and lists, may be more effective in dominant-party contexts. But institutional barriers have limited effect if executives have their minds set on "appointing cadres to the bench."

There are few significant *differences with regard to tenure and conditions of service*. Despite the 2001 impeachment incidence in Malawi, protection for tenure is generally considered as adequate. But judges who negotiate conditions with the government represent a potential vulnerability. Ugandan judges have comparatively strong protection for salaries and benefits, whereas in Zambia (and to some extent in Malawi) the salaries and perks of judges have improved significantly while politically important cases have been pending.

Tanzanian courts have the least *financial autonomy* and can most easily be "starved" by the government. As elsewhere, possibilities for direct donor funding reduces dependence on the government (but adds to administrative burdens). The general trend has been toward more administrative autonomy, although legislation going in the opposite direction was proposed in South Africa (Gordon and Bruce, 2007). The South African judiciary—particularly the Constitutional Court—is far better resourced than the other courts analyzed here, which are all to varying degrees hampered by resource constraints.

The court structure varies considerably. South Africa has a separate Constitutional Court at the apex, hearing constitutional cases on appeal from lower courts or the Supreme Court of Appeal (the highest court in nonconstitutional cases). Elsewhere, the Supreme Court is the apex court for both constitutional and other cases. "Constitutional courts" are here panels of High Court judges (in Uganda, of the Court of Appeal) hearing constitutional cases in the first instance. Constitutional courts develop deeper competence in constitutional jurisprudence and an awareness of constitutional principles and values, boding for an enhanced accountability function. However, dealing exclusively with constitutional matters, they are also prone to being more politicized, potentially making them more politically cautious as they look to secure their long-term institutional position.[108] The two African cases with specialized constitutional courts are situated at different ends of the accountability spectrum. While the South African Constitutional Court's performance is characterized by a consistent pattern of careful, well-researched, but often cautious and "politically balanced" judgments—consistent with the assumed structural advantages of a separate court specializing in constitutional jurisprudence—Mozambique's Constitutional Court has not yet developed a significant accountability function. That the SACC—reflecting an apparent trend among constitutional courts—includes legal academics and is broader in terms of background than most supreme courts (and certainly those scrutinized in this chapter) also serves to bolster its skill pool. The SACC is also comparatively privileged in terms of resources, allowing judgments based on better research); hence, it is difficult to determine how important the constitutional court model as such is to explain the accountability function of courts.

Another potentially significant aspect of the legal structure is *the disciplining force of the judicial hierarchy*. Where the accountability performance of courts is low or shows dramatic ruptures (Zambia, Uganda, and, as we shall see, Mozambique), chief justices have been more politicized and are perceived to be closer to the executive. This may affect the accountability functions of courts since lack of trust in the political independence of courts may discourage litigation ("demand-side failure"). Judges may also be more cautious if they believe that the chief justice will punish independent-minded judgments ("supply-side failure"). In Uganda, historically, chief justices have changed with new presidents, contrary to formal norms and sometimes violently. Perceived close links between the chief justice and the executive can partially explain the lapse in time from the passing of the Ugandan Constitution in 1995 to the judiciary's strengthening its accountability functions.

The accountability performance of courts is stronger or more consistent where chief justices are more delinked from party politics, serving until retirement and under several presidents. In Malawi, the norm (recently broken) of appointing the chief justice on a seniority principle may have been conducive to the broad individual variation among Malawian judges and helps explain why the courts have managed to maintain legitimacy in broad sectors of society despite their increasingly central political role, and at times, apparently partisan individual judges (VonDoepp 2006).

Court procedure is another factor. Neither of these courts can initiate cases, and the cases brought before them depend on the courts' legitimacy, as well as court procedure and rules of standing (who can bring what type of cases before which court). Some Latin American countries (Colombia and Costa Rica) have a very low threshold for access, at least for some cases, with courts aiding litigants in preparing arguments (see Chapters 3 and 4; Gargarella, Domingo, and Roux, 2006). This is not true for these African cases. Access to the higher courts is easier in Uganda and South Africa, where public interest litigation is allowed,[109] than in Malawi, where restrictions on standing hampers civil society organizations' ability to litigate. Procedures and cost remains a barrier everywhere. However, once cases are accepted (particularly cases related to elections), Malawian courts are quick and frequently use injunctions to stop government action.

Differences in *jurisdiction and review powers* are also significant. In South Africa, the inclusion of a broad range of social and economic rights as justiciable constitutional rights has given the SACC the widest jurisdiction. This is reflected in its accountability function, which is particularly significant in cases relating to public policy including housing and health. Provisions limiting the application of constitutional rights may also explain some differences. In Tanzania, the courts' jurisdiction is most limited; in particular, the ability to protect the integrity of the electoral channel is hampered by the election law, which limits the courts' jurisdiction in presidential petitions. Ugandan courts face a threat to their jurisdiction from the government's use of military courts for political purposes. In contrast, Malawi and South Africa have constitutional provisions preserving the right of the highest courts to decide what falls under their jurisdiction, thus protecting them against encroachment.

Differences in the institutional structure explain some of the variation in the African judiciaries' accountability function, but cannot systematically explain the observed variation across countries and over time.

Actor-based Explanations

Does it matter who the judges are? A large literature, particularly focusing on the United States explains differences in the accountability functions of courts vis-à-vis the government with differences in the judges' background, or political or ideological orientation. Does this explain the variation—over time or across countries—in African courts' behavior?

Very few statistical analyses of ideological voting patterns among African judges exist, partly due to limited access to systematic data. However, analyzing how judges in Malawi and Zambia vote in political cases, VonDoepp (2006, 2009) finds that variables normally considered important, such as who appointed the judge, or judges' previous record, are not significant.

Identities such as ethnicity, region, and religion are politically significant in many African countries; thus, the question is whether they also affect the judiciary. In Malawi, judges' regional identity appears to exert some influence in the sense that judges from the president's region are more likely to decide for the government (VonDoepp 2006, 2009).

While these are interesting findings, they should be interpreted with caution. The judiciaries in these countries are small in size. With the exception of South Africa, with over 200 judges in the higher judiciary, they number less than 50 judges.[110] This means that personalities take on a special role, and individual judges can make a significant difference to overall performance.[111]

Our cases suggest that judges from academic backgrounds tend to exercise an activist democracy-enhancing accountability function more assertively.[112] Concerning gender, some of the judges who are most consistent in their accountability performance are women.[113] This is notable given their small number; however, some of the female judges are also very supportive of the executive.

Two particularly important factors, given the hierarchical structure of the judiciary, are the chief justice's personality and the degree of politicization of the office. In the context of a new democracy, chief justices have an important role in developing the judicial culture, and in particular the judges' conception of their own role vis-à-vis the executive and the political domain. In Malawi, we have suggested that the appointment of the chief justice according to seniority contributed to depoliticizing the office. But whether a diversity of legal mindsets is tolerated if not encouraged might be as much a reflection of the personality of the chief justice. In Tanzania, with few structural or contextual changes that can account for the gradual (albeit modest) strengthening of judicial independence, the chief justices' growing attention to issues of judicial independence has been noted as a factor encouraging the accountability functions of courts (Gloppen 2004; Widner 1999).

Furthermore, actors' behavior is influenced by the social, legal, and political context discussed in the previous section. Two arguments pertain to the way in which contextual factors influence judges' incentives to act independently (*internal* contextual explanations). First, "strategic defection" (see Chapter 2; Helmke 2002, 2003, 2005) assumes that judges are primarily concerned with their future, individually and as an institution. When the political context becomes uncertain, typically before a competitive election, judges are likely to shift their allegiance away from the sitting regime and perform a stronger accountability function (strategic defection).

The second explanation focuses on judges' normative orientation, and its activation in political contexts creating a sense of urgency, such as a "need to save democracy." This is linked to the legal culture and professional norms within the judiciary, but independent-minded judges who were interviewed also referred to the regional and international professional community of judges (with shared professional norms and where judges' standing among their peers depend on adherence with these) as a source of commitment to judicial independence.

The cases furnish some evidence for this reasoning. Particularly in Uganda but also in Malawi and Zambia, brave judgments from an accountability perspective have been forthcoming in preelection contexts, while the courts seem more cautious after the vote.[114] This supports the strategic defection argument: If it is uncertain who will be in power after the election, judges have an incentive to distance themselves from the "old regime," and conversely, when the winners have been declared, they tend to fall in line.

Conclusion

No single factor can by itself explain the variation in the accountability performance of the five African high courts examined in this chapter. Nor is one set of variables—institutional structure, social and political context, or the nature of the actors—sufficient to account fully for the observed variation over time and across countries.

Nevertheless, certain factors seem to carry particular explanatory force. Helmke's theory of strategic defection appears consistent with the general pattern observed in Malawi and Zambia.[115] In fluid political contexts, the accountability functions of the courts seem to fluctuate with the electoral cycle. Strategic defection also correctly predicts the more stable pattern that we see in the accountability performance of courts in South Africa and Tanzania, where there is little or no likelihood of a change of power in the short or medium term. However, other factors are also needed to explain why the judiciaries sometimes still hold their governments to account. To understand the dynamics at play, it is important to combine the various factors and investigate how, within a particular social and political context, specific aspects of the institutional structure (such as appointment procedures or time limits on presidential petitions) acquire particular significance, or how a particular opportunity situation facilitates the extraordinary influence of individual personalities.

The five countries analyzed here share a common law influence on their legal system. It is difficult to assess the importance of this for their accountability performance beyond the fact that this heritage is part of the judges' expressed identity and reflected in their perception of themselves as part of an international community of judges with whom they share professional norms and values. Whether and how the legal tradition matters is the main question to be explored in the following chapter. How do the courts' accountability functions in Mozambique differ from that of its neighboring common-law countries? Is it less developed, as the literature would predict? And if so, is this a consequence of its colonial, civil law heritage?

CHAPTER 6

Does Legal Tradition Matter? The Emerging Accountability Functions of Mozambican High Courts

Similar to the African cases discussed in the previous chapter, Mozambique's judiciary suffers from a lack of staff, funds, and other resources. Not unlike Uganda, Mozambique has emerged from a context of prolonged civil war preceded by colonial rule, and for a long time, formal court structures simply were not functional. Similar to its neighbors in the north, Mozambique has inherited formal court structures and a large body of legislation from its colonial power. Today, it has a court structure resembling that of Portugal, where three different high courts constitutionally rank as the highest bodies of competence in different judicial areas. However, the Mozambican case differs from the other African countries analyzed in this book on one important dimension: In contrast to their common law systems, Mozambique—a former Portuguese colony—employs a civil law tradition much like Angola, Guinea-Bissau, Cape Verde Islands, and São Tomé and Príncipe Islands.

Consequently, this chapter examines the extent to which the civil law tradition has influenced the accountability function of the three highest courts in Mozambique since the passing of the 1990 Constitution till 2007. The main emphasis lies on the relationship between the three highest courts (the Supreme Court, the Administrative Court, and the Constitutional Council) on the one hand, and the remaining state structures on the other. To assess the accountability functions of the courts, we examine a small number of court cases dealing with electoral matters and alleged corruption. The cases were selected on the basis of panel interviews with core actors in Mozambique's legal system, who rated them as "important accountability cases." Where relevant, we comment on the internal hierarchy of the court system and the relationship with lower courts. We first provide a brief history of the system and a snapshot of the legal–political and social context in which the courts operate. We then outline the institutional structure of the Mozambican judiciary, with a focus on formal powers and independence of the judiciary. Next, we consider the extent to which the courts have exercised any meaningful accountability function by focusing on selected cases. We proceed to analyze why the courts have failed to exercise a stronger accountability function before concluding.

Legal–Political Context

Judicial accountability is a rather novel idea in the Mozambican context. In fact, the idea that the courts constitute one of three autonomous and independent state branches was only launched in 1990. Prior to 1990, courts were considered rather like administrative structures, subservient to the executive. Mozambique may, therefore, be characterized as a "new" or "emerging" state based on the classic notion of separation of state powers, and state institutions are still in a process of formation, development, and institutionalization. As in the rest of the region, the formal state structures exist alongside numerous traditional legal and judicial practices (de Sousa Santos 2006).

The Courts under Portuguese Rule (1890–1975)

Under Portuguese colonial rule from 1890 to 1975, the Portuguese legal system operated as the formal legal system in Mozambique.[1] Belonging to the civil law tradition, this system was based on a mixture of Roman and French laws. Legislation was the primary source of law. Judges were considered interpreters, not makers, of the law, and precedent did not play a significant role. The Portuguese Supreme Court had jurisdiction over the entire Portuguese territory. As was the case in the British colonies, Mozambique constituted one judicial district with a high court. Notably, the Portuguese system functioned principally for the white settlers and their descendants, as well as for a minority of black citizens who were assimilated into Portuguese colonial rule, known as *assimilados*. The ordinary Mozambican, whether Muslim, Christian, or of traditional faith, was left to solve disputes in the informal court system, according to customary law. There was thus one structure with two sets of laws: Portuguese and customary law. In some cases, both kinds of laws could be applied, but chiefs' courts were not recognized by the central state structures (AfriMAP and OSISA, 2006; Blom 2002: 131). The latter part of the colonial period was dominated by the military authoritarian Salazar regime in Portugal (1926–1974), and we find no evidence in the literature that the Portuguese Supreme Court played a role in holding the power holders in Maputo accountable when overstepping their powers.

Postindependence and the Popular Justice Period (1975–1990)

Following the end of colonialism, the attempt to install a Soviet-style one-party state and planned economy led to a gradual destruction of existing court structures. The 1975 Constitution declared a unitary state, where the courts were formally subordinated to the executive. Frelimo (*Frente para a libertacão de Moçambique*) was the only legalized party. To install a "new legal order," Frelimo insisted on destroying existing judicial structures, which it perceived as part of the colonial-capitalist apparatus. Rather than operate with a dual legal system—the formal Portuguese system, on the one hand, and traditional legal authorities on the other—the Frelimo government wanted the same law to apply to all citizens of the country. This marked not only a move away from colonial judicial structures, but also a break with traditional authorities and legal pluralism, which Frelimo regarded as incompatible with access to justice for the majority of the population. So-called "people's courts" (*tribunais populares*) were set up all over the countryside to provide access for as many people as possible (Sachs and Honwana, 1990: chapter 3). The Frelimo experiment with people's courts failed, largely as a result of the bloody civil war. The one-party state under the Frelimo leadership was challenged by the guerrilla opposition, Renamo (*Resistencia Nacional Mocambicana*), during a bitter civil war that according to an estimate of a UN report killed over 900,000 people, over half of whom were children, and led to the internal displacement of approximately 5 million people (Abrahamsson and Nilsson, 1995: 66). Large parts of the countryside were ravaged during the war, which resulted in the destruction of most structures such as hospitals, schools, and other public buildings including the few court buildings that had existed outside the capital. In fact, courts did not operate in large parts of the country during much of this period.

The Modern Courts (1990–2007)

The end of the civil war resulted in the creation of a new constitution, the introduction of multipartyism, market capitalism, and a new judicial system. The 1990 Constitution and the 1992 Organic Law of the Judicial Courts (*Lei Orgânica dos Tribunais Judicias*, Law 10/92) introduced fundamental changes to the Mozambican courts system including a formal accountability function vis-à-vis the two other state branches. The constitution abolished the one-party state and instead introduced multi-partyism that allowed political opposition, separation of powers, a state founded on the rule of law, and guaranteed numerous rights.[2] The new constitution focused on individual rights, but also afforded the president powers much more extensive than in many other African postcolonial states. In contrast, the parliament was granted relatively weak powers. Although the constitution is reputed to strongly advantage the executive, the courts were now considered formally autonomous and independent. Because formal court structures had been lacking or mostly inoperative for so long, the justice system had to be rebuilt almost from scratch. Old structures from the colonial period were once again used including a large body of laws dating back to the nineteenth century. Importantly, Mozambique's new Frelimo government copied the Portuguese system of three parallel high courts (a Supreme Court, an Administrative Court, and a Constitutional Council), albeit in a slightly modified version.

Constitutional revisions in 2004 brought some important substantive as well as structural changes to the courts system. Rather than breaking with the past, the 2004 Constitution "sharpened and clarified a number of provisions related to human rights protection and also recognized some new rights" (AfriMAP and OSISA, 2006). Most importantly, the constitutional revisions introduced the right of popular action (*direito de acção popular*).[3] Furthermore, the constitution imposed a time limit of eight days within which courts must respond to writs of *habeas corpus* (provided for in the 1990 Constitution) and recognized, for the first time, the existence of legal pluralism (*pluralismo judicial*) in Mozambique.[4] In many ways, this latest revision has merged the concerns of the 1975 Constitution with people's access to justice and the importance of legal plurality with the 1990 Constitution's concerns with the rule of law, formal structures, and accountability. As the ensuing analysis shows, this complicated history and a mixture of old and new ideas have presented particular challenges for the court system in Mozambique with respect to its accountability function.

In addition, other organs and institutions that might perform an accountability function are weak or nonexistent: civil society is weak; a Human Rights Commission was only established in December 2008, but is yet to start its work; and the country does not yet have an ombudsperson's office despite the provisions in the 2004 Constitution and the subsequent bill introduced in 2006.[5]

Institutional Structure: Judicial Powers and Independence

The theoretical framework presented in this book posits that several factors determine courts' structural independence, such as the structure of the court system, the scope of jurisdiction and review powers, appointment procedures of judges, the tenure and conditions of service of judges, and the financial and administrative autonomy of the courts. This section applies these factors to the accountability functions of courts in Mozambique.

The Structure of the Formal Court System

The 1990 Constitution set up a three-tiered system of formal courts: at the highest level, the Supreme Court (SC) is the final court of appeal in civil and criminal matters and in other cases expressly provided for by law. The Administrative Court (AC) is at the same level as the Supreme Court but with different jurisdiction. The Constitutional Council (CC) has special jurisdiction on legal questions that arise from or related to the constitution. At the provincial level, 11 provincial courts exist: one for each of the ten provinces plus one for the city of Maputo. At the lowest level, district courts rule, and in theory, one court is in place in the capital of each of the 128 districts. In addition, provisions were made for the establishment of several specialized courts: courts-martial, customs courts, fiscal courts, maritime courts, and labor courts. These structures were maintained after the 2004 constitutional revisions; however, they are only partially operational.[6]

The SC, the AC, and the CC all enjoy formal independence though the actual independence of judges may be compromised in various ways (discussed later). These three higher courts wield substantial administrative power over the lower courts, which may diminish the independence of lower court judges. The three higher courts are responsible for exercising accountability functions in different areas, as defined by the constitution, laws, and the review powers of courts.

Scope of Jurisdiction and Review Powers

Article 212 of the 2004 Constitution states that "It shall be the function of the courts to guarantee and strengthen the rule of law as an instrument of legal stability to guarantee respect for the laws, to safeguard the rights and freedoms of citizens, as well as the juridical interests of other legal entities." This, at the outset, should bode well for *formal* judicial independence and thus for a strong accountability function.

Mozambican laws, in principle, provide for holding the executive and other government officials accountable. There are "a number of criminal and civil sanctions stemming from the Criminal Code and Civil Code that can be applied to members of government. Legislation in the form of statutes applicable to holders of high government office has reinforced the sanctions provided in these codes."[7] The 2004 constitutional revisions strengthened provisions against the president, who had previously enjoyed immunity from both civil and criminal proceedings. Importantly, the revisions also set out the right to compensation and state responsibility for damages caused by violation of fundamental rights, or by illegal acts of state officials during the exercise of their duties.[8]

The AC, situated in Maputo since 1992, is potentially important in matters of accountability and has specialized jurisdiction in three areas: to oversee the legality of administrative acts *(actos administrativos)*,[9] to ensure the enforcement of regulations issued by the public administration, and to oversee state accounts and public expenditure. The AC has constitutional status as "the highest body in the hierarchy of administrative, fiscal and customs courts" and is therefore the ultimate body of appeal in several important legal matters. However, many of the lower court structures, from which decisions will be appealed, are still not in place. As a general rule, cases can be presented to the AC only after all other avenues for redress within the public administration are exhausted. If the court accepts the case and finds the government act in question illegal, the court can declare the act null or nonexistent.[10] Access to the AC was greatly improved with the passing of the Administrative Litigation Law in 2001.[11]

Prior to the 2003 establishment of the CC, its functions were carried out by the SC. According to the 2004 Constitution, the CC has special jurisdiction to "administer justice in matters of a legal-constitutional nature"; to rule on the constitutionality of laws and the legality of "normative acts" of the executive; to settle conflicts arising between sovereign public offices; and to make prior evaluations of the constitutionality of referenda. The CC is also responsible for evaluating electoral complaints and appeals in the last instance.

In the specific area of elections, the 1990 Constitution granted the CC the powers to (i) supervise the electoral process; (ii) verify the legal prerequisites required of candidates for the post of president of the republic; (iii) rule as an appellate body on electoral complaints; and (iv) validate and declare the final results of the electoral process. The decisions of the CC are final and cannot be appealed. The 2004 constitutional revisions limited the CC's powers in electoral matters to "evaluate electoral complaints and appeals in the last instance, and validate and proclaim electoral results, in terms of the law." Since the CC can recommend repeating an election entirely or partially (for instance in some provinces), its potential political impact is large. Note that whereas the CC prior to the 2004 revisions was obliged to publish its decision, no mention was made of this in the constitutional revisions—an obvious drawback with respect to its accountability function.

The 1990 Constitution granted the following bodies the power to request the CC to consider the constitutionality of a law: the president of the republic, the president of the parliament, the prime minister, and the prosecutor general. Access to the court was expanded in the 2004 Constitution to include the National Assembly (with the support of at least one-third of its members), the ombudsperson, and citizens (with the support of a petition with at least 2,000 individual signatures). Despite this expansion, access to the CC in Mozambique remains relatively difficult.[12]

The president of the Republic may also request the CC to undertake a prior evaluation of the constitutionality of legal instruments approved by the National Assembly that have been sent to him for ratification—which is referred to as "abstract review." If the CC declares a law or normative act of the executive unconstitutional or illegal, it will automatically lose its legal force, and thus any legal effect that it may already have produced will not be considered (AfriMAP and OSISA, 2006; Gloor 2005). Formally, then, the CC has extensive powers to check acts issued by the executive. This should, in theory at least, provide the CC with a strong accountability function.

Appointment and Disciplinary Procedures

Similar to many other African countries, elected judges play a central role in the Mozambican justice system. According to law, all judicial courts should include both professional judges with legal training *(juizes professionais)* and elected judges from the local community *(juízes eleitos)*. This is a carry-over from the system of popular justice in place prior to the 1990 Constitution.[13] The appointment, promotion, and dismissal processes for professional judges are established in the Statute of Judges of the Judicial Courts, the Organic Law of the Judicial Courts (Law 10/92), and the 2004 Constitution.

The SC is composed of seven professional judges and 17 elected judges. The president of the republic nominates the SC president and the vice president in consultation with the Supreme Council of Judges (the *Conselho Superior da Magistratura Judicial*, CSMJ), the organ formally in charge of promoting, disciplining, and removing judges.[14] The president of the Republic also nominates the other professional judges of the SC on the recommendation of the CSMJ, which presents a recommendatory list on the basis of the candidates' curricula, which in turn is based on a public tender (AfriMAP and OSISA 2006, 86–87). The list should include judges with at least ten years of experience at the bar or in teaching law. The parliament elects the other judges to the SC.

The CC, which arguably functions more like a political than a judicial body, consists of seven judges. Its structure is peculiar to the Mozambican case. The president of the republic appoints the CC president. The parliament chooses five judges proportionately to the parliamentary seat share of each party. Once six members of the CC are chosen, they meet as a group to choose the seventh member. The AC is divided into three sections (*salas*), each of which has three judges. The president of the republic appoints all the judges on the court, including its president.[15]

In sum, three general points about appointment powers and procedures regarding professional judges are noteworthy: most importantly, the president of the republic enjoys extensive powers to appoint the president and vice president of the SC as well as the other professional judges on the court, the president of the CC, and the president of the AC. Second, the president of the republic may also appoint, exonerate, and dismiss the attorney general and the deputy attorney general of the republic, which are considered parts of the courts system in a civil law system. In short, all the top positions in the highest judicial institutions are controlled by the president. Third, presidential choice is somewhat restricted by a requirement that parliament has to confirm the appointments of most of these top positions.

Tenure and Conditions of Service

Supreme Court judges are appointed for life, which gives them a certain amount of autonomy and independence. The SC president and the vice president, however, are appointed for five years subject to reappointment (renewal without limits), but cannot be removed from office by the president.[16] The mandate of the president of the AC too is for renewable five-year terms.[17] The seven judges on the CC serve five-year, nonrenewable terms. Note also that the presidency of the CCMJ is for five-year renewable terms. The fact that many of the judges in top positions on the three highest courts in the country are not appointed for life may potentially present a problem for their independence—and hence for the accountability function of the three courts.

As far as the conditions of service are concerned, the Mozambican judiciary is understaffed, underbudgeted, and has serious absorption capacity problems. Currently, there are only approximately 190 judges and 160 prosecutors to serve a population of over 20 million.[18] To have an effective justice system, at least 500 judges are needed, according to estimates from the SC.[19] More than 80 percent of the 800 lawyers in the country live in the capital Maputo, meaning that access to legal aid is not meaningful to large parts of the population. Judges are generally lowly paid, especially at the district and provincial levels. It should, however, be noted that the courts in Maputo are the best staffed and best equipped by national standards. The salaries of high court judges have recently been raised to attract the best jurists to these positions. Yet, it is commonly thought that a crucial lack of resources may encourage corruption and impede the independence and hence the accountability functions of courts.

Financial and Administrative Autonomy

There is no provision in the Mozambican Constitution guaranteeing the courts a fixed percentage of the state budget. State allocations to the judiciary have been very small since the early 1990s (estimates range from 1.9–2.3 percent of the state budget), but have somewhat increased recently.[20] Because the judiciary has been notoriously underfunded and understaffed and has been struggling with absorption capacity problems, a wide range of donors have been involved in assisting the judicial sector over a number of years, among them the Danida, the Swedish International Development Agency (SIDA), Portugal, Ireland, the World Bank, United Nations Development Programme (UNDP), and United States Agency for International Development (USAID). The heavy donor involvement potentially has implications for the accountability function of the courts, though we have found no evidence in the literature to support this hypothesis.

The SC has significant autonomy in administrative as well as judicial matters. In terms of budget control, the SC can sign financial agreements with donors without the government's knowledge.[21] The SC also takes part in the discussions of budgets, equipment, and other administrative matters with judges at the provincial level. The practice of provincial judges having to travel to Maputo once a year for briefings and instructions in various court and administrative matters is thought to interfere with internal independence of lower court judges. The SC has control over various reform initiatives, including the physical construction of new court buildings.

It might appear that the SC commands a substantial amount of power and autonomy. Yet, in a context where the entire justice sector suffers from weak capacity and financial transparency at the central as well as the provincial level, it appears that SC judges have become administrators of the judicial system, giving them little time to pass judgments.[22] Consequently, the SC's backlog is reported to be large and growing. Mozambican lawyers estimate civil procedures to take 9 to 11 years to reach a court of first instance and up to 11 years if appealed to the SC, whereas criminal procedures can take between two and five years to reach trial in the courts of first instance, and up to 10 to 20 years on appeal to the SC. In 2005, the SC was able to decide only ten percent of cases awaiting judgment (AfriMAP 2006b). Several interviewees reported that the SC has earned a reputation as "the cemetery of court cases." Partly due to case overload, the SC has not prioritized publishing its judgments.[23] Hence, the judgments are not available to lower court judges, which is detrimental to the development of legal jurisprudence, nor to the public, which diminishes transparency and accountability.

Accountability in Practice

To what extent have Mozambican courts succeed in executing their accountability functions? In other words, to what extent do we find evidence that the courts have managed to hold power holders accountable when they have overstepped their powers?

Similar to the other African countries analyzed in the previous chapter, the timeframe available for assessing the accountability function of courts in Mozambique is relatively short. The contrast between "new democracies" and well-established democracies, such as Chile or Costa Rica, is stark. More importantly, the starting point for the Mozambican analysis resembles a zero-point more so than is true for the other countries since court structures were largely inoperative prior to 1990. Another substantial problem is that the case material available for evaluating the accountability function of courts in Mozambique is thin. A third problem is that expert analyses of court material are rare.[24] The following section illustrates how the courts have executed their accountability function in two main fields, electoral matters and areas of corruption and power abuse.

Electoral Matters

As illustrated in Chapter 5, one area in which the courts may play an important checks-and-balances role relates to elections. Since the adoption of the 1990 Constitution, Mozambique has held three national elections (1994, 1999, and 2004) and two local governmental elections (1998 and 2003), which have been proclaimed relatively free and fair by international election observers. Nonetheless, widespread evidence points the contrary—including in cases where the SC and the CC (after its founding in 2003) have been involved.

The opposition party, Renamo, disputed the presidential as well as the parliamentary elections in 1999 (both of which were a close race between the two parties and their presidential candidates) and petitioned the SC to declare the elections null and void. A month after Renamo lodged a 24-point complaint, the SC unanimously upheld the elections, rejecting all of Renamo's 24 points (Hanlon 2000; Mozambique News Agency 2000; Williams 2004).

Renamo also disputed the outcome of the 2004 national election on the basis that a series of irregularities had allegedly taken place, but did not win support internationally for its demand to have the elections annulled. The final results presented by the Frelimo-dominated National Election Commission (CNE)[25] were validated by the CC. The CC rejected all allegations of fraud stemming from both Renamo and the smaller opposition parties on procedural grounds, arguing that the opposition had failed to respect deadlines for presenting its complaints.[26] However, Hanlon (2005) notes that the CC rejected the protest because "by law, it can only consider complaints which would change the results of the elections" and further that had they been taken seriously, the complaints would indeed have changed the election results (albeit in only one district). Thus, it remains unclear whether or not the CC should have upheld the election results on procedural grounds. The CC could certainly have chosen to be tougher on the CNE, although it criticized it strongly regarding the management of the December 2004 general elections,[27] as it had similarly done for the CNE's management of some aspects of the November 2003 local elections (Mozambique News Agency 2004).

Although the SC and the CC validated the 1999 and 2004 national elections respectively, there is obviously no guarantee that the elections were indeed free and fair. For instance, there were reports of police oppression, use of physical violence, and poll riggings, and personal accounts indicated that opposition members as well as electoral observers were detained and imprisoned during the run-up to the 2004 presidential election.[28] International observers too pointed out extensive irregularities in the 2004 elections, but the election results were not disputed as the Frelimo candidate Armando Emílio Guebuza won a landslide victory over his Renamo opponent, Dhlakama.[29]

In sum, both the SC and the CC have rejected all complaints regarding electoral disputes after 1990. The relatively small number of cases concerning electoral matters actually brought to the court may suggest that the executive and parliament largely comply with the constitution. We have not been made aware of misuse of presidential decrees, for instance—a problem typical of many Latin American countries. Apart from postponing the first municipal elections, eventually held in June 1998, former Frelimo President Nyimpine Joaquim Chissano is not reported of having made attempts at manipulating electoral rules or postponing general elections (in contrast to Angola, for example, where the presidential and general elections first promised for 2003 were only held in 2008). Chissano's resignation at the end of his term in December 2004—admittedly after 18 years in power—in favor of another presidential candidate from the same party, Armando Guebuza, could also be considered a positive anomaly in the African context.[30]

However, the few decisions that the SC and the CC have made concerning electoral matters have always favored the ruling party, Frelimo. It is evident that "irregularities" have taken place. Although the legal and procedural reasons for not accepting the various Renamo complaints appear valid, it has been speculated that the electoral complaints might have been heard more seriously by a less partisan judicial organ. Our tentative conclusion, therefore, is that the SC and the CC have, to some extent, employed their accountability function with respect to elections.

Corruption and the Abuse of Power

Whereas in the years after independence the Mozambican government was renowned for being virtually free from corruption, corruption has become a substantial problem since the privatization process initiated following the passing of the 1990 Constitution (Austral Consultoria e Projectos 2005; USAID 2005). In sub-Saharan Africa, Mozambique is only surpassed by Angola and Zimbabwe in terms of widespread corruption and misuse of public funds (Austral Consultoria e Projectos 2005: 5); Transparency International ranks Mozambique among the ten most corrupt countries in the world (World Bank 2004). Corruption has also infected the judicial sector (USAID 2005). The government's commitment to fighting corruption is reflected in its new strategy for poverty reduction (Parpa II),[31] in its 2002 establishment of an anti-corruption unit within the Office of the Prosecutor-General, in the Council of Ministers' approval of Mozambique's first Anti-Corruption Strategy in April 2006, and by the parliament's unanimous ratification of the anticorruption conventions of the African Union and of the United Nations on April 26, 2006 (Mozambique News Agency 2006b). However, so far the courts appear to have been rather passive in taking power holders to account in matters of corruption.

The AC has taken action in only one important case that directly addresses the issue of accountability. In the 2002 case of *Luís Timóteo Matsinhe v. President of the Supreme Court of Mozambique*, the AC questioned the close institutional links between the CSMJ and the SC. In essence, a judge from a judicial court in Maputo was suspended from his position by the CSMJ, and he took his complaint to the AC, arguing that it would be unconstitutional that his case be heard by the SC as long as the SC chief justice was simultaneously heading the organ, CSMJ, that had issued disciplinary action against him. The AC ruled in favor of the suspended judge, and at the same time criticized the close link between the SC and the CSMJ,[32] thus providing some evidence of its ability and willingness to exercise its accountability function.

Apart from this case, the AC has so far largely restricted itself to present audit reports on the government's financial matters to parliament once a year. According to interviews, the reports included several critical points. Although the media has widely reported on these audits, parliament has apparently not followed up on the criticisms. The AC may take punitive action in cases in which it discovers irregularities, but has so far refrained from using its powers in this manner. We may thus question the extent to which the AC has exercised its accountability function, although the transparency element inherent in such processes should perhaps not be underestimated. Obviously, courts cannot properly enact their accountability function unless their decisions are respected and implemented by other government branches.

Just as the actual performance of the AC apparently varies in different types of cases, so do the opinions on the functioning of the AC. One legal scholar referred to it as "very critical in its reporting," another called its work "transparent" and the "best functioning court in Mozambique."[33] Others have called it a "toothless organ." One legal scholar called it an "anachronism" inherited from the Portuguese and argued that its auditing functions would be better performed by the attorney general's office.[34] In sum, the available evidence does not clearly indicate the extent to which the AC has succeeded in pushing court cases against the government in corruption matters and thus is exercising an accountability function.

The ordinary courts in general and the SC in particular have also been very cautious in handling cases of financial mismanagement or corruption against government officials. Apparently, "no investigations with conclusive findings against high-level officials during their time in office" were conducted (AfriMAP and OSISA, 2006: 68–69). This is supported by long-term research by Mozambican and Portuguese scholars who conclude that "on the one hand, there is an almost total absence in the courts of cases of corrupt practices imputed to citizens who exercise political, economic and social power. On the other hand, in cases of corruption practices by magistrates and state officials who stand trial, the defendants are usually condemned" (Trinidade and Pedroso, 2006). Numerous reports expose instances in which judges have been "encouraged" or even "instructed" by higher court judges to drop a case. Alternatively, judges let the case in question "stall" in the judicial system, never to reach a solution.[35] This seems to fit well with a legal culture characterized by hierarchy, party loyalty, and deference to those higher up in the system.

Compelling evidence on cases when a judge has been instructed or forced to rule in a certain way is not easily available. The following section discusses three cases where courts have been forced—or alternatively have neglected—to press charges against government officials or against individuals who are well connected at the top level of the political system. Although these three cases arguably could be classified as common criminal cases, they also address important aspects of accountability.

One much cited and much debated court case, which contains the ingredients of massive fraud and political murder, is the internationally known *Cardoso case*.[36] The November 2000 murder of a prominent critical Mozambican journalist, Carlos Cardoso, was connected to him being responsible for uncovering a fraud scandal involving two large Mozambican banks in the 1990s. The Maputo City Judicial Court arrested and tried six individuals with murder, all of whom were found guilty and received jail sentences up to over 28 years.[37] One of the men was tried in absentia having escaped three times from a high-security prison in Maputo. The SC ruled that the sentence issued by the Maputo City Judicial Court was not valid because the defendant was not present. A retrial at the SC began in December 2005 and was concluded in February 2007, when the SC upheld the original verdicts.

The main suspect, incriminated by other convicts in the same case of having masterminded the murder of Carlos Cardoso, was the oldest son of then President Chissano, who was not among those originally arrested. Many Mozambicans believe that the judiciary let him go free because he was the president's son. Interestingly, the president dismissed the attorney general as well as the deputy attorney general during the trial process, suspected of deliberately having sabotaged the preparation of the criminal case against the defendants (World Bank 2004). Others, including Cardoso's lawyer, were not convinced that Chissano Jr. was involved at all. After President Chissano's resignation in May 2006, the public prosecutor's office decided to file charges against Chissano Jr., arguing that evidence indicated that he had paid the assassins to kill Cardoso (Mozambique News Agency 2004). Chissano Jr. denied any involvement in the murder and was never arrested before his death in Maputo in November 2007 after a kidney transplant (Mozambique News Agency 2006a).

Despite revelations of massive fraud and corruption in the wake of the investigations, the Cardoso case has been referred to as "a high momentum for the justice sector."[38] Not unlike the trials of the *junta* generals in Argentina after the return to democracy in 1989, or the hearings of the Truth and Reconciliation Commission in South Africa in 1990, the Cardoso case was widely covered by both television and the print media in Mozambique and subject of much public debate. The trial of six people could be considered a triumph for the independence of the judiciary; alternatively the initial failure to prosecute the president's son could be interpreted as a blatant lack of independence of the judiciary (including not only the courts, but also the police, and the prosecution). The prosecutor's office's final decision to charge the former president's son with murder certainly points to the existence of accountability. However, it could also be argued that it was politically too sensitive for the courts to bring charges against the sitting president's son—meaning that the close connections between the judiciary and the executive made it difficult for the courts to exercise their accountability function.

A related case, the so-called *Siba-Siba case*, had a very different outcome. In essence, António Siba-Siba Macuácua, a young economist at the Banco de Moçambique and provisional chairman of the board of the Austral Bank, was murdered in August 2001. The murder was allegedly committed "by people who were opposed to the Austral Bank passing into 'non-manipulable' hands, and who desperately thought that the killing could reverse the re-privatization process" (*People's Daily* 2001). Apparently, Macauácua was killed just before he was due to present a report "which would probably have identified senior political figures who had stolen millions of dollars from the bank" (Hanlon 2001). As part of his task to investigate and uncover corruption at the bank, Macuácua had published a list of 1,200 debtors in the Maputo-based daily paper *Noticias* shortly before he was murdered. The list included key figures in the Frelimo party and part of the president's family. Apparently, investigation of the murder was repeatedly blocked and delayed. In April 2003, the police arrested a member of the elite presidential guard, suspecting him of having taking part in Macuácua's murder. More than five years later, nobody was charged in the case.

The fact that the murder of Macuácua was never investigated with the same fervor as the Cardoso murder may suggest that the media and judicial attention given to the latter was partly due to pressure from his Norwegian wife, Nina Berg, and a number of international journalists. The successful prosecution of several culprits in the Cardoso case may thus be attributed primarily to the fact that the international community—and important donors to the justice sector—were eagerly awaiting a serious investigation and trial. The failure to uncover the Macuácua murder may also suggest that some authorities might be more afraid of court procedures when individuals with connections high up in the political system are implicated.

A third case, known as the *Vilanculos case*,[39] involves the economic interests of ministers and governors. This case deals with property rights and land rights. In brief, in 1994, a company, Cabo do Mar, bought up land in the popular Vilanculos area in the Province of Inhambane on the northern coast of Mozambique to develop it for tourism. The Minister for Co-ordination of Environmental Affairs, in partnership with the Coastal Wildlife Sanctuary of Vilanculos, invaded the plot of land, annexed it to their area of 25,000 ha (almost 62,000 acres) and resold the plot to the owners of Nyati Beach Lodge for $200,000. To justify the annexation of the land, the minister had the governor of the Inhambane Province declare Cabo do Mar's purchase null and void. The Cabo do Mar Company, in protest, took three cases to court, denouncing the unlawful invasion of land and the destruction of property respectively, one with the AC in Maputo and two with the judicial court in Inhambane.

In the first case, the AC, in Judgement 8/04, annulled the order of the governor of the Province of Inhambane. The new governor of Inhambane complied with the court's orders and ordered the land to be handed back to Cabo do Mar. In the second case, Cabo do Mar submitted Action 36/03 to the judicial court in the Inhambane Province, claiming damages for destroyed infrastructures. The court ruled in favor of Cabo do Mar on March 23, 2004 and ordered the plot of land to be handed back to Cabo do Mar. Parallel with Case 36/03, Cabo do Mar also initiated criminal charges against the new buyers of Nyati Beach Lodge for other crimes including the destruction of property. This case was also heard by the judicial court of the Inhambane Province, which ruled in favor of Cabo do Mar. In the meantime, however, the Minister of Agriculture and Rural Development had granted a special license to Nyati Beach Lodge. The Nyati Beach Lodge Company then launched an appeal to the SC—and won. In February 2005, the SC overturned the restitutive effect of the appeal and ordered the plot of land to be handed over to Nyati Beach Lodge.[40] It is important to note that the handing over of the piece of land to Nyati Beach Lodge was undertaken in the month of February, when the courts in Mozambique are not in session.

How can this case be interpreted? It is of course possible that the expropriation of land was carried out according to the law and that the Minister of Coordination of Environmental Affairs was in his right to act as a private person in the buying and reselling of land. However, legal experts in Mozambique have questioned both the decision of the SC and the speed at which the court issued its ruling in this case (normally such a case takes 12 years to reach a solution). It thus might seem suspicious that the court acted so promptly and that it arrived at a conclusion different from both the judicial court of Inhambane and the AC—in favor of high-level political figures (ministers and governors). Consequently, this might be an example of corrupt behavior, although it is impossible to know the details due to the complex process of the judicial chain leading from the presentation of a case to its ruling. We can tentatively conclude that *if* there has been misuse of political power for personal benefits, the SC has failed to keep the power holders accountable. However, evidence to that effect is not conclusive.

Together, these three cases suggest that it is difficult for the SC and AC to take appropriate action in concrete cases involving possible corruption or abuse of powers, especially when central figures in the political system are involved.[41]

A Broader Assessment of the High Courts' Accountability Functions

It is difficult to assess the SC's accountability function due to the lack of available case material, as court rulings are not publicly available. The CC, though active in electoral matters, has not been fully tested in questions of legality yet. The two constitutional cases it has handled so far concern electoral disputes during the 2003 and 2004 elections. Apparently, no cases of enacted legislation have been challenged before the CC (AfriMAP and OSISA, 2006: 34). However, in two cases the president of the republic has referred legislation to the CC for evaluation prior to enactment: the Islamic Holidays Law *(Lei dos Feriados Islâmicos de Idul-Fitre e Idul-Adhah)* in 1996 (AfriMAP 2006b: 34)[42] and the Family Law *(Lei da Família)* in 2004.[43] The CC may have been expected to rule on more issues, given its wide review powers and the fact that a wide range of actors may request a declaration of unconstitutionality from the CC.

The AC, too, appears to have used its wide formal powers to exercise its potential accountability role rather sparingly and carefully. For instance, the second section of the AC, responsible for tax and customs litigation, managed to judge an average of fewer than eight cases per year in the four-year period from 1998–2001 (World Bank 2004: 34). Apparently, it has so far not concluded any cases based on investigation into irregular financial management.[44] Additional cases were pending at the end of 2005, but information on the rulings in these cases is not available at the time of writing.

Explaining the Accountability Function of Mozambique Courts

The 2004 Constitution granting formal power and independence, relatively broad review powers, and relatively broad standing to the courts, provides for a potentially strong accountability function. Interviewees report that the lack of resources is not the reason for why the accountability function of courts has been limited as the available resources would have been sufficient. Why then have the courts in Mozambique not exercised their accountability functions more effectively since the introduction of the new judicial structures in 1990? In line with the theoretical framework of this book, we explore potential explanations from the legal–political context, institutional design, and actor-based explanations.

Social, Legal, and Political Context

Evidently, the legal and political context in which the courts operate may determine the accountability function of judges or courts. One central feature is the strong tradition of a one-party state and the practice of clientelism, dating back to preindependence time. Salazar's authoritarian regime in Portugal exerted considerable influence on its African colonies. The colonizers allied themselves with traditional chiefs, thus securing vertical power structures in all parts of the country (Blom 2002). When the Portuguese government and Frelimo signed the peace agreement in 1975, Frelimo was the only viable political force in the country. Renamo has never seriously threatened the hegemony of the ruling party, with the exception of the 1999 election.[45] Although Frelimo has always fallen short of securing the two-thirds majority in parliament, which would have allowed it to amend the constitution, Mozambique has for all practical purposes remained a strong one-party state throughout the first quarter of a century after independence. Neither a strong and vibrant civil society, nor active accountability institutions have challenged the state.

This strong one-party legacy continues to penetrate the political as well as the judicial system, blurring the division between the two despite formal judicial independence. Frelimo's hegemony has extended well beyond the political arena. The legacy of the one-party state has manifested itself in at least two different ways pertaining to our argument: First, it has had strong implications for the political profile of the people appointed (and elected) to serve in the judicial system, thus creating strong ties between politicians and judges. Second, it has influenced the legal culture, for instance with respect to how judges and politicians think about the way courts should operate.

Most importantly, practically all the people in higher judicial positions (provincial level and above) are reportedly Frelimo supporters, if not party members. Despite the lack of availability of official data, several individuals working both inside as well as outside the legal sector have asserted this fact.[46] This makes the political links between the executive, the parliament, and the judiciary potentially extremely tight. As the intellectual elite is still very small in Mozambique, numerous strong family ties may play a role in political and judicial matters. Doing each other favors is a prominent feature of Mozambican culture, which means that formal rules are not always followed.

Also, the judicial or legal culture is clearly influenced by the existence of a one-party state. Historically, the idea that courts should perform an accountability function has received little support. The weak link to a broader legal tradition may, in part, be explained by the poor integration of Mozambican citizens in the colonial culture and the Portuguese legal tradition. From the end of colonialism until 1990, access to justice for the people was determined as a broader social goal, whereas the checks-and-balance function that courts ideally should have assumed was not an issue at all. Loyalty to the party was the central goal. The courts and the prosecution were formally subordinate to the executive under the 1975 Constitution, thus functioning more like administrative bodies. During this period, the courts typically reported to the executive on the number of cases and the types of cases they handled. Although substantial progress has been made in raising acceptance for the ideas of judicial independence and the rule of law after the 1990 Constitution, some of the old ideas of executive subservience and party loyalty are still reflected in the legal culture.[47] There is, for instance, still an eagerness to please those higher up in the system and to assimilate to the prevailing way of thinking. Judges as well as lawyers report on how new recruits to the courts frequently enter with liberal ideas and specific work ethics, which are rapidly eroded as they conform to the prevailing ways of doing business. This is not encouraging for judicial independence or accountability—neither at the individual nor at the collective level.

Though hard to prove, the civil law tradition has probably not been helpful in promoting the accountability function of the courts. This legal tradition, where cases do not possess the binding authority they have in common law systems and are therefore not considered a source of law, may have encouraged the (mal)practice of not publishing judgments, which, we would argue, has been detrimental to transparency and the exercise of an accountability function.

Institutional Design

The institutional setup of courts reinforces their links with the president. The provisions for structural independence are mixed. On the one hand, the constitution and laws guarantee each of the bodies in the higher levels of the judiciary autonomy and independence. On the other hand, the president of the republic appoints all the top positions in the three high courts. Furthermore, the president of the SC also serves as president of the CSMJ (which nominates the other SC judges appointed by the president of the republic); as head of the Higher Council of the Judicial Magistrature (the collective body responsible for supervising and disciplining the corps of judicial magistrates); and as head of the Coordinating Council for Legality and Justice (CCLJ), which is the judicial sector's main coordinating body (composed of the heads of the Ministry of Justice, the Attorney General's Office, and the AC). This institutional framework provides the president of the republic with direct access to influencing the courts through the SC president. Whether or not this in fact takes place will depend on the two individuals elected/appointed to the two offices at any given time.

Within this institutional construct, where party politics seems to play such a central role, the practice of renewable terms for SC, AC, and CSMJ presidents may further compromise the accountability function of the high courts. We do not have data for all the judgeships and the number of judges whose terms were renewed, but the three-times renewal of the SC president's term appears as potentially problematic. Apparently, Renamo has attempted to change the rule of renewable five-year terms but failed to gain parliamentary approval.

The institutional setup of the high courts and their control organs have wielded undue influence in legal matters to some key individuals. Our analysis suggests that too much power is concentrated in the role of the SC president, who simultaneously serves on several other high judicial organs. This problem is compounded by renewable terms for this office. The current president of the SC, Mario Mangaze, has held the presidency of the SC since it was first established in 1988; prior to this, he had been president of the former Supreme People's Court since 1978. The close relationship between him and former President Chissano is undisputable. Mangaze will continue to complete his fourth term under the president in office, Guebuza. This powerful position has been recognized as problematic by core individuals both within and outside the legal system (USAID 2005). Many think it will be hard to reform the judicial system— including increasing its transparency and enabling the high courts to carry out their accountability function—as long as Mangaze controls this central position.

Actor-based Explanations

To explain the behavior of judges, it is necessary to consider both their values and preferences (according to the attitudinal model) as well as to identify their strategic self-interest, given the incentive structure they face (rational choice approach). No analysis is available on this. However, it seems quite clear that Mozambican high court judges operate in an environment that demands conformity with existing hierarchical rules and dominant judicial practices, rather than innovative thinking and radical application of the law.

The following story may illustrate this point: An SC judge who left the court to set up a training school for judges and other judicial personnel (the CFJJ), known to be liberal in its profile and unanimously praised by donors as well as more progressive voices within the legal sector, was requested by the SC president at the end of his first term to return to his position as an SC judge. He was replaced by a person who enjoys the confidence of the SC president. Many have voiced great concern with the future of the CFJJ and the consequences for the professionalization of Mozambican judges.

Conclusion

The three high courts have exercised an emerging, albeit limited, accountability function since the introduction of the modern court system and the principles of judicial independence and accountability in 1990. The CC appears to have operated conscientiously in electoral matters; the AC upheld a ruling against a high-level politician in the *Vilanculos case*; and corruption and murder charges were brought against the former president's son by the judicial court in Maputo in the wake of the *Cardoso case.*

However, the courts are still not fully able and willing to exercise their accountability function in a fair and an effective manner. Although the civil law tradition is the main feature distinguishing the Mozambican case from the other African cases analyzed in this book, this factor seems to be of only modest explanatory value. Rather, the most important factors impeding the exercise of an effective accountability function seem to be the legacy of one-partyism and a culture of clientelism, reinforced by the institutional framework and the influence of strong individuals within the hierarchy of courts. The structures for a satisfactory performance in the future are partly in place and operational, building on well-known principles of a state based on the rule of law, but it is still unclear whether the existing potential for a more active judiciary will be fully realized.

CHAPTER 7

Conclusion: Multifactor Explanations

This book has addressed the puzzle of why, over the last two decades, some superior courts in less developed, democratic countries have increasingly exercised an accountability function, while others have remained relatively deferential to the popular branches of government. Our examination of the high courts in ten countries on two continents has shown that similar judicial and/or constitutional reforms have produced dissimilar outcomes. At one end of the spectrum are the highly assertive superior courts of Costa Rica and Colombia demonstrating a willingness and ability to hold political power to law in controversial political cases.[1] At the other end, superior courts in Chile, Tanzania, and Mozambique have remained politically deferential. Our ten case studies also reveal that superior courts' exercise of their accountability functions is not constant over time, within countries, across the regions, or in the areas of accountability actions taken by courts. In this concluding chapter, we first discuss the observable patterns that emerge from our cases both within and across regions. We then draw some conclusions to explain the variance in judicial behavior.

Patterns of Superior Court Accountability

Given the qualitative and context-sensitive nature of our analysis, it is not possible to *measure* the accountability functions of courts in a strict sense. Nevertheless, for heuristic purposes, and to facilitate a comparison of the accountability functions of courts over time and across contexts, we have combined the various aspects of the assessment into an impressionistic accountability scale, ranging from a "high accountability function," in which the courts contribute significantly towards the well-functioning of the democratic system, to a "low accountability function," in which their impact is negligible or negative. As with Table 1.1 in Chapter 1, Figure 7.1 maps variation on the dependent variable of our analysis. Figure 7.1 should thus not be taken to imply a formal scale, neither in terms of the individual country graphs nor the distance between them. The idea is merely to visualize the qualitative assessment of the accountability function of the ten courts as a heuristic device. Each graph reflects the descriptions and analyses provided in the corresponding country studies by sketching a simplified pattern of the performance of courts. Time is relative to each country, as the reforms started in the late 1980s in some countries and elsewhere in the mid-1990s, with some reforms in some countries set in motion through abrupt institutional changes, while others were emanating more gradually. With these caveats in mind, Figure 7.1 may facilitate comparison across cases and over time and reveal patterns across regions.

Perhaps the most striking pattern in Figure 7.1 is the divergence between countries where the accountability performance of courts has been relatively stable and those vacillating between the exercise of a strong accountability function vis-à-vis the executive and political deference. The first stable group of countries includes both the highest performing courts (Colombia and Costa Rica) and the lowest performing courts (Mozambique, Tanzania, and

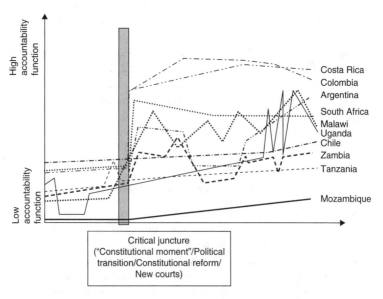

Figure 7.1 Fluctuations in courts' accountability functions

Chile) with South Africa in-between. The second, unstable group includes Argentina, Malawi, Zambia, and Uganda. In most of the countries, the critical juncture that serves as the starting point for the analysis corresponds with a significant rise in the accountability functions of courts.[2] However, in some countries, this is not the case (Chile, Tanzania, and Mozambique) or it manifests itself only after several years (Uganda). This raises interesting questions about causes of judicial assertiveness, to which we will return.

None of the ten countries had highly active courts prior to the reforms, but the level and pattern of activity differed. In Malawi, for example, the courts started to play a more significant role prior to the constitutional reforms and were themselves a force in the political transition. In Uganda and Tanzania, on the other hand, where courts had previously exercised an occasional accountability function, the constitutional reforms brought no immediate increase in court accountability function. In some countries, the introduction of new constitutional courts or panels is associated with a sharp rise in accountability function (Colombia, Costa Rica, and South Africa) while elsewhere extant superior courts have taken on a stronger political role (Argentina, Malawi, and Zambia).

Equally striking is how some expected patterns have not emerged including the lack of clear differences between courts operating in different legal traditions. Courts in civil law countries include the highest performers to the lowest, while courts in common law countries are found in the middle to low range. This is contrary to the expectations in the literature concerning the deferential influence of the civil law tradition. Similarly, there is no clear pattern between courts exercising strong accountability functions and the level of economic development. Stronger and weaker courts exist in all the regions and are as likely to be found in poorer as in richer countries.

Concerning differences at the regional level, Latin American superior courts vary widely in their behavior. As detailed in Chapters 3 and 4, these courts exercised little or no accountability function and exhibited high levels of deference toward popular branches of government before the judicial and constitutional reforms starting in the late 1980s. The four Latin American countries examined here share common colonial and independence histories, civil law legal traditions, and relatively similar constitutions. Yet, their superior courts have, in the last 30 years, exercised their accountability functions in very dissimilar manners. The Chilean Supreme Court remains manifestly passive and is still one of the most deferential courts in Latin America. On the other hand, the Colombian and Costa Rican Constitutional Courts have become world-renowned for the exercise of their accountability function. Finally, the Argentine Supreme Court's accountability record is mixed—weak in some periods and strong in others. More recently, the court has been increasingly willing and able to hold other branches of government to account. Why court behavior in these four countries varies so dramatically demands an explanation.

Our six African countries present a similar puzzle. All the countries experienced extended periods of authoritarian rule with strong executives and with their democratic transitions of the 1990s; they all promulgated constitutions vesting their judiciaries with stronger powers and broader jurisdictions. Yet, these six superior courts responded differently to the new legal and political context with variation in the overall level of account-ability, the degree of consistency, and the trend of judicial development. In Mozambique and Tanzania, for example, the judiciary has remained largely deferential to the other branches of government, while their counterparts in Malawi, South Africa, Zambia, and Uganda have all issued some bold accountability decisions. The greatest fluctuations and inconsistencies are found in the behavior of courts in Malawi and Uganda, which combine some remarkably strong judgments with deferential ones. While fluctuations between strong and weak decisions have marked the entire post–Banda era in Malawi, in Uganda strong decisions holding the government to account in politically sensitive cases only started to emerge five years after the new constitution gave the judiciary increased independence and powers. South Africa's Constitutional Court, established after the transition from apart-heid rule, started out with several strong accountability decisions, but has since stagnated. Also, the Zambian Supreme Court produced some remark-able decisions in the immediate post-transition period, but then experienced a downward trend, which now appears to have been reversed. Thus, as in Latin America, the manner in which superior courts in African countries responded to the new political and legal context varies significantly across countries and within countries over time. The remainder of this chapter draws conclusions from the ten countries to explain these variations.

Explaining Patterns of the Accountability Function of Higher Courts

In accordance with the theoretical framework developed in Chapter 2 (Table 2.1), our ten cases have been examined through three distinct, but interrelated lenses: *the social and political context* in which the courts operate (legal–political culture and history, political balance of power, civil society strength, and litigiousness); *institutional design* (judicial institutional struc-tures, legal basis for court decisions, powers and competences, appointments and tenure, protection of the judiciary's political and financial independence, and access to the court); and *actors-based explanations* (ideological, social, and professional characteristics of judges, collectively and individually).

Each of these represents approaches employed in the literature to account for patterns of judicial accountability, and in the previous chapters we have examined their significance in explaining the patterns revealed through our country cases and regional comparisons.

The findings suggest that no single overarching, parsimonious theory is able to account for the exercise of the accountability function of superior courts across our cases. Existing theories offer compelling explanations for increased levels of accountability exercised by high courts for specific countries at given points in time, but they tend not to travel well across time within a country, or across countries or geographic regions. Rather, understanding superior courts' exercise of accountability functions requires an in-depth understanding of the local political and legal context and the interrelations between institutional, sociopolitical, and actor variables.

As Table 2.1 indicates, the institutional structure and the sociopolitical context combine to form the country-specific political and legal opportunity structures within which the judges (as well as prospective litigants and other political actors) operate; that is, the incentives and constraints they face in making their decisions. Our broad conclusion is that the country-specific opportunity structures are crucial to understanding superior courts' accountability function. Actor variables influence how justices respond, but the willingness and ability of superior courts to hold power to account depends, to a significant extent, on the political and legal conditions and limiting parameters under which they operate in a given country. The combination and interaction between the various elements of the opportunity structure is the key factor. When factors that seem to explain judicial accountability functions in one context are insignificant—or work the other way—in another context, this may be explained by other aspects of the opportunity structure that enhances, distorts, or compensates the effect.

To facilitate a cross-regional comparison of judges' opportunity structure and motivation to act, Table 7.1 systematically lays out differences between the countries regarding their sociopolitical context, legal institutional structure, and judicial actor variables. We emphasize aspects assumed to be most central for the superior courts to develop and sustain accountability functions vis-à-vis the executive. With regard to institutional design, we focus on appointments and security of tenure, court structure, jurisdiction, and ease of access to the superior courts. The most significant aspects of the political context are assumed to be the case load, political balance of power and civil society activism, the courts' protective constituencies, and the legal culture. The central actor variables are the nature of the superior court judges and their (social/ political/professional) background. The table systematizes variation across our cases on the dependent variables.

Table 7.1 Explaining superior courts' accountability functions (variation on independent variables)

Country	Institutional design					Sociopolitical context		
	Appointments (insulation from executive influence)	Tenure and conditions	Court structure, jurisdiction	Access	Case load	Balance of power, civil society, protective constituencies	Legal culture	Actor variables (Nature of judges)
Costa Rica	Very strong insulation from presidential influence. Congress appoints CC magistrates by two-thirds majority.	Moderate. 8-year terms, renewable; two-thirds majority of Congress required to deny renewal. Full SC can remove magistrates. Well resourced.	Unitary. CC (chamber of SC) highest court for constitutional and individual rights issues (can be first instance court).	Very easy: direct access, simple, free, court prepares cases, broad standing, informal.	Extremely high.	Competitive elections. Weakening parties, highly legitimate elections, low social mobilization.	Legitimacy for courts, especially the CC. Civil Law, but increasingly using precedent .	Small judiciary, individuals not very important; CJ no more significant actor than other magistrates
Colombia	Strong insulation. CC judges are elected by the Senate from lists presented by the president, the SC, and the Council of State.	Strong. Members of the CC are appointed for eight years and cannot be reelected. Well resourced.	Separate SC and CC. Tradition of conflicts between the two courts regarding scope and limits of their functions.	Very easy. Simple procedures, free, easy access to litigant support. Broad standing, informal.	Extremely high.	Competitive multiparty elections. New parties after 1991 and 2003 reforms. Weak civil society, high political violence. Context of violence and	Legitimacy for courts, especially CC. Culture of legalism (abuses during state of emergency). Civil law, increasing influence of CC precedents.	Relatively small CC. Individuals matter decisively. Some CC magistrates drawn from academia.

South Africa	Moderate insulation. President appoints judges from nomination lists made by the JSC after public hearings, but chooses the CJ freely. Politically constituted JSC.	Strong. Long, nonrenewable terms for CC judges (up to 15 years), otherwise life tenure. CC well resourced.	Separate CC and SC. Some conflicts over jurisdiction. CC became apex court. Decentralized constitutional review.	Broad standing. Direct access provision, but in practice long appeals process. Formalism. Some litigant support from LSOs.	Very low for CC.	intimidation to judges. Dominant party, little room for opposition. Strong civil society. Political opposition and civil society use courts.	Culture of legalism. Strong legal profession. (Mixed common-civil law—plural legal system)	Largest, most professional judiciary in Africa. Eleven judges on CC several from academia, CJ head of CC.
Malawi	Moderate insulation. President appoints judges (JSC nominates candidates with 10 years practice); free to appoint SC judges among sitting judges. Selects CJ subject to confirmation by two-thirds members of parliament.	Moderate. Life tenure (65 years), but political impeachment incident. Parliament approves service conditions. Resource constraints.	Unitary. SC highest constitutional authority. CC (rotating High Court panel rotating) is first instance for constitutional interpretation.	Restrictive standing. Formalism. Quick process in many political cases. Frequent injunctions. No litigant support - few LSOs.	Moderate, but many significant political cases.	Competitive elections, but weak opposition and weak parliament. Political actors use courts as arena. Weak civil society apart from churches. International donors have acted as protective constituency.	Legitimacy for the courts' role in the democratic process. Common law (plural legal system).	Small judiciary, individuals matter. Tradition of "un-political" appointments of chief justice (until 2007).

Continued

Table 7.1 Continued

| Country | Institutional design | | | | Case load | Sociopolitical context | | Actor variables (Nature of Judges) |
	Appointments (insulation from executive influence)	Tenure and conditions	Court structure, jurisdiction	Access		Balance of power, civil society, protective constituencies	Legal culture	
Argentina	Weak insulation until 2003. President now appoints SC in agreement with two-thirds of the Senate, in a public process with civil society participation.	Formally strong. Life tenure, but history of instability—every new government appoints its own majority. Well resourced.	Unitary structure. SC highest constitutional authority.	Formalism. Relatively restrictive standing that slowly began to change after the 1994 Constitutional reform and the more open and liberal criteria that prevail in the current SC	Extremely high.	Competitive elections with one relatively dominant party. Strong civil society.	History of "judicial dependence" and low social legitimacy. The SC is working to recover social support. Civil law.	Small judiciary. Present composition of SC combines career judges and academics, many with strong legal viewpoints.
Uganda	Strong insulation. President appoints judges subject to JSC nomination and parliamentary confirmation. Strict criteria (10 to 20 years of practice).	Strong. Life tenure, strong formal safeguards for conditions. Resource constraints.	Unitary structure, SC highest constitutional authority, CC (rotating Court of Appeal panel) is first instance for	Moderate access, good in election cases, relatively lenient standing. Appeals process. Formalism. No litigant	Moderate, increase in important political cases.	Dominant party, increasingly competitive elections. Fragmented opposition. Moderately strong civil	Turbulent legal history. Courts historically at times assertive. Almost wiped out under Idi Amin. Common law	Small judiciary, individuals matter. History of politicized chief justices, current is long-serving, increasingly independent.

			constitutional cases.	support beyond LSOs.		society — protective constituency (sometimes, also donors).	(plural legal system).	
Chile	Strong insulation. "Endogamic" appointment procedure to SC. President appoints but decisive participation of the court, which processes a slate of five candidates, and Senate (reviews and ratifies). Several organs appoint to the CC: the president (3), the SC (3) and the Congress (4).	Strong. Life tenure. In the case of CC's members judges are appointed for a period of nine years. In both cases, there are disciplinary procedures of removal, rarely used. Well resourced.	Separate SC and CC. Historically both participate in controlling the validity of laws. After 2005, task of controlling the validity of the laws in CC.	Relatively easy access to the SC (The CC designed to allow parliament to consult, but open to litigants entitled to ask the CC to review laws validity).	Extremely high at the SC, and relatively low—though increasing after 2005—at the CC.	Competitive elections. Multi-party system, two dominant coalitions. Relatively weak civil society, but tendency towards more civic activism.	Formalist legal culture. Judges with "low political profile." Tradition of stability. Civil law.	Small court. Judges coming from the legal profession. Tradition of deferential judges.
Zambia	Relatively strong insulation. President appoints subject to parliamentary confirmation. JSC nominates	Moderate. Life tenure. Executive influence on conditions. Resource constraints.	Unitary structure, SC highest constitutional authority.	Relatively poor access. Appeal process, save for election cases. Formalism.	Moderate but significant political cases.	Competitive elections. Fragmented opposition. Moderately strong civil society. Lack	Common law (plural legal system). Courts relatively low	Small judiciary, individuals matter. Politicized chief justices.

Table 7.1 Continued

Country	Institutional design				Case load	Sociopolitical context		
	Appointments (insulation from executive influence)	*Tenure and conditions*	*Court structure, jurisdiction*	*Access*		*Balance of power, civil society, protective constituencies*	*Legal culture*	*Actor variables (Nature of Judges)*
	(among judges with 10 years of practice).			No litigant support beyond LSOs.		strong protective constituencies.	legitimacy in political cases.	
Tanzania	Weak insulation. President has wide discretion in appointing judges. JSC nominates but closed process and lenient criteria (5 years practice).	Moderate. Life tenure, but executive influence on conditions and retirement options. Resource constraints.	Unitary structure. CA highest constitutional authority. High court panel (rotating CC) for all application of rights. Limited jurisdiction on election law.	Poor access in constitutional rights cases. Restrictive standing, appeals. Formalism. No support for litigants, few LSOs.	Low but significant political/constitutional cases.	Dominant party, very weak opposition, weak civil society. Courts lack strong protective constituencies.	Common law (legitimacy).	Small judiciary, individuals matter. Long serving, increasingly independent chief justices.

Mozambique	Moderate insulation. President Appoints SC and AC judges in consultation with CSMJ. Top judicial positions require parliamentary confirmation. Parliament chooses CC judges (8 years practice).	Moderate. Weak for top positions. Life tenure for SC judges; 5 years nonrenewable terms for CC; 5 years renewable terms for AC judges, and SC and AC president. Resource constraints.	Separate CS, CC, and AC (with different functions) participate in controlling the validity of laws. Relatively wide formal powers.	Moderate/high (after 2004) access to CC in constitutional cases. Moderate access in other cases to SC and AC. Formalism.	Very low but significant political/constitutional cases.	Increasingly dominant party system, weak opposition, very weak civil society. Donors protective constituency.	Civil law (plural legal system). Emerging legitimacy for courts' role in democratic process.	Small judiciary, individuals matter. Tradition of politicized SC president, reappointed multiple times.

* *Abbreviations*: CC (Constitutional Court); SC (Supreme Court); AC (Administrative Court); CJ (Chief Justice); JSC (Judicial Service Commission); CSMJ (Judicial Council); LSO (Legal support organization).

Opportunity Structures of Judges—Interaction of Sociopolitical Context and Institutional Design

Our analysis examines how the opportunity structures of superior courts judges are created in interplay between the formal institutions and the social and political context in which they operate. This analysis starts from some central assumptions regarding the effects of legal institutional design, that is, the incentives flowing from specific institutional arrangements.

Structural Insulation: Appointment and Tenure

As discussed in Chapter 2, various schools of thoughts share the assumption that judges' decisions are influenced by who appoints them.[3] Given that executive dominance is the central challenge, the ability of courts to hold political power to account is seen to depend on institutional rules that limit executive influence over judicial appointments. Table 7.1 shows that all ten countries have judicial appointment procedures that grant significant roles to other political actors through vetting and nominees' selection, in the appointment procedure itself and/or in ratification. These roles are generally regarded as sufficient to protect the judiciary from undue executive influence. Yet, our case studies show that the strongest limitations on executive influence on judicial appointments include superior courts that exercise a consistently strong accountability function (Costa Rica and Colombia), the weakest (Chile and Mozambique), and courts whose accountability function has varied significantly over time without changes in the formal selection provisions (Zambia and Uganda). Our case studies provide little support for the assumption that selection procedures are decisive for judicial assertiveness in political cases. A notable exception is Argentina, where a change in the formal appointment process during this period corresponds with a strengthening of the accountability function of the SC.

A closer look at the cases, though, reveals that formal rules designed to enhance judicial independence, such as the vetting and nomination of candidates by a judicial selection commission or council, or a legislative approval requirement for superior court justices, is a promise of independence that only holds under certain political conditions. If, for example, opposition political parties are weak, legislative approval may not provide an effective insulation from the executive, or a dominant political party might be able to exert strong government influence over the composition of the judicial nominating body. The judicial selection process in the cases of Uganda, Zambia, and Argentina are all illustrative of this point.

In situations where institutional checks have little effect, other aspects of the appointment process that receive less attention in the literature—such as the use of public interviews or hearings related to nominations, public lists, and strict selection criteria—may have a more constraining effect. Selection criteria (standards regarding years of service, professional background, diversity) limit and shape the pool of prospective candidates, effectively limiting executive discretion, particularly in countries where the pool of potential candidates is small. Where, as in Uganda, 15 years of legal practice is required for appointment to the superior court (ten for judges in lower courts and 20 for the chief justice), the president's choice is limited to candidates that are firmly embedded in the norms of the legal culture. It was thus not surprising when President Museveni sought to lower the judicial appointment requirement to five years of practice as part of the 2005 constitutional reforms. This change would allow him to fulfill his stated goal of aligning the judiciary more closely with the ideals of the "Movement" (the NRM-O party) appointing his cadres to the bench. It was also not surprising that his strategy was resisted by the judiciary and the legal community at large.

The professional judicial hierarchy is commonly brought in to counterbalance executive influence on the selection process, either through nominations or directly (as in Chile, where the SC selects its own new members). This may strengthen the political insulation, but might also hamper the development of a stronger accountability function by perpetuating the judicial culture and increase the influence of the top judicial hierarchy. Where the president exerts strong influence over the chief justice and other top judicial officers, a strong gatekeeper function for the judiciary may strengthen internal mechanisms for control in ways that undermine judicial independence of (particularly lower level) individual judges, and promote only the most loyal lower court judges to the superior courts. In Mozambique, where the president enjoys considerable discretion in the appointment, and reappointment, of the chief justice and thus maintains close ties to the chief justice, this is a major restraining force on judges throughout the judicial hierarchy. Our findings suggest that selection procedures do influence to what extent the courts develop accountability functions, but that the effects of particular formal procedures cannot be determined outside their political context.

Tenure conditions for justices are another institutional variable that influence judges' opportunity structure. Life tenure or long nonrenewable terms are assumed to be necessary to prevent judges from unduly considering the political reactions to their decisions. Again, Table 7.1 shows that most of the countries satisfy these criteria. Only two countries have renewable terms for superior court judges: Costa Rica and Mozambique. Interestingly, these courts are on opposite sides of our accountability scale. However, on closer examination, conditions of tenure vary considerably. While there is a real concern for the tenure of top judicial personnel in Mozambique, this is much better safeguarded in Costa Rica, where a two-thirds congressional majority is required to prevent reconfirmation, which has never actually happened in the court's 20 years of existence.

Impeachment is the ultimate mechanism by which judges themselves are held accountable in cases of gross misconduct. It is an important "emergency brake," particularly in the context of increasing judicial power. But impeachment—or threats of such—may also be used politically to instill a sense of insecurity in the judiciary regarding their tenure.[4] In most of the countries analyzed in this book, impeachments are rare, and there are few charges of politically motivated impeachments. However, there are some exceptions. In 2001, three Malawian judges were impeached (but later pardoned) in what was widely considered a politically motivated process. In Argentina, SC tenure has in practice been less than secure, as new administrations regularly have changed the court's majority (particularly with military/civil regime shifts). In some countries, chief justices in practice follow the political cycle as incoming presidents have appointed their own chief of the judiciary despite formal provisions for life tenure. Both in Zambia and in Uganda this has served to align the judiciary more closely with the political elite, at least in the public's perception.

Tenure insecurity can also be caused by other means. Historically in Uganda, politically brave judges have not only lost office, but have also on at least one occasion been killed. In this context, the demonstration of military force on court premises during a highly politicized trial sent signals that go far to undermine the country's strong formal protection of judicial independence and tenure. Less dramatic, but also damaging for judicial independence, is the lack of regulations to prevent the executive from influencing judges' remuneration, service, and retirement conditions. When Zambian judges repeatedly receive pay raises while a presidential election petition is before the court, this is damaging to (at least perceptions of) judicial independence. And when retirement conditions in Zambia, Malawi, and Tanzania are so poor that judges rely on the government for other work or permission to remain on the bench, concerns are that this may affect their independence toward the end of their tenure. Generally, governments' ability to influence their judiciaries through the purse strings are higher in Africa, where the judiciary has less protection for and autonomy over their budget than in Latin America, where the judiciary commonly secures a fixed share of the budget. Again, the formal institutional protection of tenure and service conditions matter, but how much and which incentive structures it creates depends on the social and political context.

The formal and practical independence (financially and politically) of superior courts from the popular branches of government influence the opportunity structure of courts or the scope of action (they perceive to be) open to them. Yet, judicial independence is a necessary rather than a sufficient condition for superior courts to develop their accountability functions. That Costa Rica's judicial branch enjoyed political and financial independence for over three decades before aggressively exercising its accountability functions is a striking example of this. Thus, even with high levels of judicial independence, Costa Rica's SC lacked the willingness and/or ability to act as a countermajoritarian agency.

Our examination of Mozambique demonstrates most clearly the very real gaps that can exist between formal judicial independence (which exists) and practical independence (which does not). All the formal independence and powers granted to the Mozambique superior courts are rendered mute by the long history of one-party rule. Although the 1990 Constitution formally ended the practice and instituted formal controls to afford the court high levels of political independence from the executive, the weakness of opposition parties allow the executive's party to continue to govern as if it were a one-party state (which is also the case in Tanzania, South Africa, Tanzania, and Uganda). Close ties between the president and the chief justice renders the court a mere cipher given to supporting executive actions. Thus, despite institutional rules designed to limit the executive's control of the court, the nature of the political system has allowed the executive to influence the court.

Legal Powers, Jurisdiction, and the Legal System
The structure of the legal system and, in particular, whether there is a special constitutional court are also assumed to be important for the development of strong judicial accountability functions. Table 7.1 reveals that the three most consistently assertive courts are all specialized constitutional courts or panels (Costa Rica, Colombia, and South Africa). On the other hand, the other cases where special constitutional tribunals serve as the superior court for constitutional matters, Chile and Mozambique, are low in terms of judicial assertiveness. While the effect is not universal, it is interesting that special constitutional courts seem to be such a strong factor, particularly since the system of separate constitutional tribunals stems from the civil law tradition,[5] which has traditionally been assumed to work against the development of a strong accountability function (Merryman 1985; Rosenn 1987). This is not to say that constitutional courts are integral to civil law systems. Many civil law countries, including Argentina, have unitary superior courts without a specialized constitutional bench. And specialized constitutional courts exist in countries influenced by the common law tradition, such as in South Africa. (Given that South Africa's legal tradition is mixed, with

Roman Dutch law as one pillar, the establishment of a specialized constitutional court could be understood in this context. However, this reflects a general trend of cross-fertilization and a less clear-cut division between legal traditions.)

Traditionally, in civil law countries, with little or no use of precedent, superior courts often have very large case loads. In this context, the specialization provided by a separate constitutional court or chamber, facilitating the development of a stronger constitutional jurisprudence, seems particularly conducive to a strengthening of the accountability function of courts. Yet Argentina, a civil law country without special constitutional courts, has developed a stronger (albeit less consistent) accountability function than several civil law countries with constitutional courts. Thus, there is considerable variance that the presence of a constitutional court does not explain. The relatively deferential behavior of the court in Chile remains unexplained, as is the increasing assertiveness of the Argentinean court.

Our hypothesis is that this is closely related to the composition of the constitutional court bench, which in turn is related to the appointment process. In countries where constitutional courts are most assertive, they tend to be broadly constituted with academics as well as career judges and without a strong gatekeeper role for the judicial hierarchy. Hence, the professional culture of courts is less likely to be decisively influenced by the dominant judicial culture than for example in Chile, where superior court recruitment is endogenous and controlled by the judicial hierarchy. Again, design—in this case a separate constitutional court—is in itself not sufficient to explain the observed variation, but in interaction with other variables, it carries explanatory potential.

The likelihood that superior courts will exercise a strong accountability function is assumed to increase when their formal powers are strong, and they enjoy wide jurisdiction. Jurisdictions differ among the courts, depending on whether they are specialized constitutional courts or the final court of appeal for all cases, and to what extent there are special courts, hearing election cases, for example. As already discussed, specialization in the form of a constitutional court seems to encourage an accountability function. Other limitations on jurisdiction of courts undermine a strong accountability function, such as when parts of the electoral law in Tanzania are shielded from judicial review, or when the court martial is used as a parallel system for political cases in Uganda.

Superior courts seem more prone to limit executive or legislative overreach when they have a clear constitutional mandate to do so, and popular branches cannot easily overturn or ignore court decisions. In the absence of constitutional review powers or with high barriers to the court's use of the powers, the courts are less likely to exercise an accountability function. The case of Costa Rica is illustrative; before the creation of the Constitutional Chamber of the SC, the SC had judicial review powers, but required a two-thirds vote of the court *en banc* to declare executive and legislative assembly actions and also laws unconstitutional. This supermajority was very difficult to muster and resulted in the court declining to exercise its accountability function even though it had enjoyed significant levels of political and financial independence from the popular branches for many years.

Still, jurisdiction is not only a matter of formal regulation. Judges themselves, through their interpretation, play a role in shaping their jurisdiction.[6] In South Africa, the constitutional court's first certification judgment struck down what it perceived as an attempt at "immunizing legislation from constitutional scrutiny."[7] Who the judges are—their ideology and competence, and the opportunity structure they face in terms of political independence and norms of appropriateness—matters for the way in which they interpret the law, which, in turn, matters for their powers and jurisdiction.

In all our case studies, courts are empowered by liberal-democratic, rights-rich constitutions, but significant differences exist concerning the constitutional status of social, economic, and cultural rights. South Africa's Constitution, for example, explicitly states all social and economic rights are justiciable, but for other African countries, these rights are seen merely as "principles to guide policy" and explicitly not justiciable. Latin American constitutions, on the other hand, generally include long lists of social rights (Chile is an exception), but normally they are more ambiguous regarding enforceability (more so in Argentina than in Colombia). This differential status of constitutional rights impacts whether and how courts exercise accountability functions related to public policy. But again formal provisions are only one aspect, and judicial interpretations arguably matter even more. For example, Costa Rica's Constitutional Court exercises a strong accountability function on policy issues, particularly in health policy, even though there is no explicit constitutional right to health. Over a number of years, the court has constructed a constitutional right to health through its jurisprudence based on other constitutional provisions including the right to life (21), social security (73), and various international conventions (Wilson 2009).

Access to the Superior Courts

Access to courts is one aspect of constitutional design we have found to be significant in explaining accountability functions. Even when the institutional conditions are in place for the superior courts to hold the other branches to account, they are unlikely to act without a significant level of demand for judicial solutions to political questions. Provisions for direct and easy access to the superior courts for litigants impact radically on the flow of constitutional cases, which in turn enables the court to build a strong accountability function. Costa Rica's Constitutional Chamber is a striking example of the link between widening access and court accountability. In our ten case studies, the most assertive courts are also the most accessible in terms of direct access provisions, broad standing, inexpensive and un-bureaucratic procedures, and even court internal support structures for litigants. Conversely, the most inaccessible ones generally have weaker accountability functions. Mozambique is an interesting case as it has medium accessibility (increased with constitutional revisions in 2004), but few litigants have used their constitutional rights to bring cases before the courts.

As the Mozambican case clearly demonstrates, the flow of cases to the court is not only a function of access provisions. To better understand what influences the demand-side pressure on the courts, we need to consider the overall opportunity structure of the litigants. The exponential growth in *tutelas* in Colombia (in 2005, there were over 80,000 cases in the area of right to health) may for example indicate that other parts of the political system are not functioning adequately (Yamin and Parra Vera, 2008).

Demand-side Pressure, Litigants' Opportunity Structure, and Civil Society

Whether or not individuals, political actors, and organized interest in civil society choose to go to court when the government is acting contrary to its constitutional mandate depends, obviously, on the available alternatives. The legal route is more likely to be an attractive alternative in which credible institutional guarantees for judicial independence are present and in which previous performance signals independence and a certain likelihood of success. Choosing the courts is also more likely where the political system functions poorly and is less responsive to civil society interests, and where there are few chances of being heard through other channels, such as the media or collective action, or through quasijudicial institutions.

In Colombia and Costa Rica, where civil society is weak, important social and political issues not addressed by parliament have been taken to the courts. Indeed, in Costa Rica, even deputies from smaller political parties have harnessed the Constitutional Court's capacity and willingness to exercise its accountability function to strengthen their policy bargaining positions within the Congress (Wilson 2005). We see a similar dynamic in South Africa, where the dominance of the ANC in the legislature made the courts a useful avenue for the political opposition. Due to the increasing centralization of the ANC party leadership and its unresponsiveness on important issues such as HIV/AIDS, the grassroots members of the party have also taken claims to the court.

Where civil society is closely linked to organized interests vying for state power, political mobilization might often be a more fruitful option. This is particularly so if the political opposition has real influence on policy making, or a chance to gain state power. It is also true where corporatist or other arrangements exist that allow civil society to influence the ruling party directly (or that "buy" and neutralize civil society). This close link between civil society and political parties, though, might not be stable over time. Both in Argentina and South Africa, civil society organizations sought solutions through political parties in the first period after the transition, but have later sought legal remedies through the courts.

Whether court action is within prospective litigants' opportunity structures also depends on whether the litigants possess the resources needed to access the court. Given that court activism depends on individuals or organized interests turning to the courts, it has been assumed that if civil society is too weak, this is less likely to happen. This is supported by empirical studies, among others in India (Epp 1998) and South Africa, where, in the context of a relatively high threshold, but with liberal provisions for standing, deep-pocketed civil society organizations have been able to successfully hold the government accountable by sustaining expensive litigation strategies (Gloppen 2005). Yet, our cases demonstrate that even countries where civil society is weak (Colombia, Costa Rica, and Malawi), courts are successfully called upon to protect individual rights against state abuse (Wilson 2009).

To understand this seeming contradiction in the relationship between civil society strength and court assertiveness, it is important to take into account the factors beyond the litigants' own individual and collective resources that motivate and enable successful use of the courts (the responsiveness of the political system; the threshold of access into the judicial system; the nature of the bench). Colombia is an illustrative case where civil society is weak with poor political linkages and the threshold for political mobilization is heightened due to the violence that makes political activism dangerous. Before the creation of the constitutional courts, large sections of civil society were excluded from the political process and unable to seek judicial solutions from the courts because of a lack of a legal opportunity structure. When the legal opportunity structure was changed by a radical lowering of the threshold for taking cases to court, the judiciary became a more attractive avenue, and the number of cases increased exponentially. In addition to the lowering of the threshold of access to court (judiciaries generally have considerable influence on procedures for the lodging of cases and their interpretation of standing criteria etc affect the threshold of entry), the judgments of the Colombian Constitutional Court showed considerable assertiveness and activism, particularly in the area of social rights. Hence, the court encouraged further litigation. Why the new Constitutional Court went a route that ran counter to the rest of the political and legal establishment has been explained mainly by actor variables: the Constitutional Court comprised judges, including legal scholars, with a strong commitment to the new constitution and its ideals of social justice (Nunes 2009). When other avenues were closed, they saw it as their role to act as agents of social transformation. In other words, in the case of Colombia, the very weakness of civil society becomes an explanation of court activism (Uprimny 2007).

This does not, however, help us understand the combination of weak civil society and (periodically) high accountability function in Malawi, where access to court is not particularly easy with strict standing and procedural requirements (although the liberal granting of injunctions do provide a quick and easy legal solution). There is no large flow of constitutional cases from individuals or civil society organizations. Instead, political actors use the legal arena to fight over the rules of the political game and dispute compliance. Thus, the openness and relevance of the courts to actors in political society makes it an important accountability institution in the context of a weak, executive-dominated political system, similar to several of the other African countries.

It is thus important not to conflate courts' *activity* (number of cases/ share decided against the government) and their accountability function vis-à-vis political authorities. The scale of litigation matters less than the nature of the cases (who uses the courts and for what). We focus here on cases in which the courts are called on to protect against abuse of power that threatens to undermine the functioning of the political system and the principles of democracy. One such case, in which the political stakes are high, may be more important in terms of accountability than hundreds of routine cases. The Constitutional Court of Colombia has become less assertive on important political power issues than it was in its first period, demonstrated most notably in the 2005 presidential reelection case. Its accountability function has clearly weakened despite the growing number of cases and rulings against the executive in social rights cases.

Considering the demand-side pressure on the courts, it also matters that the type of cases that are central to democracy differ between countries and over time. Courts' horizontal accountability function depends on the historical context in which the institutions are created or reformed (Przeworski 2006: 326). At the critical juncture—the point of creation or reform of contemporary courts—social and political context across the regions examined in this book varied considerably as did the concerns that motivated the design of the court institutions and rules of operation. This, in turn, influenced incentives for litigants and the nature of the cases reaching the courts. Throughout much of Latin America, for example, a major concern has been keeping the executive branch in check and breathing life into moribund, rights-rich constitutions. Electoral issues were generally not a concern as well-regarded agencies, such as the Tribunal Supremo de Elecciones in Costa Rica, already functioned as courts of appeal for all electoral questions. In contrast, in our African cases, the lack of credibility and weakness of the relatively new electoral commissions pushed election cases onto the SC dockets, which produced some of the clearest examples of superior courts' exercising—or failing to exercise—their accountability functions as a way of keeping the channels of electoral competition and political succession open and honest. While numerous other cases are handled by the superior courts in Africa including important rights cases, election-related cases are the most potent from an accountability perspective.

Political Power, Protective Constituencies, and Strategic Defection

The nature of the political system and civil society strength are important for the opportunity structure of potential litigants and thus for the demand-side pressure on the courts to hold executive power to account. But the political context also influences the judges' opportunity structure and their ability and willingness to exercise an accountability function.

A comparison of the lines in Figure 7.1 with the "balance of power" column in Table 7.1 reveals that countries with a consistently low accountability function are countries where the ruling party is dominant, and where a formal multiparty democracy has not challenged the pretransition ruling party's hold on political power (Tanzania, Mozambique, Uganda until the 2006 elections). The countries with an inconsistent and vacillating pattern (Malawi, Zambia, Argentina, and Uganda) have more viable opposition parties and elections that represent a genuine contestation for power. Interestingly, in Uganda, the strengthening of the court's accountability functions came not with the 1995 Constitution, which strengthened the powers and independence of the judiciary (while elections remained restricted to individual candidates within a "no-party system"). Rather, the assertiveness of the courts grew in the period leading up to the adoption of a multiparty system and more competitive, although not fully democratic, elections in 2006. The courts with a consistently strong accountability function are predominantly found in competitive party systems. But, while a competitive political context is conducive for courts to assert their accountability functions, this is neither required nor sufficient: South Africa is a dominant party system, but still has an assertive constitutional court, while Chile has a competitive party system, but lacks a politically assertive court.

What can this tell us about the way in which the political context influence judges opportunity structure? If we assume, as is common, that judges care about the fate and effect of their judgments, as well as about their own fate and that of their institution, they will stand up against executive abuse of power when they have reason to believe that their decisions will be accepted, and that the effort to hold government to account will not result in sanctions against them personally or that will harm the institution. The political balance of power is assumed to influence the way power-holders view the courts in the sense that the government might be more willing to tolerate adverse judgments or at least not react aggressively, where there is a viable opposition. Particularly if politicians fear being voted out of power in the not so distant future, they may recognize the "insurance value" of independent courts. This "thin strategic" argument has been widely offered as an explanation for variations in judicial independence, not least in Latin America (Helmke 2005). Our analysis suggests that the government's tolerance of judicial independence is likely to influence how judges perceive their opportunity structure, which might explain why countries that lack significant political opposition also have courts with the weakest accountability function. But, it does not explain the variation between the countries with a viable opposition, nor the uneven pattern in some countries. The "insurance" or "thin strategic" approaches are also insufficient to account for African cases, where executives seem particularly prone to strike down on judicial independence when their power is being threatened. As VonDoepp (2009) shows, to lose power in neopatrimonal African states is simply too dangerous. Rather than count on the insurance of an independent judiciary, executives under threat will seek to eliminate potential opposition from the courts, often with little effect. Also in Africa, the most assertive courts exist where the political struggles are strongest. How can this be explained?

It is argued that particularly in weakly institutionalized democracies with uncertainty over rules—for example, whether judicial tenure will hold under changing political circumstances—judges are more likely to keep an eye on the political contest, including what is likely to happen in the future. This effect is most systematically captured in Helmke's (2005) strategic defection theory. Helmke argues that Argentine SC magistrates acted rationally when they began challenging the decisions of the sitting government, even though they had little independence from the executive branch "because they fear being punished by the government's successors" (2005: 20, 155). This also seems to capture the rising assertiveness of the Ugandan judiciary in the run-up to the 2006 multiparty elections, and some of the shifts that we see in accountability function in Malawi and Zambia. It also seemingly explains why African superior courts that demonstrate a willingness to hold all sides—including the executive and the ruling party—accountable in the run-up to elections seem incapable of deciding presidential election petitions against the incumbent (VonDoepp 2009).

But again, this leaves other questions unresolved, for example, why in some cases significant assertiveness occurs in the absence of a realistic chance of an electoral turnover (South Africa), or why Chilean SC judges, in a country with a similar history of human rights abuses as Argentina and a similar democratic transition, failed to engage in strategic defection.

A more complete explanation of judicial behavior can be ascertained through an examination of not only the present (and likely future) government, but also other actors that might act as *protective constituencies* for the court, making it difficult or costly for governments to sanction the court or individual judges. Even in the absence of a likely regime change, the political costs of oppressing a judge or the superior court may rise if the courts are supported by a significant political opposition (who may see the court as way to protect their right and an arena for political contestation). A strong civil society or politically significant sections, such as the business community, the legal community, and churches that are supportive of the courts may play a significant protective role. In other contexts, international donors or organizations may serve a similar function. Indeed, being in the "international public eye," for example, in the run-up to an election, may provide significant protection and change the way judges perceive their opportunity situation. The combination of a strong civil society and consistent international attention serving as protective constituencies goes a long way toward explaining the relatively strong performance of the South African Constitutional Court in the context of a dominant single-party system.

These varieties of rational choice approaches consider how institutional and sociopolitical factors combine to provide an incentive structure to which judges react. Still we concur with Weyland (2002) that while this approach offers some general explanatory promise, it remains problematic as an overarching explanation for judicial behavior. These rational choice theories do not lend themselves to construct general explanations about when specific types of behavior are in the rational interests of the actors. That is, there is no systematic analysis of how context shapes self-interested behavior. Either it excludes, a priori, the possibility of possible motivations for judicial action other than the self-interest of judges (most importantly, actions responding to norms of appropriateness and moral urgency), or broadens the notion of rational action to the point where it risks becoming tautological (where the fact that an action was taken means that it was rational in relation to some motive). As this book's cases illustrate, the incentives provided by the institutional, political and legal context are important in constraining the possible actions of justices. But our cases also identify other influences on judicial motivations including "doing what the law says" or "doing the right thing to save democracy."

Legal Tradition

Judicial "norms of appropriateness" differ between legal systems and provide the lens through which judges interpret their opportunity structure and what is possible and appropriate to do in a given situation—including what is the proper separation of powers and what belongs in the constitutional domain as opposed to the domain of politics. Judicial norms of appropriateness can also be seen as an aspect of the opportunity structure itself, in the sense that there are costs involved in going against the judicial culture or peers whose recognition is valued. The broader legal culture in a society frame how other actors relate to the court, and whether judgments are likely to be complied with.

The legal tradition (civil versus common law) has historically been a major factor to account for a lack of accountability function by superior courts in civil law countries, where judges are framed as technocratic appliers of legal codes rather than independent cultivators developing the law to serve new contexts, as in the common law tradition (Merryman 1985: 35; Rosenn 1987). As summarized in Figure 7.1, when compared with the "Legal tradition" column in Table 7.1, our results discount the importance of legal traditions. First, across all our cases, the existence of a common law legal system has little explanatory power to understand superior courts' use of their accountability function. Second, and perhaps more importantly, the use of a civil law legal tradition does not, in and of itself, preclude an active role for superior courts. Third, our cases demonstrate that attributing the lack of accountability to the civil law tradition without closer analysis may lead to wrong conclusions.

First, our case studies reveal considerable variation across common law countries' superior courts exercise of accountability functions. Among the African common law systems examined here, South Africa (a mixed system) and Malawi exhibit a far higher level than Tanzania. Generally, it seems as if the twin colonial experience of a deferential common law judiciary and a Westminster tradition of parliamentary sovereignty combined with a postcolonial experience in which the judiciary was either dominated or marginalized, has left African judges very concerned with the separation of powers. Because these judiciaries are generally small and young, the nature of individual judges and the personality of the chief justice are also much more important than they might be in larger, more established, democracies.

A second lesson drawn from our analysis is that hyperactive courts exist even in civil law legal systems, such as Costa Rica and Colombia. Thus, a commonly held assumption concerning civil law traditions as a major limitation on court behavior is not supported by the evidence from our case studies.

Third, we caution against attributing a lack of accountability function to legal tradition per se. The relative lack of accountability function exercised in Mozambique or Chile might superficially be explained with reference to their civil law legal traditions. That is, without knowing anything else about courts or politics in these countries, legal scholars regularly conclude that deferential behavior from these courts should be expected. However, upon closer scrutiny, explanations for lack of accountability need to be sought elsewhere. The Mozambican judiciary no doubt failed to exercise its accountability functions to any significant degree, even after the creation of the new courts in 1990s and increased levels of democratic governance. Yet, the inactivity of the superior courts is better explained by the near-eradication of a professional judiciary during the country's postcolonial experience of one-party governance. This provided little support in the legal culture for a strong accountability function for the courts. This factor, combined with the presence of powerful reactionary individuals, with close ties to the executive in key positions in the judicial hierarchy, has hindered the courts' ability and willingness to hold power to account. Executive control over the judicial hierarchy is supported by the appointment procedures and conditions of tenure for the chief justice—the president has total discretion in the selection and can keep the chief justice on a short leash, while securing continuity though a system of five-year terms with possibility for renewal.

Comparing Mozambique, with its Portuguese colonial heritage and civil law legal tradition, more closely with the five common law African countries demonstrates that although the differences in the legal tradition may have had some implication for the formal institutional structures, this does not seem to explain the observed variances in judicial behavior across the countries. In the African context, what seems more important is the state of the political system and the political balance of power, and, in particular, the presence of protective constituencies for the judiciary (with significant internal or external actors) and other functioning mechanisms for holding the government to the rules of play.

We conclude then that legal tradition is not a good predictor of superior courts' willingness and ability to exercise an accountability function; examples of hyperactive and deferential superior courts abound in both civil and common law systems. Indeed, the empirical evidence from our cases supports Jacob's (1996: 4) observation that both legal systems have tended to adopt aspects of each other's system, making them no longer "as distinct as they were during the nineteenth and early twentieth centuries."

While legal tradition in and by itself does not seem to carry much explanatory force with regard to the superior courts' ability and willingness to exercise their accountability function, it can be quite significant in an interplay with other factors. We discussed earlier how the strong gatekeeper role of the Chilean judiciary over judicial appointments has perpetuated the politically deferential corporate legal culture in a far more effective way than where the appointment process encourages a broader composition of the bench. This brings us to the importance of the actors—the nature of the judges on the superior courts—for whether these institutions develop strong accountability functions vis-à-vis the political branches.

Judges' Interests, Norms, and Ideology

The focus on the opportunity structure to explain judicial assertiveness implicitly assumes that all superior court judges react in the same manner when faced with the same context. Our findings do, however, also indicate that judges react differently to similar contexts. Indeed, judicial "norms of appropriateness" also commonly differ within a country's legal community depending on factors such as professional background and competence, ideology, identity, and personality. Such actor variables, in turn, affect the way they approach their judicial accountability functions. On the other hand, the impact of actor variables is context-dependent.

In Argentina, where presidents routinely packed the SC with their own handpicked judges, the political leanings of the judges have historically been an important variable in explaining the court behavior. On the other hand, in Costa Rica even with the complete turnover of magistrates on the Constitutional Court, few significant changes in the pattern of the court's jurisprudence have occurred. A *magistrado suplente* on the *Sala IV* recently noted that for many important accountability cases, such as health rights, there would be no significant change no matter who sat on the court.[8] In Colombia in recent years, on the other hand, magistrates retiring after their single eight-year terms have been replaced by magistrates more in line with the views of the sitting government. The result seems to be a decline in the accountability rulings from the Constitutional Court. The ongoing debate over allowing sitting president Uribe to seek an unprecedented (and at this point unconstitutional) third term has in part raised the possibility of his "stuffing" the Constitutional Court (Shifter 2009).

The significance of the role of judicial actors appears to vary with the level of a judiciary's institutionalization, both in terms of normative cohesion and internal operating rules. Where, as in Colombia, a new type of judge is brought into the superior courts, with different judicial values, this may significantly change the nature of the institution. Similarly, in several African cases in which the judicial institutions are weakly developed, the role of individual judicial personalities, in particular, the chief justice may take on more import, as the Mozambique case illustrates well. This is exacerbated by the size of the judge pool. In most of our African cases, the judge pool is small, and a handful of judges write a majority of the accountability judgments.[9] This enhances the position of personalities and gives individual judges disproportionate influence over court behavior. But also in more institutionalized cases, it seems to be important who the judges are. In particular, it seems that broadly constituted superior courts that also include academic constitutional scholars are more likely to develop a strong accountability function regardless of legal tradition and level of institutionalization. We see this in several of our cases most notably in South Africa and Colombia. A good analysis of the impact of ideational variables on the voting pattern of judges on the Colombian Constitutional Court is provided by Nunes (2009).

Concluding Comments

Our analysis demonstrates that, in spite of very different historical trajectories, different legal traditions, and varying levels of economic and institutional development, there are commonalities across countries in different regions of the world that help explain variations in judicial accountability functions. More specifically, three sets of explanatory factors—the sociopolitical context and tradition, the institutional structure, and personal motivations—demonstrate how these factors interact in different contexts to provide different opportunity situations within which judges and other actors act and interact. Changes in the political context may impact directly on judges' incentives to hold political power to account, but may also do so indirectly, by changing litigants' opportunity structures and the flow of cases in ways that present new opportunities and motivation for the courts to act. Shifts in the superior courts' pattern of decisions may in turn serve to encourage further litigation (or the opposite). Our comparative study emphasizes the significance of specific legal reforms for strengthening the accountability function of courts. We demonstrate, in particular, procedural reforms that facilitate access to courts by reducing legal formalities to litigate, or the potential of broadening legal standing for inducing changes in judicial behavior in substantially different contexts.

In sum, the accountability function of courts is a complex phenomenon and has to be studied as such. This is of consequence also for international agencies and legal reformers, whose work would be made easier if single changes in judicial institutions would lead to predicted outcomes in the performance of judicial systems regardless of context. Further research on additional cases may help us in specifying more clearly under what conditions specific factors influence the performance of legal systems in specific ways. For now, we have gained the knowledge that the performance of legal systems is best understood by considering the complex contexts in which they operate.

Notes

1 Introduction: Power and Accountability in Latin America and Africa

1. In some cases (e.g., Costa Rica), we refer to constitutional revisions rather than regime changes or the adoption of a new constitution. The extent to which the countries are democratic varies. In Uganda, the first multiparty elections were held in February 2006 under conditions favoring the incumbent (see Kiiza, Makara, and Rakner 2008).
2. Tanzania was under German rule from 1880 to 1919, but the influence of British colonialism on the judiciary and the legal culture is comparable to that of Zambia, Uganda, and Malawi. South Africa gained independence in 1910, but it continued under white minority rule until 1994. Besides the common law tradition, South Africa is influenced by Roman Dutch law and, as in all the countries, African legal traditions. For an analysis of South Africa's legal culture, see Chanock (2001).

2 Accountability Functions of Courts: A Framework for Inquiry

1. Apart from periodic elections, few "vertical" institutional mechanisms for the control of the representatives through the participation of the public are retained in modern democracies (i.e., mandatory instructions and the right to recall). Political mandates have also been extended in their duration (less frequent popular elections).
2. On the concept of "veto players," see Tsebelis (1995, 2002).
3. The distinction is less clear in practice. Although horizontal accountability relations in principle are politically neutral, at least in a party-political sense, political judgement does enter into legal interpretation and judgment.
4. For example, the existence of reasonably satisfactory elections does not automatically equal "democracy" in the sense of participation of the people. In highly professionalized political democracies with low voter turnouts, it is crucially important to provide guarantees through legally enforceable constraints on political actions and decision-making.

5. Most countries also elect representatives to subnational representative bodies and offices.

6. However, exceptions exist: In the United States, many state-level judges are in fact elected.

7. We acknowledge that the notion of "protecting the law and the constitution" raises difficult questions regarding interpretive theory (i.e., what is really required by the constitution?); democratic theory (what are the limits on the actions of a court in relation to the other branches in a democratic system that is committed to respect the principle of the separation of powers?), and so on, but these questions are put aside for now.

8. An excellent study on the topic is Elster and Slagstad (1988).

9. In the past decades, there has been a growing ideological consensus in the international community that has seen democracy in terms of liberal, constitutional democracy, with a strong emphasis on rights protection and institutions to check government power while leaving courts with a more prominent role. See Ackerman (1997); Bugaric (2001); Choudhry (1999); Gloppen, Gargarella, and Skaar (2004); Klug (1997); Tate (1997).

10. This statement follows the so-called most famous footnote in the history of constitutional law, where the U.S. Court defined the scope of its own institutional role, and from which Ely (1980) developed his view on legal adjudication and democracy, which we take as a starting point: "There may be narrower scope for operation of the presumption of constitutionality when legislation appears on its face to be within a specific prohibition of the Constitution, such as those of the first ten Amendments, which are deemed equally specific when held to be embraced within the 14th. [Case citations deleted] It is unnecessary to consider now whether legislation which restricts those political processes which can ordinarily be expected to bring about repeal of undesirable legislation, is to be subjected to more exacting judicial scrutiny under the general prohibitions of the 14th Amendments than are most other types of legislation... Nor need we enquire whether similar considerations enter into the review of statues directed at particular religious... or national... or racial minorities; [or] whether prejudice against discrete and insular minorities may be a special condition, which tends seriously to curtail the operation of those political processes ordinarily to be relied upon to protect minorities, and which may call for a correspondingly more searching judicial inquiry..." (Footnote 4 in the case *United States v. Carolene Products* 304, U.S. 144, 1938).

11. Ely's (1980) view is also based on a particular conception of democracy, namely a (so-called) pluralist approach to democracy. However, and given that in this respect his position refers to some core and widely shared democratic values, we think that such a view on legal adjudication may be (with few modifications) fully endorsed by other people who rely on different conceptions of democracy. Nino (1996), for example, endorsed such a view (or one that was almost identical) from a deliberative notion of democracy.

12. This includes "discrete and insular" minorities, but also other disadvantaged groups (see Ackerman 1985).

13. Unelected judges nullifying elected representatives' decisions gives rise to a countermajoritarian dilemma. Legalization of politics may empty the political sphere and thus produce a democratic deficit.

14. Our use of the term "constitutional moment" is similar to Sieder, Schjolden, and Angell's (2005: 10) concept of "critical juncture," which includes "the election of a constituent assembly and the subsequent drafting of a new constitution," or "the transition from a authoritarian government to elected constitutional rule involving the continuation or restitution of a previous constitution." It differs somewhat from Ackerman's (1991) concept of "constitutional moment."

15. The civil law originated in Roman law and spread and developed among other countries in continental Europe and Latin America. Common law was born in England (around the eleventh century) and developed in the United States, Australia, Canada, and other countries of the British Commonwealth.

16. While judicial independence and accountability are linked, they are not the same. Judicial independence is assumed to be a condition for courts to perform an accountability function, while the manifestation of such an accountability function can be seen as an indication of judicial independence.

17. Most notably the "Basic Principles on the Independence of the Judiciary" (United Nations 1985).

18. See, for example, "The International Foundation for Election Systems" (IFES) (n.d.).

19. The model holds "that the Supreme Court decides disputes in light of the facts of the case vis-à-vis the ideological attitudes and values of the justices. Simply put, Rehnquist votes the way he does because he is extremely conservative; Marshall voted the way he did because he is extremely liberal" (Segal and Spaeth, 1993: 65).

20. Bickel (1967) popularized this view, according to which judicial review generates a "counter-majoritarian difficulty," given the fact that (Supreme Court) judges, who are not directly elected or removed by the people, have the power to invalidate legislation created "here and now" by those who directly represent the people.

21. On "nested games" see Tsebelis (1990). Nested games arguments—actors engaging repeatedly with the same institutional players think beyond the individual case and may sacrifice short-term gains for long-term benefits—are also made in relation to attitudinal approaches.

22. VonDoepp has carried out similar analyses in an African context (Malawi, Zambia, and Namibia), although with emphasis on what makes power holders try to reign in judges (see VonDoepp 2005, 2006, 2009; VonDoepp and Ellett, 2008; see also Ellett 2008).

23. There are exceptions, however, that combine institutional and political context variables. See, for example, Brinks (2005) on judicial independence in Brazil and Argentina; Ansolabehere (2007) on Argentine and Mexican courts; Taylor (2008) on judicial involvement in Brazilian policymaking; and Wilson (2005, 2009) on Costa Rica and Colombian judicial politics.

24. Proponents of strategic explanations tend to do this, as we will demonstrate in the following chapters.
25. Curiously, these approaches have mostly grown in the United States where the following, conditions exist: judicial review has not been limited by Congress, even when Congress could have limited it; no successful impeachment process and practically no impeachment processes at all is found; the size of the Supreme Court and its budget have basically not suffered from extortive changes. Also, views such as the separation of powers model "underestimates the Court's freedom to act by completely eliminating the Court's ability to react to congressional action" (Segal 1997: 32).

3　The Accountability Functions of Latin American Courts

1. Unless stated to the contrary, references are to the highest courts of the country: the Supreme Court in Argentina and Chile and the Constitutional Court in Colombia. The starting point of the analysis is 1983 (the return of democracy) for Argentina, approximately 1990 for Chile, and 1991 (the creation of the Constitutional Court) for Colombia.
2. Argentina, for example, has an unusually high record of social and political mobilization. The country used to have the strongest trade unions in the region and has preserved a practice of intense social mobilization even after the neoliberal reforms of the 1990s. In contrast, Chile is characterized by its low level of political activism, even though some recent events seem to point in the opposite direction. The case of Colombia is distinctive. On the one hand, Colombia has some of the highest levels of political violence in the region, which explains, at least in part, the existence of a low level of civic organization. However, the very presence of a highly activist court that preempts politics may provide a better explanation. On the other hand, Colombia is the only country where *guerrilla* groups are still pursuing political change through violent means.
3. However, our study focuses on the activity of courts during democratic periods. On the Allende period, see Velasco (1976a, 1976b, 1976c).
4. On October 16, 1998, the London police arrested Pinochet and a complex judicial process began to determine whether Pinochet could be extradited from the United Kingdom to Spain. After various decisions and appeals, the House of Lords declared that Pinochet did not enjoy legal immunity and could therefore be extradited. However, a medical examination was then carried out and concluded that the ex-dictator was not mentally capable for facing a trial, a decision that finally allowed Pinochet to return to Chile. This final decision adopted by British authorities obviously disappointed many, particularly human rights activists and victims of Pinochet's abuses.
5. Another important antecedent is the constitutional reform of 1936, which established the social function of property.
6. However, voter turnout was relatively low.

7. The cases include an analysis of the criminalization of the consumption of drugs, the right to euthanasia, abortion, legal pluralism, the rights of indigenous groups, the rights of homosexuals, the rights of people affected by AIDS, and the rights of religious minorities. Also, the court acted in highly politicized cases, such as those related to the reelection of the president, the expansion of the executive powers; emergency powers (and other situations related to the declaration of "states of exception" and "state of siege"); the illegal financing of political campaigns, or the rights of the *desplazados* (those who are forced to leave their home and properties as a consequence of the armed war the country is still involved in).

8. Since the 1991 constitutional reform, the Constitutional Court has been the main tribunal to exercise an accountability function in Colombia. Therefore, we focus our attention on this court rather than on the Supreme Court. However, recently—and particularly after a series of political scandals (referring to the existing links between members of the National Assembly and paramilitary groups)—the Supreme Court acquired a new and unexpected political role.

9. As a reaction against this decision, Congress passed a new law with lower penalties, which found a more favorable reception within the court—see for example, *Dicapua* (*Fallos* 312: 1892).

10. In this respect, probably the most significant decision was *Aramayo* (*Fallos* 306–73), where the court, opposing a long and contrary line of judicial decisions, firmly distinguished between democratic legislation adopted by democratic authorities and de facto norms that were approved by military regimes and declared the supremacy of the democratic norms.

11. The *Opus Dei* came to have at least two representatives in the court, namely Antonio Boggiano and Rodolfo Barra.

12. These conservative views were also ratified in cases such as *Ekmedjián* (*Fallos* 315: 1429), in which the court surprisingly recognized the right to reply, in a case that involved a speech that the court considered offensive to the Virgin Mary. See also the court's conservative views regarding the validity of de facto laws (e.g., *Godoy*, CSJN 19990: 27/12).

13. See also its decision in *Granada* (*Fallos* 307: 2284), validating a polemic *state of siege* decided by President Alfonsín.

14. Simon, Julio y otros s/ privación ilegitima de la libertad—causa 17.768.

15. The "Full Stop" law was also promoted by President Alfonsin in order to establish a time limit regarding the prosecution of past human rights crimes.

16. See, for example, the cases involving Judge Del Castillo; Attorney General Ricardo Molinas (*Fallos* 314: 1091), or General Prosecutor Andrés D'Alessio.

17. The only significant case that was solved at the time was the famous Letelier case, probably as a consequence of pressures coming from the United States.

18. See, for example, the cases of Judge René García (1990); Judge Carlos Cerda Fernánde (1991); or Judge Gloria Olivares (1992) (Hilbink 1999b: 325–6).

19. The court maintained that the amnesty constitutes an act of legislative power, which has the objective effect of suspending the declaration of criminality

under any other law, as a result of which the offense cannot be punished because the penalty associated with the illicit acts is eliminated, which prevents and paralyzes definitively or forever the exercise of any judicial action that is intended to prosecute them. This means that since the amnesty law has been upheld as valid, the courts must apply it pursuant to the provisions of Articles 107 and 408 Number 5 of the Code of Criminal Procedure without regard to the provisions of Article 413 of that code, which require that a decree of definitive dismissal is conditional upon having exhausted all investigative attempts to produce the *corpus delicti* and to determine the identity of the guilty party.

20. Aylwin pressed for the investigation of all cases involving "missing people," and maintained that tribunals should at least look at the facts and define who was responsible for these actions.

21. In fact, already in 1995, the court had proposed a narrow interpretation of the amnesty law. Moreover, in 1996, the argument was made that kidnapping was a continuous crime until the victim, already appeared in the opinion of one of its members. In 1998, after some repeated decisions upholding the amnesty decree, the court recognized that the Geneva Conventions applied in the Chilean case because the same military government had declared that it was in a "state of war" and required the reopening of investigations. In 1999, in a case related to "disappearances" in the south of Chile, the court maintained that this crime was "a permanent one" (Human Rights Watch 1999: 9).

22. The name refers to military collaboration between the dictatorships of Argentina, Brazil, Chile, Uruguay, and Paraguay, aimed at "disappearing" dissidents from each other's countries.

23. See, for example, the 1998 case involving the newspaper *La Tercera*.

24. Some of the most problematic situations refer to cases that involve criticisms against public officers, and particularly those including members of the judicial branch. See, for example, the so-called *El Termómetro* case.

25. See, for example, the case involving Francisco Cuadra, a former member of the military regime, which was met with heavy international criticism (i.e., from Human Rights Watch and the Center for Justice and International Law, CEJIL).

26. See also the so-called *Chilevisión* case.

27. One of the most famous cases referred to the prohibition imposed against the book *Impunidad diplomática* by Francisco Martorell, which included information about the scandalous activities of Oscar Spinosa Melo, Argentina's former Ambassador in Chile. The court's decision maintained the prohibition on selling the book. In its decision of *Martorell v. Chile, Caso* 1997 f. 1230, the CIDH recommended the end of the state of censorship that affected Martorell's book.

28. The third important case was related to the film *The Last Temptation of Christ* by Martin Scorsese, which was censored following judicial decisions by both the Court of Appeals of Santiago (January 20, 1997) and the Supreme Court (June 17, 1997). The CIDH also recommended that Chilean national authorities put an end to the prohibition against the film and maintained that the

decisions by the Chilean high tribunals contradicted the American Convention of Human Rights.

29. Its decision T-231, 1994, presents a good example. In that decision, the court established that the judicial branch has to adequate its decisions to the constitution, which implies not only to ensure individuals' access to justice, but also their access to decisions with particular content. Judicial decisions have to respect strictly the rights and principles of the new constitution, which makes all sentences disrespectful of those contents revisable before the Constitutional Court. In *Decision* C-578, 1995, about military criminal justice, the court made it clear that military officers were not allowed to obey orders that violated human rights, and in *Decision* C-358, 1997, the court maintained, among other things, that military officers who violated human rights were subject to civil rather than military justice.

30. For example, in *Decision C-283, 1995,* the court contributed to delimiting the powers of Congress and the president regarding the preservation of public order and tried to preserve the autonomy and authority of the latter. Also, in *Decision T-683, 1999,* the court argued for the superior authority of the executive in issues concerning public order. This allowed the president to decide freely how to deal with an extremely difficult situation that involved a mass kidnapping in Cali (while the plaintiff wanted the court to seek alternative solutions that the president was not willing to explore). And in *Decision C-048, 2001,* the court validated a law that allowed the president to withdraw national armed forces from certain areas of the country to facilitate the president's strategy in the promotion of peace.

31. See *Decision C-027, 1996,* which came after the assassination of a presidential candidate, Alvaro Gómez, and Samper's declaration of a state of "internal commotion." Taking into account the social impact of this dramatic event, the court recognized, at least in part, the validity of the President's decision (Uprimny 2004: 59).

32. In a subsequent decision (*Decision C-1153, 2005*), which concerned the *Ley de Garantías,* the court partially moderated the impact of its reelection sentence. Here, and through its self-defined power to "modulate" the laws through its interpretative powers, the court rewrote the law in order to increase the opposition's chances to participate in a fair electoral process.

33. There were three rulings concerning the UPAC system, the first of which was issued in May 1999, *Decision C-383, 1999.*

34. We find the same problem (and may find a similar response) when we explore Helmke's (2005: 134): difficulties in explaining the court's "surprising" ruling in considering some of Alfonsín's pardon laws as constitutional.

4 Explaining the Rise of Accountability Functions of Costa Rica's Constitutional Court

1. The autonomous institutions (adopted from the Uruguayan model) have policy and (frequently) financial autonomy from the elected branches.

2. This stood in stark contrast to the pattern of close elections across Latin America, for example in Mexico in 2006 or Honduras in 2005, where the losing party refused to accept the final result.

3. All constitutional references are from the 1949 Constitution (1998 edition).

4. One notable scholar of Costa Rica constitutional history notes that this was a period of "constitutional obscurantism" during which Supreme Court "magistrates exercised constitutional control with excessive timidity" (Gutiérrez 1999).

5. *Amparo* guarantees everyone, without limitation, the right to appeal to the court to maintain or reestablish all rights established in the Constitution (individual and social guarantees sections IV and V) not already included under the *habeas corpus* provision (article 48 of the Constitution).

6. Law no. 7,128 amended articles 10, 48, 105, and 128 of the Constitution.

7. Authors' interviews with a former justice minister (San Pedro, 1998) and former deputy (San José, August 1997).

8. Studies reveal that most deputies express an interest in returning to Congress after their enforced four-year sabbatical, but very few actually win reelection. Indeed, the average number of "freshmen" deputies was approximately 80 percent from the 1950s through the 1990s, increasing to 88 percent in the 2006–2010 Congress. These data are based on calculations by Michelle Taylor-Robinson, personal correspondence, April 24, 2006.

9. Authors' interview with a Magistrate of the *Sala IV*, San José, November 2007.

10. Cases of unconstitutionality, though, have more formal requirements including the need for legal representation. But, as noted above, the overwhelming majority of cases filed are writs of *amparo*.

11. The president can only set the Assembly's agenda during special sessions of the parliament. In regular sessions of the Congress, the president needs to rely on co-partisans to place bills high on the agenda.

12. Public expenditure in state education, for example, cannot be less than 6 percent of gross domestic product (GDP) (article 78).

13. The executive was also instructed to contact the *Casa Real Española* to correct their Web site concerning the information about Costa Rica's military.

14. In both cases, the necessary two-thirds vote to prevent the automatic reelection was not obtained.

15. With the collapse of the PUSC and the rise of smaller parties in the Congress, this compromise on who to elect to the *Sala IV* has become still more pronounced.

5 The Accountability Functions of African Courts

1. Although, as VonDoepp (2009) points out, Nuglube was not Chiluba's favorite candiate for the job.

2. Survey data indicate that Zambians have considerably less trust in their courts than Malawians, indeed, the least of the African countries analyzed (see footnote 7).

3. President Banda, who ruled Malawi from 1961 to 1994, sidelined the formal judiciary through a parallel system of "traditional courts" with broad jurisdiction and very limited independence (Kanyongolo 2004).

4. See Ellett (2008); Gloppen and Kanyongolo (2006a, 2006b, 2007); VonDoepp (2009). The Afrobarometer surveys (2005–2006) report higher trust in the courts in Malawi than in any other of the 15 counties surveyed. Seventy-four percent of the respondents indicate that they trust the courts "a lot" and only 8 percent do not trust them at all. In Uganda and Mozambique, 60 and 59 percent of the population report that they trust the courts "a lot," as do 39 percent in Tanzania, 32 percent in South Africa, and 23 percent in Zambia. (The average for the 15 African countries surveyed is 37 percent.) In Malawi, trust in the courts has been steadily rising: in 1999, 50 percent of Malawian respondents indicated that they trusted the courts "somewhat/most times" or "a lot/always," while in 2002, 61 percent indicated that they trusted the courts "a lot" or "a very great deal" (Afrobarometer n.d.).

5. An injunction requires someone to stop (or take) specific actions, or face civil or criminal penalties. Preliminary injunctions temporarily restrain actions until the court has made a final decision after a trial. Injunctions are based on equity or natural justice and are normally viewed as extraordinary measures taken when the law does not provide adequate remedies (see Cornell Law School, n.d.). Injunctions are also sought by the government against the opposition and in conflicts where the government is not involved, for example in party-internal conflicts (see Gloppen, Rakner, and Svåsand, 2007).

6. Authors' interview with a Malawian judge, July 2004.

7. Corruption is endemic and the quality of the democratic process has declined (see Gloppen and Kanyongolo, 2006a; Gloppen, Rakner, and Svåsand, 2007).

8. This includes the Public Affairs Committee (PAC), a civil society body formed by a number of the country's faith communities. For the role of Malawi's civil society and faith communities, see Englund (2000); Ross (2004); Svåsand and Patel (2007); VonDoepp (2002).

9. On the role of the South African judiciary under apartheid, see Dyzenhaus (1991) and Ellmann (1992, 1995).

10. It also provided for horizontal application, making constitutional rights applicable to relations between private individuals, not only between citizens and state institutions.

11. Contrary to expectations that COPE might challenge the ANC's dominance, the party only won 7.4 percent of the vote in the April 2009 elections against 65.9 percent for Jacob Zuma and the ANC (EISA 2009).

12. CCM has won all elections under the multiparty system (1995, 2000, 2005). In the last presidential election, the CCM's candidate, Jakaya Kikwete, received 80 percent of the vote and the party won 206 of the 232 directly elected seats of the National Assembly (see EISA, n.d.).

13. Strong allegations of political influence are levied at the courts on Zanzibar, where political power is hotly contested. While Zanzibar's Chief Justice is seen

to merge the political will of the executive with the disciplining force of the internal court hierarchy, the Court of Appeal, which Zanzibar shares with the mainland, is considered a safeguard.

14. Authors' interviews with Tanzanian High Court and Court of Appeal judges, August 2002.

15. This is elaborated in Chapter 2. See Corder and van de Vijver (2006); codes for judicial independence (such as the Bangalore Principles) and norms for assessing judicial independence (e.g., IFES Judicial Integrity Principles).

16. A merger between the two courts has long been discussed and is a priority of the Zuma administration (Minister of Justice Jeff Radebe in Alcock 2009b). Concerns have been that the Constitutional Court would lack expertise to deal with everyday "black letter" law, and that a merger would detract from the quality of constitutional jurisprudence—the 11 Constitutional Court judges with their light case load and generous research facilities apply ample attention to develop the legal arguments in each case.

17. In Tanzania the Supreme Court of Appeal hears appeals directly from the High Court on the mainland. Zanzibar has its own appellate court from where decisions can be appealed to the Supreme Court.

18. In Tanzania, since 1994 and in Malawi since 2004. The Zambian government rejected a proposal by the 1996 Mwanakatwe Constitution Review Commission for a high-court level Constitutional Court (Chanda 2007).

19. "I used to collect 2–3 cases a week, but after 1994 . . . we have maybe 1–2 human rights cases a year" (Authors' interview with legal scholar, Dar es Salam, July 2002; Peter and Kijo-Bisimba, 2007).

20. RSA Constitution, § 33 obliges government institutions to provide written reasons to those affected by a decision.

21. In addition, military courts are used extensively, also for charging civilians and their jurisdiction and when relations to the civil court hierarchy are disputed. The General Court Martial has refused to accept the authority of the High Court and the Constitutional Court.

22. According to the Malawian Constitution, Article 103(2), the establishment of parallel judicial institutions is prohibited. Courts have jurisdiction over all issues of a judicial nature, and exclusive authority to decide whether an issue is within its competence. Some sections of the constitution, including protection of judicial independence and jurisdiction, can only be amended through a referendum.

23. All SACC judges have been lawyers, but some are appointed from academia. Legal academics are also found on the court elsewhere, notably in Uganda, but these are practicing lawyers, satisfying the formal criteria.

24. Authors' interview with JSC staff, Kampala, December 2005.

25. In the 2006 constitutional review process, the Ugandan government proposed to cut the qualification for judicial appointment to five years, which was widely seen to be part of a plan to "transform" the judiciary.

26. Justice Kalaile was, however, considered weak. As head of the Electoral Commission, he was perceived as politically dependent and had to resign after the 2004 elections.

27. Its five members are the Chief Justice (Chair); the Chair of the Civil Service Commission; Judge or Justice of Appeal; and a legal practitioner and a magistrate appointed by the president after consultation with the Chief Justice.

28. Only Uganda has a fixed (four-year) term for JSC commissioners, but with the possibility of reappointment.

29. The JSC consists of the Chief Justice, the Deputy Chief Justice, the Minister of Justice (all presidential appointees), and four members chosen by the president after consultation with the leaders of the other parties. Ten commissioners are parliamentarians (at least three from the opposition). Six are from the legal profession, nominated by their profession (§178). The JSC (without the ten parliamentary representatives) advises the government on matters relating to the judiciary and the administration of justice (§178(5)).

30. Authors' interviews indicate that the president has on occasion appointed judges from outside the list.

31. The process should be in accordance with principles of natural justice, which includes that the judge in question is heard. The limited possibility for the judges be heard was a point of criticism (Martin 2002).

32. At the time of writing, this has led to politicization of the JSC after its recommendation to impeach Western Cape Judge President Hlope for trying to unduly influence two Constitutional Court judges in a case involving President Zuma (Alcock 2009).

33. In South Africa, legislation and constitutional amendments tabled in late 2005 proposed to reduce the financial and administrative autonomy of the judiciary, placing it more under the control of the Ministry of Justice. A huge public outcry and resistance from civil society, the legal community, and the judiciary itself led to the withdrawal of the legislation in June 2006 (see Albertyn 2007; Gordon and Bruce, 2007).

34. Political cases are broadly defined as "any case whose outcome had implications for the ability of governments to exercise or retain power or had any impact on the political fortunes and activities of actors in civil and political society" (VonDoepp 2006: 392).

35. The Public Order Act, defamation, and criminal libel suits have been used to harass journalists (Freedom House 2006).

36. The article by Arthur Simuchoba (editor) and Chali Nondo appeared in the August 16–19, 2002, edition of *The Monitor* (Zambia) and is cited in Amnesty International (2003). The incident is also reported in MISA (2002).

37. *A.M. Lewanika and others v. F.J.T. Chiluba* 1998 SCZ 8/EP/4/96.

38. Court rulings restrained police efforts to halt an opposition rally with prominent ruling party politicians challenging Chiluba's program to amend the constitution and forbade Chiluba and his allies from expelling from MMD some members opposing the constitutional amendment (Van Doepp 2004, 2009). Regarding Chiluba's abandonment of his reelection bid, see Cauvin (2001).

39. *Godfrey Miyanda and Others v. Attorney General, the Electoral Commission and Returning Officer for Presidential Elections* 2001 HP 1174). See also VonDoepp (2009).

40. The president opted for a new constitution to be adopted by parliament—after the 2006 elections.

41. A new electoral law had been put in place, and international observers judged the 2006 elections the best since 1991 (Freedom House 2007).

42. Parliament lifted Chiluba's immunity, and in 2007 the Supreme Court ordered him to stand trial despite pleas that he was too ill (see BBC News Reporter 2007; Times of Zambia Reporter 2007). The verdict in the case is expected on July 20, 2009 (Dugger 2009).

43. The High Court in *The People v. Senior Chief Inyambo Yeta and 7 others* (1996 HCZ) in November 1996 dismissed a treason charge against members of a main opposition party.

44. *Nkhwazi v. Referendum Commission* 1993 Civil Cause 96.

45. *Aaron Longwe v. Attorney General* 1993 Miscellaneous Civil Application 11.

46. *Du Chsiza jnr v. Minister of Education* 1993 Civil Cause 10.

47. The judiciary also upheld laws that hampered the democratization process, notably in *Chakufwa Chihana v. The Republic* (1992 Criminal Appeal 9), which involved a sedition charge against the leader of a promultiparty pressure group; and *Muluzi and Thomson v. Attorney General* (1993 Civil Cause 66), in which opposition members were denied an injunction to prevent the police from stopping their publicity for a public meeting.

48. In *Re Nomination of J.J. Chidule* (1995 Civil Cause 5), the High Court held that to qualify for nomination to contest for a parliamentary seat, a person must be registered, but not necessarily in the constituency in which (s)he intends to contest. Election petitions include *Chikweza v. The Electoral Commission* 1994 Civil Cause 1061 and *Phoso v. The Electoral Commission* 1996 Civil Cause 1271.

49. *Chakuamba and Chihana v. The Electoral Commission* 1999 Civil Cause 25.

50. *Phambala v. Chairman* 1999 Electoral Commission Civil Cause 34.

51. *Khembo v. Electoral Commission* 1999 Civil Cause 70.

52. *Mungomo v. Electoral Commission* 1999 Civil Application 23.

53. Other decisions upheld the Electoral Commission's authority. *The Attorney General v. Chakuamba, Kalua and Mnkhumbwe and Kafumba v. Electoral Commission* 1999 Civil Cause 30.

54. 1999 Civil Cause 30.

55. *The Republic v. Chikhadwe and Chikhadwe* (2004 First Magistrates Court LL/CR/60/1/2004).

56. *National Democratic Alliance (NDA) v. Electoral Commission, MBC and TVM* 2004 Constitutional Cause 3.

57. *The Attorney General v. Chakuamba, Kalua and Mnkhumbwe* 1999 Civil Cause 1.

58. In *Public Affairs Committee v. Attorney General* 2002, the right of MPs to freely associate with civil society groups in political advocacy campaigns was upheld.

59. The first petitioner withdrew after being given a cabinet post, while the second petitioner was ruled out of the case in July 2005.

60. *The Malawi Supreme Court of Appeal at Blantyre* 2006 MSCA Civil Appeal 22.

61. The quote is attributed to several former presidents, including Brazil's Getulio Vargas, Peru's Oscar R. Benavides, Mexico's Benito Juarez, and former Spanish dictator Francisco Franco.

62. Mwawa was reportedly taken to the maximum security prison after the trial (IOL 2006).

63. The two also reconciled in the wake of the May 2009 elections. President Mutharika has also arrested other political opponents on charges of treason, but most of these cases fizzled without coming to trial (*Tribune Reporter* 2008).

64. *August v. Electoral Commission* 1996 CCT 8/99.

65. The South African floor-crossing provision, unlike the one in Malawi, applies not only apply to voluntary defections to other parties, but also to deputies who are expelled or become independent. This enhances the provision's usefulness as a disciplining mechanism for the party leadership.

66. For an overview, see BBC News (2009).

67. Zuma admitted intercourse with a family friend, but claimed it was consensual. He was acquitted, but politically damaged, particularly after statements indicating that he believed taking a shower would protect against HIV transmission (Harber, de Plessis and Kupe, 2006; Kapp, 2006).

68. In November 2007, the SCA ruled in favor of the National Prosecuting Authority with respect to various search and seizure exercises and rejected four appeals made by Zuma's defense team. The Constitutional Court confirmed this in July 2008 (Mabuza 2008).

69. *National Director of Public Prosecutions v Zuma* (573/08) [2009] ZASCA 1 (January 12, 2009).

70. *Government of the Republic of South Africa and Others v. Grootboom and Others* 2001 SA 1/46/CC.

71. For further information and analysis regarding this case, see Gloppen (2005) and Roux (2004).

72. For an analysis of this case and its political dimensions, see Gloppen (2005) and Heywood (2005).

73. *Julius Ishengoma Francis Ndyanabo v. The Attorney General* 2001 CA 64, judgment on February 14, 2002.

74. *Peter Ng'omango v. Gerson M.K. Mwarangwa and another* 1992 High Court of Tanzania at Dodoma (reported in Peter 1997b, 309). See also *Pumbun and Another v. Attorney-General and Another* 1992/1993 Court of Appeal of Tanzania at Arusha.

75. *Rev Christopher Mtikila v. Attorney General* 1993 High Court of Tanzania at Dodoma (Peter 1997b:674).

76. *Pumbun and Another v. Attorney-General and Another* 1993 Court of Appeal of Tanzania at Arusha 2/LRC/317.

77. *Mbushuu, Dominic Mnyaroje, and Kalai Sangula v. Republic* 1994 Court of Appeal of Tanzania at Dar es Salaam, Criminal Appeal 142 (reported in 1995 LRC 1).

78. In *Attorney-General v. W.K. Butambala* 1993 TLR 46, the Court Appeal indirectly referred to a High Court Judge as an "Ambulance Chaser"; see also

Mbushuu Dominic Mnyaroge and Another v. R 1995 TLR 97 (Peter and Kijo-Bisimba, 2007).

79. *Paul Kawanga Ssemogerere and Another* v. *Attorney General* 2000.
80. *The New Referendum (Political Systems) Act* 2000(9).
81. *James Rwanyarare and Badru Wegulo* 2000 Petition 4. The Petitioners sought an interim order to prohibit the holding of the referendum until the final disposal of the case.
82. *Ssemwogerere and* Zachary *Olum v. Attorney General* 1999 Constitutional Petition 6.
83. *Ssemogerere and Anor v. Attorney General* 1999 Constitutional Petition 7.
84. *Ssemogerere and Anor v. Attorney General* 2002 Constitutional Appeal 4.
85. *Attorney General v. Ssemogerere and Others.*
86. *Paul Kawanga Ssemogerere and 5 others v. Attorney General of Uganda*
87. *Okello Okello, John Livingstone, and 6 Others v. Attorney General and Electoral Commission* 2005 Constitutional Petition 4. The reference to nonexisting system referred to the judgment in the PPOA case (earlier text) in which the court found that Uganda in fact was a one-party state (which it was argued, is in breach of fundamental rights and not a constitutional option).
88. JSC staff, in Gloppen, Kasimbazi and Kibandama (2008).
89. 2002 Constitutional Appeal 2.
90. Andrew Mwenda, political editor in *The Monitor* and KFM talk show host.
91. *Weekly Observer* editor James Tumusiime and reporter Semujju Ibrahim Nganda.
92. 2005 Constitutional Petition 6.
93. The judgment quoted Liberman (1988: 128), "Even when constitutional rights are asserted, some questions are too political for the courts to give legal answers. This 'political question' doctrine is another way of saying that over certain issues, the Constitution commits complete discretion to the other branches."
94. Documented by observers, including the NGO Election Monitoring Group-Uganda (Redfern 2001)
95. Justices Oder and Tsekooko supported Besigye's petition. Chief Justice Odoki, Justices Karokora and Mulenga ruled in favour of Museveni. See Supreme Court of Uganda (2006) *Rtd. Col. Kizza Besigye v. The EC and Yoweri Kaguta Museveni* (Presidential Election Petition 1 of 2006); the full case is cited in *The Monitor* (2006).
96. *Miria Matembe, Ben Wacha, and Hon. Abdu Katuntu v. A.G.* 2005 Constitutional Petition 5.
97. *Rtd. Col. Kizza Besigye v. The EC and Yoweri Kaguta Museveni* 2006 Presidential Election Petition 1.
98. The claims of illegal campaigning practices by Museveni personally, or by his agents with his knowledge and consent, were dismissed by a majority of five judges.
99. For example, after the Constitutional Court ruling that found the 2001 referendum unconstitutional, and when a minority on the Supreme Court voted to overturn the 2001 presidential election. Museveni accused judges of supporting

Besigye, drawing strong reactions from the judiciary (Sunday Monitor Team 2006). Besigye's team has also questioned the independence of the judiciary, and of named judges.

100. Similar paramilitary presence in court a year later caused very little reaction, nationally or internationally.

101. *Asol Kabagambe and Faraj Abdullah v. EC* 2006 Constitutional Petition 1. Here, the court declared that the Electoral Commission, as an independent institution, was not obliged to follow the advice of the Attorney General (who had suggested to the EC that the nomination should be dismissed).

102. A partial exception is Tanzania, which experienced a period of judicial activism in the late 1980s.

103. In an internal memo in July 2005, Deputy Chief Justice Kikonyogo stopped dissenting rulings in the *Okello Okello* case (earlier text).

104. The 2001 impeachment of Malawian judges drew reactions from the international community—unlike when the chief justice resigned in 2007. In Uganda, the international community reacted strongly to the military action in the Kampala High Court prior to the 2006 election, but not at all to a similar incident a year later.

105. Interviews with authors, Kampala, February 2006.

106. Donors need to stay on good terms with the government to secure good projects (authors' interview with donor representatives, Kampala, 2005–2006).

107. Authors' interview, April 2005.

108. To isolate "political" matters, preventing "contamination" of the remaining legal system, is a central argument for separate Constitutional Courts. That political considerations often influence their composition may be an advantage: "(T)hat a court's members have political views broadly sympathetic to those of the governing elite may be a necessary condition for them to assert their independence …" (Roux 2004: 94).

109. Access to the SACC is more difficult in practice than reflected in the legal provisions (Dugard 2006).

110. In 2006, South Africa had 218 judges (see Government Communication and Information System 2006).

111. In Tanzania, one High Court Justice, Mwalusanya, made a string of assertive judgments on human rights issues in the 1980s and early 1990s. His retirement marked a sharp downturn in judgments challenging the government (Peter and Kijo-Bisimba, 2007). Similarly in Malawi, Judge Mwaungulu has delivered a number of judgments against the government in political cases. VonDoepp (2006) finds, however, that the pattern is robust, even when controlling for the effect of individual judges.

112. Examples here include notably SC Judge Kaneyhamba in Uganda and SACC Judge Kate O'Regan in South Africa. Similarly, a higher share of the more assertive judges seems to receive academic training abroad.

113. Including Justices Mpangi Bahigeine (Uganda), Kate O'Regan (South Africa), Anastasia Msosa and Jane Ansah (Malawi), and Eusebia Munuo and Kimaro (Tanzania).

114. In Malawi, very significant accountability judgments came in the aftermath of the 2004 election, but this was also a political context marked by uncertainty regarding who would be the long-term power holders.

115. VonDoepp's (2006) study of the judiciary in Malawi and Zambia, using "strategic defection," also finds that this has considerable explanatory value.

6 Does Legal Tradition Matter? The Emerging Accountability Functions of Mozambican High Courts

1. Note that Mozambique's independence coincided with the fall of the Salazar regime in Portugal in 1974 and the introduction of democratic rule in the former colonial power. For an account of the influence of colonial Portuguese law and courts system on national and traditional legal practice in Lusophone Africa, see Coissoro (1984).

2. Mozambique's constitutional developments are analyzed in Hall and Young (1991).

3. Both as an individual or as part of a group, citizens now possess the right to claim compensation as well as the right to act in defense of public health, consumer rights, environmental conservation, cultural heritage, and public property.

4. Community courts were once again recognized as legal structures, with jurisdiction at the lowest level in both civil and criminal matters.

5. For more details on the ombudsperson's office and expectations for such an office, see Global Integrity (n.d).

6. Of the specialized courts, only the Customs Court has been established (in 1992) and many of the district courts have either not been established or are not operational (AfriMAP and OSISA, 2006b).

7. Law 4/1990, and Law 7/1998 and corresponding regulations, approved respectively by Decree 55/2000 and Decree 48/ 2000. See also the Anti-Corruption Law 6/2004 (cited in ibid.).

8. Accountability and review mechanisms are further discussed in (AfriMAP and OSISA, 2006: 66–70).

9. "Administrative acts are decisions or regulations specifically pertaining to a particular individual or a group of individuals (including contracts), as opposed to legislative acts which refer to a general abstract body. Administrative acts are issued by the executive and its agencies, as opposed to the legislature" (AfriMAP, and OSISA, 2006b: 37, fn. 70).

10. For more details on contesting government acts before the AC, see (ibid., 67).

11. *Lei do Contencioso Administrativo* (Administrative Litigation Law, 2001 9/ BR/27, I Série).

12. Compared to, for example, Costa Rica's Constitutional Chamber (discussed in Chapter 4), access is much more limited in Mozambique. However, compared to high courts in other countries not analyzed in this book, such as the Supreme Court of Norway, many more agents have access in Mozambique. Note that access should not be discussed in isolation, but rather in relation to standing and docket control.

13. Since elected judges are to participate only in first instance trials and in discussions regarding verification of matters of fact (not in interpretation of the law), they do not play a central role in exercising the type of accountability function that is the focus of this chapter and will therefore not be discussed any further.

14. The CSMJ is composed of the president of the SC, the vice president of the SC, two members nominated by the president of the republic, five members appointed by parliament (based on proportional representation), one SC judge, two provincial court judges, one district court judge, and four court officials.

15. The details of the structure and composition of the AC are laid out in "The Administrative Court of the Republic of Mozambique" in Law 5/92 (see Rainha 2009).

16. Statute of the Judicial Magistracy (Law 10/91 of July 30, article 43) (see ibid).

17. The AC of the Republic of Mozambique in Law 5/92 (see ibid).

18. Population according to the 2007 census carried out by the *Instituto National de Estatística* (INA) in Mozambique was 20,530,714 (see Instituto Nacional de Estatística 2009).

19. Statement by Mario Mangaze, president of the SC, interviewed in the first week of September 2006 issue of the Mozambican weekly paper *O Pais*.

20. For more specific figures for the 2005 state budget see AfriMAP and OSISA (2006b).

21. While this may raise questions about financial accountability and transparency, this is a different issue that we will not address here.

22. However, this may change with the new Organic Law for the courts submitted to the Legal Affairs Committee of the Parliament in 2006. The Organic Law of the Judicial Courts (Law 24/07 of August 20, 2007) transferred the construction competence from the SC to the Ministry of Justice in an attempt to relieve the judges of some of their administrative burden. It still remains to be seen how the Ministry of Justice manages its increased portfolio of administrating the courts (Antonopolous, Maputo, 2006, personal communication).

23. Note that this practice runs contrary to what the SC is legally bound to do. During colonial times, the judgments were in effect published annually in books. This practice stopped in 1975 and has not been resumed despite considerable donor pressure to the contrary (authors' interviews with individuals in the legal sector, including an SC judge, in Maputo, November 2005).

24. A ten-year research project on law and justice in Mozambique concluded in 2006 that data are not readily available, lamented the inadequacies of official statistics, and noted "the chaos of judicial archives, where they existed...." (de Sousa Santos, Trinidade, and Meneses, 2006).

25. The CNE, established in 2002, is the organization responsible for elections in Mozambique. The CNE, composed of both Frelimo and Renamo members (proportionate to the parties' vote share in the assembly), has been accused of being Frelimo-friendly due to the Frelimo majority of the membership.

26. Mozambique News Agency (2004); Mozambique News Agency (2005); see also The Carter Center (2005); Gloor (2005). All the sentences issued by the CC in connection with the 2004 presidential and parliamentary elections are compiled in República de Mocambique, Conselho Constitucional (2004).
27. 2004 16/CC/04, 14 (re Proc. 14/CC/03); Decision 5/CC/2005 (re Proc. 30/CC/2005).
28. Authors' interview with leading personnel of the Liga Mocambicana dos Direitos Humanos (LDH), Maputo, November 18, 2005.
29. afrol News (2005). See also reports from one of the international election observers, The Carter Center (2005a, 2005).
30. The fact that Renamo lost the elections by a landslide and thus never threatened the hegemony of the ruling party may have facilitated Chissano's resignation in favor of Guebuza.
31. See Republic of Mozambique (2006: section IV, A) for information on the justice sector.
32. Luís Timóteo Matsinhe v. President of the Supreme Court of Mozambique 2002 78, Acórdão 5/2002/1/a, I Section of the AC.
33. Authors' interview with law professor, Eduardo Mondlane University, Maputo, November 16, 2005; and a private lawyer, Maputo, November 17, 2005.
34. Authors' interview by the author, Maputo, November 2005.
35. This information is compiled from lawyers, judges, and donors (Maputo, November 2005).
36. See a series of articles appearing in the Mozambican press compiled in Hanlon (2001). See also biweekly reports on the Cardoso case from Mozambique News Agency for the period December 2002–May 2004 (Mozambique News Agency 2003). Note in particular Mozambique News Agency (2004).
37. Tribunal Judicial da Cidade de Maputo, 10a Secção. Acórdão (unnumbered and undated, on file with authors). The judge issuing the sentence, Judge Augusto Paulino, is now the country's attorney general.
38. Authors' interview with a legal advisor to UNDP, Maputo, November 17, 2006.
39. The details of the Vilanculos case are to be found in "Resumo do Litigo entre a Sociedade Cabo do Mar Limitada e as Sociedades Santuario da Fauna Costeira de Vilanculos e Nyati Beach Lodge" (document in Portuguese on file with authors, including English translation).
40. Supreme Court of Mozambique (Secção Cível do Tribunal Supremo), Vilanculos case 2006 Acórdão.
41. Our conclusion is supported by other research (AfriMAP and OSISA, 2006b).
42. Prior to the implementation of the CC, its functions were carried out by the SC, and hence the Islamic Holidays Law was referred to the SC. Apparently, it took seven years for the judgment to be published.
43. Family Law 2004 10/04/BR/34, I Série, Suplemento.
44. Authors' interview with a law professor, Eduardo Mondlane University, Maputo, November 16, 2005.

45. For an insightful account of the recruitment basis for Renamo as well as the transformation of Renamo from a guerrilla movement to a political opposition party, see Manning (1998).
46. Summary of evidence from authors' interviews in Maputo, November 2005.
47. Authors' interview with an SC judge, Maputo, November 24, 2005.

7 Conclusion: Multifactor Explanations

1. These include cases where executives have overstepped their powers, altered the rules of the political game in their favor, or acted in breach of constitutional mandates.
2. The concept of "critical junctures" is discussed in Chapter 2.
3. For example, attitudinalists assume the appointing authority selects judges who share their ideology or background to create propensities for "friendly" voting, even when judges vote their sincere preferences. Rational choice scholars, on the other hand, assume the appointing authority influences judges' incentive structures and their strategic calculations.
4. (Threaths of) subjecting the judiciary to corruption investigations have a similar function, particularly in contexts where anti-corruption bodies are effectively under executive control (VonDoepp 2009). Such "warnings" have been issued in Uganda, Zambia, and Malawi (and carried out in Kenya). Of course, legitimate reasons for corruption investigations may exist, but when the executive orders corruption investigations that follow adverse judgments, it signals intimidation.
5. On constitutional courts in the tradition of Kelsen, see Shaprio (2004). A central concern is here to prevent politicization of the rest of the legal system by isolating the more overtly political constitutional cases.
6. The most famous example from U.S. constitutional history, is the *Marbury v. Madison,* 5 U.S. (Cranch 1) 137 (1803) ruling in which the SC established its judicial review powers.
7. Constitutional Court of South Africa: *Ex parte Chairperson of the Constitutional Assembly: in re Certification of the Constitution of the Republic of South Africa 1996.*
8. Authors' interview with authors, San José, Costa Rica, June 2008.
9. Tanzania is a case in point. When Justice Mwalusanya, who wrote a number of assertive judgments against the executive in the 1980s and 1990s, retired, the number of accountability cases declined significantly.

References

Abrahamsson, Hans and Anders Nilsson. 1995. *Mozambique, the Troubled Transition: From Socialist Construction to Free Market Capitalism.* London: Zed Books.

Ackerman, Bruce A. 1985. "Beyond Carolene Products." *Harvard Law Review* 98: 713–746.

Ackerman, Bruce A. 1991. *We The People: Foundations.* Boston: Harvard University Press.

Ackerman, Bruce A. 1997. "The Rise of World Constitutionalism." *Virginia Law Review* 83: 771–797.

AfriMAP and OSISA. 2006. "Mozambique: Justice Sector and the Rule of Law." London and South Africa: Open Society Initiative for Southern Africa.

Afrobarometer. N.d. "Afrobarometer Online Data Analysis." Available at http://www.jdsurvey.net/jds/afrobarometer.jsp. Accessed on June 2, 2009.

afrol News. 2005. "Mozambique elections will not be annulled." January 17. Available at http://www.afrol.com/articles/15327. Accessed on December 21, 2005.

Albertyn, Catherine. 2007. "Judicial Independence and the Constitution Fourteenth Amendment Bill." *South African Journal of Human Rights* 22(1): 126–143.

Alcock, Sello S. 2009a. "Hlophe on Zuma's Yellow Brick Road." *Mail and Guardian.* May 22–28, p. 10.

Alcock, Sello S. 2009b. "Tackling Transformation of the Judiciary." *Mail and Guardian.* June 12. Available at www.mg.co.za/article/2009–06-12-tackling-transformation-of-the-judiciary. Accessed on June 2, 2009.

Alcock, Sello S. 2009c. "Race for Concourt Judges." *Mail and Guardian.* June 21. Available at http://www.mg.co.za/article/2009–06-21-race-for-concourt-judges. Accessed on June 2, 2009.

Alvarado, Eduardo E. 2005. "Encontró un artículo inconstitucional: Sala frena Ley de emergencias." *La Nación.* July 7. San José, Costa Rica. Available at http://www.mg.co.za/article/2009–06-21-race-for-concourt-judges. Accessed on October 15, 2009.

Amnesty International. 2003. "Amnesty International Report 2003: Zambia." UNHCR Refworld (May). Available at http://www.unhcr.org/refworld/docid/3edb47e42.html. Accessed on June 2, 2009.

Ansolabehere, Karina. 2007. *La política desde la justicia: Cortes Supremas, gobierno y democracia en Argentina y Mexico.* Tlalpan, Mexico DF: FLACSO.

Arrieta, Aquiles. 2003. "Comentarios a la creación de jurisprudencia constitucional." *Tutela* 4(45): 1752–1785.

Asamblea Legislativa de la República de Costa Rica. Expediente N° 10.401. Proyecto de ley de reforma a los artículos 10, 48, 105 y 128 de la Constitución Política.

Atria, Fernando. 2003. "La hora del derecho: Los 'derechos humanos' entre la política y el derecho." Unpublished manuscript.

Austen-Smith, David and Jeffrey Banks.1989. "Electoral Accountability and Incumbency." In Peter C. Ordeshook, ed., *Models of Strategic Choice in Politics.* Ann Arbor, MI: University of Michigan Press, pp. 121–150.

Austral Consultoria e Projectos, Lda. 2005. "National Survey on Governance and Corruption." Maputo: Austral Consultoria e Projectos, Lda.

BBC News. 2009. "Timeline: Zuma's legal problems." April 6. Available at http://news.bbc.co.uk/2/hi/africa/7153378.stm. Accessed on June 2, 2009.

BBC News Reporter. 2007. "Zambia's Chiluba to stand trial." *BBC News*, May 31. Available at http://news.bbc.co.uk/2/hi/africa/6707621.stm. Accessed on June 2, 2009.

Bermúdez, Mario. 2003. "Sala IV se constituye en superpoder." *La República*. April 8. San José, Costa Rica, pp. 4–5.

Bickel, Alexander. 1967. *The Least Dangerous Branch: The Supreme Court at the Bar of Politics.* New Haven, CT: Yale University Press.

Blom, Astrid Benedikte. 2002. *Beyond Despotism: An Analysis of the Constitution of Chiefs' Authority through Land Dispute Processes in Angónia District, Central Mozambique.* PhD. dissertation, International Development Studies, Roskilde University, and Center for Development Research, Copenhagen.

Brand, Danie and Christof H. Heyns. 2005. *Socio-economic Rights in South Africa.* Pretoria: Pretoria University Law Press.

Brinks, Daniel M. 2005. "Judicial Reform and Independence in Brazil and Argentina: The Beginning of a New Millennium?" *Texas International Law Journal* 40: 595–622.

Bugaric, Bojan. 2001. "Courts as Policy-Makers. Lessons from Transition." *Harvard Law Review* 42(1): 247–288.

Calzada Miranda, Ana Virginia. 2008. "Legitimación democratica de los tribunales constitucionales." Available at http://www.poder-judicial.go.cr/salaconstitucional/jornadas/ponencias.htm. Accessed on March 10, 2009.

Carey, John M. 1996. *Term Limits and Legislative Representation.* Cambridge: Cambridge University Press.

Carothers, Thomas. 2006. "The Backlash against Democracy Promotion." *Foreign Affairs* 85 (2): 55–68.

The Carter Center. 2004. "Postelection Statement on Mozambique Elections, December 4." Available at http://www.cartercenter.org/doc1933.htm. Accessed on December 21, 2005.

The Carter Center. 2005. "Postelection Statement on Mozambique Elections, January 26." Available at http://www.cartercenter.org/doc1999.htm. Accessed on December 21, 2005.

Cauvin, Henri E. 2001. "Zambia's President Abandons Re-election Bid." *New York Times*. May 5, available at http://query.nytimes.com/gst/fullpage.html?res =9D00E4DB1138F936A35756C0A9679C8B63&scp=12&sq=Chiluba&st=nyt. Accessed on June 3, 2009.

Cepeda-Espinosa, Manuel José. 2004. "Judicial Activism in a Violent Context: The Origin, Role, and Impact of the Colombian Constitutional Court." *Washington University Global Studies Law Review* 3: 529–699.

Chanda, Alfred. 2000. "Public Order (Amendment) Act—Constitutionality of the Amendment Act and its Application to Date in Zambia." *The Human Rights Observer* 3 (October): 14–19.

Chanda, Alfred W. 2007. "Mwanakatwe Constitutional Review Commission." Zambia Legal Information Institute Media Directory. Available at http://www. zamlii.ac.zm/media/news/viewnews.cgi?category=2&id=1098362568. Accessed on June 3, 2009.

Chanock, Martin. 2001. *The Making of South African Legal Culture 1902–1936: Fear, Favour and Prejudice*. Cambridge: Cambridge University Press.

Choudhry, Sujit. 1999. "Globalization in Search of Justification: Toward a Theory of Comparative Constitutional Interpretation." *Indiana Law Journal* 74(3): 819–892.

CIA World Factbook. 2008. "Rank Order—GDP Per Capita (PPP)." Available at https://www.cia.gov/library/publications/the-world-factbook/ rankorder/2004rank.html. Accessed on June 3, 2009.

CIA World Factbook. 2009a. "Rank Order—Population." Available at https:// www.cia.gov/library/publications/the-world-factbook/rankorder/2119rank.html. Accessed on June 3, 2009.

CIA World Factbook. 2009b. "Country Comparisons—GDP—per capita (PPP)." Available at https://www.cia.gov/library/publications/the-world-factbook/ rankorder/2004rank.html. Accessed on June 3, 2009.

CIA World Factbook. 2009c. "Country Comparisons—Population." Available at https://www.cia.gov/library/publications/the-world-factbook/ rankorder/2004rank.html. Accessed on June 3, 2009.

Clavijo, Sergio. 2001. "Fallos y fallas económicas de las altas cortes; el caso de Colombia 1991–2000." *Borradores de Economia,* Banco de la Republica de Colombia, 173:1–43.

Coissoro, Narana. 1984. "African Customary Law in the Former Portuguese Territories, 1954–1974." *Journal of African Law* 28(1/2): 72–79.

Constitución Política de la República de Costa Rica [de 7 de noviembre de 1949]. 1998. 1ª edición (comentada y anotada por Rubén Hernández Valle). San José: Editorial Juricentro.

Contesse, Jorge. 2004. "La rebelde democracia: una mirada a la relación entre los Mapuche y el Estado chileno." In Roberto Saba, ed., *Los Limites de la Democracia*. Buenos Aires: Universidad de Palermo, pp. 240–244.

Corder, Hugh, ed., 1989. *Democracy and the Judiciary: Proceedings of the National Conference on Democracy and the Judiciary*. Cape Town: Institute for a Democratic Alternative for South Africa.

Corder, Hugh, and Linda van de Vijver. 2006. *The Judicial Institution in Southern Africa*. Cape Town: Siber Ink and Constitutional Governance Unit, Faculty of Law, University of Cape Town.

Cornell University Law School, Legal Information Institute. N.d. "Injunction." Available at http://topics.law.cornell.edu/wex/Injunction. Accessed on June 3, 2009.

Correa Sutil, Jorge. 1993. "The Judiciary and the Political System in Chile." In Irwin P. Stotzky, ed., *Transition to Democracy in Latin America: The Role of the Judiciary*. San Francisco, CA: Westview Press, pp. 89–106.

Corte Suprema de Justicia—Sala Constitucional. 1999. Reseña histórica. Available at. http://www.poder–judicial.go.cr/sala4/aniversa/historia.html. Accessed on December 22, 1999.

Corte Suprema de Justicia—Sala Constitucional. 2000. *Jurisprudencia constitucional: recopilación de las sentencias de constitucionalidad dictadas entre 1890 y 1990 por la Corte de Casación y la Corte Plena, Vols. 1–III*. San José, C. R.: Editorial Uned.

Corte Suprema de Justicia—Sala Constitucional. 2004. "Base de Datos del Centro de Documentación de la Corte Suprema de Justicia." San José: Corte Suprema de Justicia.

Couso, Javier A. and Lisa Hilbink. 2009. "From Quietism to Incipient Activism: The Institutional and Ideational Roots of Rights Adjudication in Chile." Paper presented at the 2009 conference on Judicial Politics in Latin America, CIDE, Mexico City.

Couso, Javier A. 2004. "The Politics of Judicial Review in Chile in the Era of Democratic Transition, 1990–2002." In Siri Gloppen, Roberto Gargarella and Elin Skaar, eds., *Accountability and the Judiciary: The Accountability Function of Courts in New Democracies*. London: Frank Cass, pp. 46–69.

CPJ (Committee to Protect Journalists). 2007. "Malawi: Private Radio Stations Censored Over Political Coverage." April 17. Available at http://allafrica.com/stories/200704180033.html. Accessed on June 3, 2009.

Cruz Castro, Fernando. 2007. "Costa Rica's Constitutional Jurisprudence, its Political Importance and International Human Rights Law: Examination of Some Decisions." *Duquesnse Law Review* 45(3): 557–576.

Dahl, Robert. 1957. "Decision-Making in a Democracy: The Supreme Court as a National Policy Maker." *Journal of Public Law* 6: 279–295.

Díaz, Dóriam. 2003. "Lluvia de críticas a la Sala IV." *La Nación*. April 6. San José, Costa Rica. Available at http://www.nacion.com/ln_ee/2003/abril/06/pais2.html#1796953. Accessed on October 14, 2009.

Domingo, Pilar. 1999. "Judicial Independence and Judicial Reform in Latin America." In Andreas Schedler, Larry Diamond, and Marc F. Plattner, eds., *The Self-Restraining State: Power and Accountability in New Democracies*. Boulder, CO: Lynne Rienner Publishers, pp. 151–176.

Domingo, Pilar. 2004. "Judicialization of Politics or Politicization of the Judiciary." *Democratization* 11(1): 104–126.

Dugard, Jackie. 2006. "Court of First Instance? Towards a Pro-Poor Jurisdiction for the South African Constitutional Court." *South African Journal on Human Rights* 22(2): 261–282.

Dugger, Celia W. 2009. "Ex-Zambian Leader's High Life Awaits a Verdict." *New York Times*, June 22, available at http://www.nytimes.com/2009/06/22/world/africa/22zambia.html?_r=1. Accessed on June 22, 2009.

Dyzenhaus, David. 1991. *Hard Cases in Wicked Legal Systems: South African Law in the Perspective of Legal Philosophy.* New York: Oxford University Press.

Echeverría Martín, Gloriana. 2000. "La consulta facultativa de constitucionalidad como instrumento de control político." *Revista Parlamentaria* 8(3): 213–223.

EISA (Electoral Institute of Southern Africa). 2009. "South Africa: 2009 National Assembly Election Results." April. Available at http://www.eisa.org.za/WEP/sou2009results1.htm. Accessed on June 5, 2009.

EISA (Electoral Institute of Southern Africa). n.d. "Tanzania: Elections archive." Available at http://www.eisa.org.za/WEP/tanelectarchive.htm. Accessed on June 3, 2009.

Ellett, Rachel L. 2008. *Emerging Judicial Power in Transitional Democracies: Malawi, Tanzania and Uganda.* PhD. dissertation, Northeastern University, Boston, MA.

Ellmann, Stephen J. 1992. *In a Time of Trouble: Law and Liberty in South Africa's State of Emergency.* Oxford: Clarendon Press.

Ellmann, Stephen J. 1995. "Law and Legitimacy in South Africa." *Law and Social Inquiry Journal of the American Bar Foundation* 20(2): 407–479.

Elster, Jon, and Rune Slagstad, eds., 1988. *Constitutionalism and Democracy.* Cambridge: Cambridge University Press.

Ely, John Hart. 1980. *Democracy and Distrust: A Theory of Judicial Review.* Cambridge: Harvard University Press.

Englund, Harri. 2000. "The Dead Hand of Human Rights: Contrasting Christianities in Posttransition Malawi." *The Journal of Modern African Studies* 38(4): 579–603.

Epp, Charles R. 1998. *The Rights Revolution: Lawyers, Activists, and Supreme Courts in Comparative Perspective.* Chicago: University of Chicago Press.

Epstein, Lee, Jack Knight and Andrew D. Martin. 2001. "The Supreme Court as a Strategic National Policymaker." *Emory Law Journal* 50: 583–611.

Epstein, Lee, Jack Knight and Andrew D. Martin. 2003. "The Political (Science) Context of Judging." *St. Louis University Law Journal* 47(3): 783–818.

Epstein, Lee, and Thomas Walker. 1995. "The Role of the Supreme Court in American Society: Playing the Reconstruction Game." In Lee Epstein, ed., *Contemplating Courts.* Washington DC: Congressional Quarterly Press, pp. 315–346.

Eskridge, William, and John Ferejohn. 1992. "Making the Deal Stick: Enforcing the Original Constitutional Structure of Lawmaking in the Modern Regulatory State." *Journal of Law, Economics, and Organization* 8(1): 165–189.

Ferejohn, John A. and Barry R. Weingast. 1992. "A Positive Theory of Statutory Interpretation." *International Review of Law and Economics* 12(2): 263–279.

Flemming, Roy B. and Dan Wood. 1997. "The Public and the Supreme Court: Individual Justice Responsiveness to American Policy Moods." *American Political Science Review* 41: 468–498.

Freedom House. 2006. "Freedom in the World: Zambia 2006." UNHCR Refworld. Available at http://www.freedomhouse.org/inc/content/pubs/fiw/inc_country_detail.cfm?year=2006country=7091&pf. Accessed on June 3, 2009.

Freedom House. 2007. *"Freedom in the World—Zambia 2007."* UNHCR Refworld, available at: http://www.unhcr.org/refworld/docid/473c560949.html. Accessed on June 3, 2009.

Friedler, Edith Z. 2000. "Judicial Review in Chile." *Southwestern Journal of Law & Trade in the Americas* 7: 321–347.

Frühling, Hugo. 1984 . "Poder Judicial y Política en Chile." In *La administración de justicia en América Latina*. Lima, Peru: Consejo Latinoamericano de Derecho y Desarrollo, pp. 3–29.

Galleguillos, Nibaldo H. 1997. "Checks and Balances in New Democracies: The Role of the Judiciary in the Chilean and Mexican Transitions." Paper presented at the 1997 Latin American Studies Association Meeting, Mexico City.

Gargarella, Roberto, Pilar Domingo, and Theunis Roux. 2006. *Courts and Social Transformation in New Democracies: An Institutional Voice for the Poor?* Hampshire: Ashgate Publishing.

García-Villegas, Mauricio. 2001. "Law as Hope. Constitutions, Courts and Social Change in Latin America." Paper presented at the 2001 Modernities, the New Constitution and Constitution-Making Powers Conference, National University of Colombia.

George, Tracy E. and Lee Epstein. 1992. "On the Nature of Supreme Court Decision Making." *American Political Science Review* 86(2): 323–337.

Global Integrity. (n.d.). "Mozambique: Integrity Scorecard Report 2006." Available at http://www.globalintegrity.org/reports/2006/mozambique/scorecard.cfm?subcategoryID66&countryID=23. Accessed on February 27, 2009.

Gloor, Anne. 2005. "Electoral conflicts: Conflict triggers and approaches for conflict management. Case Study Mozambique: General Elections 2004." *Peace, Conflict and Development: an Interdisciplinary Journal* 7(July): 281–303.

Gloppen, Siri. 2001. *South African Constitutonalism 1994–2000. The Difficult Balancing Act of the Constitutional Court.* PhD. Dissertation. Bergen: Department of Comparative Politics, University of Bergen.

Gloppen, Siri. 2004. "The Accountability Function of Courts in Tanzania and Zambia." In Roberto Gargarella and Elin Skaar, eds., *Democratization and the Judiciary: The Accountability Function of Courts in New Democracies*. London: Frank Cass, pp. 112–136.

Gloppen, Siri, Roberto Gargarella, and Elin Skaar, eds., 2004. *Democratization and the Judiciary: The Accountability Function of Courts in New Democracies*. London: Frank Cass.

Gloppen, Siri. 2005. "Social Rights Litigation as Transformation: South African Perspectives." In Peris Jones and Kristian Stokke, eds., *Democratising Development:*

The Politics of Socio-Economic Rights in South Africa. Leiden, Netherlands: Martinus Nijhoff, pp. 153–180.

Gloppen, Siri and Fidelis Edge Kanyongolo. 2006a. "The Role of the Judiciary in the 2004 General Elections in Malawi." *East African Journal of Peace and Human Rights* 12(2): 279–317.

Gloppen, Siri and Fidelis Edge Kanyongolo. 2006b. "Malawi." In Linda Van de Vijver, ed., *The Judicial Institution in Southern Africa: A Comparative Study of Common Law Jurisdictions.* Cape Town: Siber Ink, pp. 73–94.

Gloppen, Siri and Fidelis Edge Kanyongolo. 2007. "The Judicary." In Nandini Patel and Lars Svåsand, eds., *Government and Politics in Malawi.* Lilongwe: Kashere Publishers, pp. 109–135.

Gloppen, Siri, Emmanuel Kasimbazi and Alexander Kibandama. 2008. "Elections in Court: The Judiciary and Uganda's 2006 Election Process." In Julius Kiiza, Sabiti Makara, and Lise Rakner, eds., *Electoral Democracy in Uganda: Understanding the Institutional Processes and Outcomes of the 2006 Multiparty Elections.* Kampala, Uganda: Fountain Publishers, pp. 53–89.

Gloppen, Siri, Emmanuel Kasimbazi, and Alexander Kibandama. 2006. "The Evolving Role of the Courts in the Political Transition Process." Chr Michelsen Institute and Makerere University: Legal and Institutional Context of the 2006 Elections in Uganda Reseach Notes, January. Available at http://www.cmi.no/pdf/?file=/uganda/doc/gloppen-kazimbazi-kibandama-courts-political%20transition-research-note-Jan-06.pdf. Accessed on June 3, 2009.

Gloppen, Siri, Lise Rakner, and Lars Svåsand. 2007. "Political Paralysis in Malawi: Repercussions of Party Splits in a Weakly Institutionalised Democracy." Paper presented at 2007 European Consortium for Political Research, Pisa.

Goetz, Anne Marie and Rob Jenkins. 2005. *Reinventing Accountability: Making Democracy Work for Human Development.* Basingstoke: Palgrave Macmillan.

Gómez Bernales, Gaston. 1986. "Corte Suprema: Análisis de algunos de sus comportamientos." Unpublished manuscript, Santiago.

Gordon, Amy and David Bruce. 2007. "Transformation and the Independence of the Judiciary in South Africa." Johannesburg, South Africa: Centre for the Study of Violence and Reconciliation.

Government Communication and Information System. 2006. "Justice and Constitutional Development." In *South Africa Yearbook 2006/7.* South Africa: Government Communication and Information System Press, pp. 392. Available at http://www.doj.gov.za/about/sa%20yearbook/2006_adminjustice.pdf. Accessed on June 3, 2009.

Grant, Ruth W. and Robert O. Keohane. 2005. "Accountability and Abuses of Power in World Politics." *American Political Science Review* 99(1): 29–43.

Gutiérrez, Carlos José. 1999. "La Constitución cincuenta años después." In *Temas clave de la Constitución Política.* Editorial Investigaciones Jurídicas.

Gutierrez Sanin, Francisco, and Richard Stoller. 2001. "The Courtroom and the Bivouac: Reflections on Law and Violence in Colombia." *Latin American Perspectives* 28(1): 56–72.

Hall, Margareth and Tom Young. 1991. "Recent Constitutional Developments in Mozambique." *Journal of African Law* 35(1/2): 102–115.

Hanlon, Joseph. 2000. "Supreme Court rejects Renamo's 24 points." *Mozambique Peace Process Bulletin* 24 (January). Accessed on December 5, 2007.

Hanlon, Joseph. 2001. "Killing the goose that laid the golden eggs." *Metical* September.

Hanlon, Joseph. 2005. "Constitutional Council says CNE violated law in 2004." *Mozambique Political Process Bulletin* 32(July 15). Available at http://www.open.ac.uk/technology/mozambique/pics/d53724.doc. Accessed on June 3, 2009.

Harber, Anthony, Irma de Plessis and Tawana Kupe. 2006. "What was at Stake in the Zuma Trial? Three points of view." *Rhodes Journalism Review* 26(September). Available at http://www.rjr.ru.ac.za/rjrpdf/rjr_no26/zuma%20trial.pdf. Accessed on June 3, 2009.

Helmke, Gretchen. 2002. "The Logic of Strategic Defection: Court-Executive Relations in Argentina." *American Political Science Review* 96(2): 291–303.

Helmke, Gretchen. 2003. "Checks and Balances by Other Means: Strategic Defection and the 'Re-Reelection' Controversy in Argentina." *Comparative Politics* 35(2): 213–228.

Helmke, Gretchen. 2005. *Courts under Constraints. Judges, Generals, and Presidents in Argentina*. Cambridge, MA: Cambridge University Press.

Herrera, Berlioth. 1999. "Oscar Arias tras reelección." *La Nación*. December 2. San José, Costa Rica. Available at http://www.nacion.com/ln_ee/1999/diciembre/02/pais1.html. Accessed on June 3, 2009.

Herrera, Berlioth. 2003. "Congreso no puede cercenar derechos." *La Nación*. 17 July. San José, Costa Rica. Available at http://www.nacion.com/ln_ee/2003/julio/17/pais10.html. Accessed on June 3, 2009.

Heywood, Mark. 2005. "Shaping, Making, and Breaking the Law in the Campaign for a National HIV/AIDS Treatment Plan." In Peris Jones and Kristian Stokke, eds., *Democratising Development: The Politics of Socio-Economic Rights in South Africa*. Leiden, Netherlands: Martinus Nijhoff, pp. 181–212.

Hilbink, Lisa. 1999a. "Exploring the Links between Institutional Characteristics of the Judiciary and the Substance of Judicial Decision-Making." Paper presented at the 1999 American Political Science Association Meeting, Atlanta, GA August.

Hilbink, Lisa. 1999b. "Un Estado de derecho no liberal: La actuación del Poder Judicial chileno en los años 90." In Paul W. Drake and Ivan Jaksic, eds., *El Modelo Chileno: Democracia y Desarrollo en los Noventa*. Santiago: LOM ediciones, pp. 317–338.

Hilbink, Lisa. 1999c. *Legalism Against Democracy: The Political Role of the Judiciary in Chile, 1964–1999*. PhD. Dissertation, Harvard University School of Law.

Human Rights Watch Report. 1999. "When Tyrants Tremble." Available at http://hrw.org/reports/1999/chile/Patrick-03.htm#P349_127831. Accessed on June 3, 2009.

Human Rights Watch Report. 2004. "Undue Process: Terrorism Trials, Military Courts, and the Mapuche in Southern Chile." Available at http://www.hrw.org/reports/2004/chile1004/chile1004text.pdf. Accessed on June 3, 2009.

Iaryczower, Matias, Pablo T. Spiller, and Mariano Tommasi. 2002. "Judicial Decision Making in Unstable Environments, Argentina 1935–1998." *American Journal of Political Science* 46(4): 699–716.

Informe anual sobre derechos humanos en Chile 2004. Hechos de 2003. 2004. Facultad de Derecho. Universidad Diego Portales, Santiago, Chile. Available at http://www.derechoshumanos.udp.cl/informe-anual-sobre-derechos-humanos-en-chile-2004/. Accessed on Feb 27, 2009.

Informe Anual sobre Derechos Humanos en Chile 2003. Hechos de 2002. 2003. Facultad de Derecho, Universidad Diego Portales, Santiago, Chile. Available at http://www.derechoshumanos.udp.cl/informe-anual-sobre-derechos-humanos-en-chile-2003/. Accessed on Jun 20, 2009.

Instituto Nacional de Estatística. 2009. "Moçambique." Available at http://www.ine.gov.mz/. Accessed on February 27, 2009.

International Commission of Jurists. 2002. "Malawi: Final Report of Fact-Finding Mission and Trial Observation to Malawi." Available at http://www.icj.org/news.php3?id_article=2781&lang=en. Accessed on June 3, 2009.

International Foundation for Election Systems (IFES). N.d. "Guidance for Promoting Judicial Independence and Impartiality." Available at http://www.ifes.org/publication/0e49c032c28f9e60a181630f281eda5a/judicial_independence.pdf. Accessed on June 3, 2009.

IOL Reporter. 2006. "Former Malawi minister guilty of corruption." *Independent Online* 3 February. Available at http://www.iol.co.za/index.php?set_id=1&click_id=68&art_id=qw1138987084582B254. Accessed on June 3, 2009.

Jacob, Herbert, Erhard Blankenburg, Herbert M. Kritzer, Doris Marie Provine, and Joseph Sanders. 1996. *Courts, Law, and Politics in Comparative Perspective.* New Haven, CT: Yale University Press.

Jamali, Prince. 2008. "Chief Justice approved illegally, says activist." *Nyasa Times*, May 3. Available at http://www.nyasatimes.com/national/156.html. Accessed on June 3, 2009.

Jinesta, Ernesto. 2005. "Reforma impostergable." *La Nación.* November 6, p. 35A.

Kanyongolo, Fidelis Edge. 2004. "State of the Judiciary Report: Malawi 2003." Washington DC: IFES, State of the Judiciary Report Series.

Kapp, Clare. 2006. "Rape on trial in South Africa." *The Lancet*, 4 March, 367(9512): 718–719. doi:10.1016/S0140–6736(06)68285–8. Accessed on June 3, 2009.

Kiiza, Julius, Sabiti Makara and Lise Rakner, eds., 2008. *Electoral Democracy in Uganda: Understanding the Institutional Processes and Outcomes of the 2006 Multiparty Elections.* Kampala, Uganda: Fountain Publishers.

Kinander, Morten. 2004. "The View from Within. Analysis and Critique of Legal Realism and Descriptive Jurisprudence." Bergen: Fagbokforlaget.

Klug, Heitz. 1997. "Introducing the Devil: An Institutional Analysis of the Power of Constitutional Review." *South African Journal of Human Rights* 13(2): 185–215.

Knight, Jack. 1992. "Positive Models and Normative Theory: A Comment on Eskridge and Ferejohn." *Journal of Law, Economics, and Organization* 8(1): 190–196.

Kufa, Charles. 2007. "Munlo appointed Chief Justice." *Nyasa Times.* June 17.

Ley de la Jurisdicción Constitucional. 1989. Ley N° 7.135. October 11. Available at http://www.hacienda.go.cr/centro/datos/Ley/Ley%207135-J-Jurisdicci%C3%B3n%20constitucional-La%20Gaceta%20n.%20198–19%20OCT-1989..doc. Accessed on June 3, 2009.

Kugler, Maurice, and Howard Rosenthal. 2000. "Checks and Balances: An Assessment of the Institutional Separation of Political Powers in Colombia." Working Paper No. 9. Department of Economics and Econometrics, University of Southampton.

Liebenberg, Sanda. 2005. "The value of human dignity in interpreting socio-economic rights." *South African Journal on Human Rights* 21(1): 22.

Lieberman, Jethro K. 1988. "The Enduring Constitution. A Bicentennial Perspective." *Michigan Law Review* 101(4): 881–884.

Linz, Juan J., and Alfred Stepan, eds. 1996. *Problems of Democratic Transitions and Consolidation. Southern Europe, South America and Post-Communist Europe.* Baltimore & London: Johns Hopkins University Press.

Kalmanovitz, Salomon. 2000. "Los efectos económicos de la Corte Constitucional." Working Paper. Banco de la República, Santa Fe de Bogotá, Colombia.

Mabuza, Ernest. 2008. "South Africa: State Can Use Seized Papers in Zuma Trial." *Business Day* 1 (August). Available at http://allafrica.com/stories/200808010668.html. Accessed on June 3, 2009.

Mabuza, Ernest. 2009. "South Africa: Judges Crush Verdict That Sunk Thabo Mbeki." *Business Day* 13 (January). Available at http://allafrica.com/stories/200901140003.html. Accessed on June 3, 2009.

Mainwaring, Scott, and Matthew S. Shugart, eds. 1997. *Presidentialism and Democracy in Latin America.* Cambridge: Cambridge University Press.

Mainwaring, Scott. 2003. "Introduction: Democratic Accountability in Latin America." In Scott Mainwaring, and Christopher Welna, eds. *Democratic Accountability in Latin America.* Oxford: Oxford University Press, pp. 3–33.

Mainwaring, Scott and Christopher Welna, eds. 2003. *Democratic Accountability in Latin America.* Oxford: Oxford University Press.

Manin, Bernard. 1997. *The Principles of Representative Government.* Cambridge: Cambridge University Press.

Manning, Carrie. 1998. "Constructing Opposition in Mozambique: Renamo as a Political Party." *Journal of Southern African Studies* 24(1): 161–189.

Maravall, José María and Adam Przeworski. 2003. *Democracy and the Rule of Law.* Cambridge: Cambridge University Press.

Martin, Claire. 2002. "Malawi: Independent Judiciary." *Commonwealth Human Rights Initiative News.* February. Available at www.humanrightsinitiative.org/publications/nl/articles/malawi/malawi_independent_judiciary.pdf. Accessed on June 3, 2009.

Martz, John D. 1992. "Democratization and National Development in Colombia." *Latin American Research Review* 27(3): 216–226.

Maskin, Eric, and Tirole, Jean. 2004. "The Politician and the Judge: Accountability in Government." *American Economic Review* 94(4): 1034–1054.

Méndez Garita, William. 2000. "Procuradores Solís y Beirute 'Sala IV decide aqui.'" *La Nación*. November 13. San José, Costa Rica. Available at http://www.nacion. com/ln_ee/2000/noviembre/13/pais3.html. Accessed on June 3, 2009.

Merryman, John H. 1985. *The Civil Law Tradition: An Introduction to the Legal Systems of Western Europe and Latin America*. Stanford, CA: Stanford University Press.

Miles, Thomas, and Cass Sunstein. 2007. "The New Legal Realism." Working Paper 191. Public Law and Legal Theory. Chicago, IL: University of Chicago.

Miller, Jonathan M. 2000. "Evaluating the Argentine Supreme Court Under Presidents Alfonsin and Menem, 1983–1999." *Southwestern Journal of Law and Trade in the Americas* 7: 369–433.

MISA. 2002. "Editor, Reporter Face Contempt Charge." Media Institute of South Africa (Zambia). September 16. Available at http://www.misazambia.org.zm/ media/news/viewnews.cgi?category=2&id=1032195467. Accessed on October 18, 2009.

MISA. 2007. "Malawi: High Court Nullifies Improperly-Appointed Communications Regulatory Board." *Media Institute of Southern Africa* (Windhoek). July 20. Available at http://allafrica.com/stories/200707230869.html. Accessed on June 3, 2009.

MISA. 2008. "Malawi: Joy Radio Allowed to Resume Broadcasting." *Media Institute of Southern Africa* (Windhoek). December 17. Available at http://allafrica.com/ stories/200812171066.html. Accessed on June 3, 2009.

Mishler, William, and Reginald S. Sheehan. 1993. "The Supreme Court as a Countermajoritarian Institution? The Impact of Public Opinion on Supreme Court Decisions." *American Political Science Review* 87(1): 87–101.

Mishler, William, and Reginald S. Sheehan. 1996. "Public Opinion, the Attitudinal Model and Supreme Court Decision-Making: A Micro Analytic Perspective." *Journal of Politics* 57(4): 169–200.

Moehler, Devra C. 2006. "Public Participation and Support for the Constitution in Uganda." *The Journal of Modern African Studies* 44(2): 275–308.

The Monitor (Kampala). 2006. "The Supreme Court Ruling." April 7.

Mora, Emilia. 2000. "Niño ganó disputa a Ministro." *La Nación*. February 14. San José, Costa Rica. Available at http://www.nacion.com/ln_ee/2000/febrero/14/ pais12.html. Accessed on June 3, 2009.

Mora, Ana Lupita. 2007. "Lisbeth Quesada envió Tratado a la Sala IV." *La Nación*. April 28. San José, Costa Rica. Available at http://www.nacion.com/ln_ee/2007/ abril/28/pais1077984.html. Accessed on June 3, 2009.

Mozambique News Agency. 2000. "Supreme Court ratifies election results." AIM Reports January 5. AIM Reports 173. Available at http://www.pop-tel.org.uk/mozambique-news/newsletter/aim173.html#story1. Accessed on June 3, 2009.

Mozambique News Agency. 2003. "Long sentences for murderers of Carlos Cardoso." February 3. AIM Reports 247. Available at http:// www. poptel.org.uk/mozambique-news/newsletter/aim247.html. Accessed on September 7, 2006.

Mozambique News Agency. 2004. "Constitutional Council validates local elections." January 19. AIM Reports 268. Available at http://www.poptel.org.uk/mozambique-news/newsletter/aim268.html. Accessed on September 7, 2006.

Mozambique News Agency. 2005. "Constitutional Council rejects Renamo appeal." January 19. AIM Reports 291. Available at http://www.poptel.org.uk/mozambique-news/newsletter/aim291.html#story2. Accessed on September 7, 2006.

Mozambique News Agency. 2006a. "Nyimpine Chissano charged over Cardoso murder." May 11. AIM Reports. Special issue. Available at http://www.poptel.org.uk/mozambique-news/newsletter/Chissano.html. Accessed on November 26, 2007.

Mozambique News Agency. 2006b. "Anti-corruption conventions ratified." May 2. AIM Reports 319. Available at http://www.poptel.org.uk/mozambique-news/newsletter/aim319.html#story3. Accessed on June 3, 2009.

Murillo Víquez, Jaime. 1994. *La Sala Constitucional: Una revolución político–jurídica en Costa Rica*. San José, Costa Rica: Editorial Guayacán.

Navia, Patricio, and Julio Ríos-Figueroa. 2005. "The Constitutional Adjudication Mosaic of Latin America." *Comparative Political Studies* 38(2): 189–217.

Ng'andu, F.M. and K. C. Chanda. 2002. "The Role of the Judiciary in Promoting Transparency and Honesty in the Zambian Electoral Process." Paper presented at Political Processes in Zambia conference, Norad/CMI/Inesor, Lusaka.

Nino, Carlos Santiago. 1996. *The Constitution of Deliberative Democracy*. New Haven: Yale University Press.

Nino, Carlos Santiago. 1992. *Fundamentos de derecho constitucional*. Buenos Aires, Argentina: Astrea.

Novoa Monreal, Eduardo. 1970. "Justicia de clases?" *Revista Mensaje* 187: 108–118.

Nunes, Rodrigo. 2009. "Ideational Origins of Progressive Judicial Activism: The Colombian Constitutional Court and the Right to Health." Paper presented at the Law and Society Association meeting, Denver, April.

Observatorio de Derechos de los Pueblos Indígenas. N.d. Available at http://www.observatorio.cl/contenidos/naveg/qs.php. Accessed on June 3, 2009.

Odoki, Benjamin. 2005. *The Search for a National Consensus: The Making of the 1995 Uganda Constitution*. Kampala, Uganda: Fountain Publishers.

O'Donnell, Guillermo A. 1998. "Horizontal Accountability in New Democracies." *Journal of Democracy* 9(3): 112–126.

O'Donnell, Guillermo A. 1999. "Horizontal Accountability in New Democracies." In Andreas Schedler, Larry Diamond, and Marc F. Plattner, eds., *The Self-restraining State: Power and Accountability in New Democracies*. Boulder, CO and London: Lynne Rienner Publishers, pp. 29–51.

O'Donnell, Guillermo A. 2003. "Horizontal Accountability: The Legal Institutionalization of Mistrust." In Scott Mainwaring and Christopher Welna, eds., *Democratic Accountability in Latin America*. Oxford, Oxford University Press, pp. 34–54.

Palacios Mejia, Hugo. 2001. "El control constitucional en el trópico." In *Precedente. Anuario Jurídico 2001*. Cali, Colombia: Universidad ICESI, pp. 3–20.

PEN. 2001. "Proyecto Estado de la Nación. Auditoría ciudadana sobre la calidad de la democracia en Costa Rica." San José, Costa Rica: Proyecto Estado de la Nación en Desarrollo Humano Sostenible–Consejo Nacional de Rectores (CONARE). Available at http://www.estadonacion.or.cr/Calidad/calidad.htm.A

PEN (Proyecto Estado de la Nación). 2000. "Resumen del anexo al capitulo 5: diez años de la sala constitucional (1989–1999)." San José, Costa Rica: Proyecto Estado de la Nación, Consejo Nacional de Rectores (CONARE). Available at http://www.estadonacion.or.cr/InformesPDF/VI-Informe/Anexo-SC.pdf. Accessed on October 17, 2009.

PEN. 2006. "Proyecto Estado de la Nación en Desarrollo Humano Sostenible. XII Informe Estado de la Nación 2006 [2005]." San José, Costa Rica: Proyecto Estado de la Nación en Desarrollo Humano Sostenible–Consejo Nacional de Rectores (CONARE). Available at http://www.estadonacion.or.cr/Info2006/Paginas/carpeta.htm. Accessed on June 3, 2009.

People's Daily. 2001. "Mozambique' Bank Chief Murdered by Privatization Opposing Forces: Report." August 18.

Pérez Salazar, Mauricio. 2003. "Razones y sinrazones de un debate: La crítica económica de la jurisprudencia constitucional colombiana." *Revista Derecho del Estado* 14: 57–95.

Persson, Torsten, Gerard Roland, and Guido Tabelini. 1996. "Separation of Powers and Accountability: Towards a Formal Approach to Comparative Politics." Discussion Paper 1475. London: Centre for Economic Policy Research.

Peruzzotti, Enrique and Catalina Smulovitz, eds. 2006. *Enforcing the Rule of Law: Societal Accountability in the New Latin American Democracies*. Pittsburgh, PA: Pittsburgh University Press.

Peter, Chris Maina. 1997a. *Human Rights Case Book*. Konstanz: Hartung-Gorre Verlag.

Peter, Chris Maina. 1997b. *Human Rights in Tanzania*. Köln: Rüdiger Köppe Verlag.

Peter, Chris Maina and Helen Kijo-Bisimba, eds. 2007. *Law and Justice in Tanzania: Quarter a Century of the Court of Appeal*. Dar es Salam: Mkuki na Nyota Publishers.

Pfeiffer, Steven B. 1978. "The Role of the Judiciary in the Constitutional Systems of East Africa." *The Journal of Modern African Studies* 16(March 1): 33–66.

Przeworski, Adam. 2006. "Social Accountability in Latin America and Beyond." In Enrique Peruzzotti and Catalina Smulovitz, eds. *Enforcing the Rule of Law: Social Accountability in the New Latin American Democracies*. Pittsburgh: University of Pittsburgh Press, pp. 323–333.

Przeworski, Adam, Susan C. Stokes, and Bernard Manin, eds. 1999. *Democracy, Accountability and Representation*. Cambridge: Cambridge University Press.

Rainha, Paula. 2009. *Republic of Mozambique—Legal System and Research*. GlobaLex 2008. Available at http://www.nyulawglobal.org/globalex/Mozambique.htm. Accessed on February 27, 2009.

Redfern, Paul. 2001. "Uganda: Vote Theft, Intimidation, Dent Museveni's Image—UK Media." *The Monitor* 14(March). Available at http://allafrica.com/stories/200103140088.html. Accessed on June 3, 2009.

Republic of Malawi. 1991. *Constitution of Zambia Act.* Available at http://unpan1.un.org/intradoc/groups/public/documents/cafrad/unpan004847.pdf. Accessed on June 3, 2009.

Republic of Malawi. 1994. *Constitution of the Republic of Malawi.* Available at http://www.sdnp.org.mw/constitut/intro.html. Accessed on June 3, 2009.

Republic of Mozambique. 2006. "Plano de Acção Para a Redução da Pobreza Absoluta 2006–2009 (PARPA II)." Maputo.

Republic of South Africa. 1983. *Constitution of the Republic of South Africa.*

Republic of South Africa. 1993. *Constitution of the Republic of South Africa.*

Republic of South Africa. 1996. *Constitution of the Republic of South Africa.* Available at http://www.info.gov.za/documents/constitution/1996/a108–96.pdf. Accessed on June 3, 2009.

Republic of Uganda. 1995. *Constitution of The Republic of Uganda.* Available at http://www.parliament.go.ug/images/constitution_1995.pdf. Accessed on June 3, 2009.

Rodríguez Cordero, Juan Carlos. 2002. *Entre curules & estrados: la consulta preceptiva de las reformas constitucionales en Costa Rica, First ed.* San José, Costa Rica: Investigaciones Jurídicas.

Rodríguez Cordero, Juan Carlos. 2003. "Sala Constitucional y equilibrio de Poderes." Noveno Informe sobre el Estado de la Nación en Desarrollo Humano Sostenible. San José, Costa Rica: Proyecto Estado de la Nación en Desarrollo Humano Sotenible-CONARE.

Rosenberg, Gerald N. 1992. "Judicial Independence and the Reality of Political Power." *Review of Politics* 54(3): 369–400.

Rosenn, Keith S. 1987. "The Protection of Judicial Independence in Latin America." *The University of Miami Inter-American Law Review* 19 (1): 1–35.

Ross, Kenneth R. 2004. "Worrisome Trends: the Voice of the Churches in Malawi's Third Term Debate." *African Affairs* 103: 91–107.

Roux, Theunis. 2004. "Legitimating Transformation: Political Resource Allocation in the South African Constitutional Court." In Siri Gloppen, Roberto Gargarella, and Elin Skaar, eds., *Democratization and the Judiciary. The Accountability Function of Courts in New Democracies.* London: Frank Cass, pp. 92–111.

Sachs, Albie and Gita Honwana Welch. 1990. *Liberating the Law: Creating Popular Justice in Mozambique.* London: Zed Books.

Sala IV. 2004. "Sentencia sobre el acuerdo del poder ejecutivo en relación con la guerra en Iraq." Available at http://nacion.com/ln_ee/2004/septiembre/09/accion.pdf. Accessed on June 3, 2009.

Sala IV. 2007. "Informe de Labores 2006." Available at http://www.poder-judicial.go.cr/Informedelabores/2006/texto2.htm#12. Accessed on June 3, 2009.

Sala IV. 2009. "La Sala Constitucional en números." Available at http://www.poder-judicial.go.cr/salaconstitucional/estadisticas.htm. Accessed October 16, 2009.

Schedler, Andreas, Larry Diamond, and Marc F. Plattner, eds., 1999. *The Self-Restraining State: Power and Accountability in New Democracies*. Boulder, CO: Lynne Rienner Publishers.

Schmitter, Philippe C. 2004. "The Quality of Democracy: The Ambiguous Virtues of Accountability." *Journal of Democracy* 15(4): 47–60.

Schmitter, Philippe C. and Terry Lynn Karl. 1991. "What Democracy Is…and Is Not." *Journal of Democracy* 2(3): 75–88.

Scribner, Druscilla. 2003. "Sincere and Strategic Judicial Behavior on the Chilean Supreme Court." Paper presented at the 2003 Midwest Political Science Association Conference, Chicago, IL, April.

Segal; Jefferey 1997. "Separation-of-Powers Games in the Positive Theory of Congress and Courts." *American Political Science Review* 91(1): 28–44.

Segal, Jeffrey, and Harold J. Spaeth. 1993. *The Supreme Court and the Attitudinal Model*. Cambridge: Cambridge University Press.

Shapiro, Martin. 2004. "Judicial Review in Developed Democracies." In Siri Gloppen, Roberto Gargarella, and Elin Skaar. eds. *Democratization and the Judiciary. The Accountability Function of Courts in New Democracies*. London: Frank Cass, pp. 7–26.

Shapiro, Martin and Alec Stone Sweet. 2004. *On Law, Politics, and Judicialization*. New York: Oxford University Press.

Shifter, Michael. 2009. "Colombia's Alvaro Uribe—Return of the South American Strongman?" *Los Angeles Times*. April 16. Available at http://articles.latimes.com/2009/apr/16/opinion/oe-shifter16. Accessed on June 3, 2009.

Sieder, Rachel, ed. 1996. *Central America: Fragile Transition*. London and Basingstoke: Macmillan Press.

Sieder, Rachel, Line Schjolden, and Alan Angell. 2005. "Introduction." In Sieder, Rachel, Line Schjolden, and Alan Angell, eds. *The Judicialization of Politics in Latin America*. New York: ISA/Palgrave Macmillan, pp. 1–20.

Simwanza, Obert. 2006. "Zambia: I won't petition election results, says Sata." *Times of Zambia*. October 3. Available at http://www.afrika.no/Detailed/12873.html. Accessed on June 3, 2009.

Skaar, Elin. 2002. Judicial Independence: A Key to Justice. An Analysis of Latin America in the 1990s. Doctoral dissertation, Department of Political Science, University of California, Los Angeles, Los Angeles.

Smulovitz, Catalina, and Enrique Peruzzotti. 2000. "Societal Accountability in Latin America." *Journal of Democracy* 11(4): 147–158.

de Sousa Santos, Boaventura. 2006. "The Heterogeneous State and Legal Plurality." In Boaventure de Sousa Santos, João Carlos Trinidade, and Maria Paula Meneses, eds., *Law and Justice in a Multicultural Society: The Case of Mozambique*. Dakar, Senegal: CODESRIA, pp. 3–29.

de Sousa Santos, Boaventura, João Carlos Trinidade, and Maria Paula Meneses, eds., 2006. *Law and Justice in a Multicultural Society: The Case of Mozambique*. Dakar, Senegal: CODESRIA.

Sunday Monitor Team. 2006. "Kikonyogo refuses to quit Besigye case." *Sunday Monitor*, Kampala, 1(1). Available at http://www.monitor.co.ug/sunday/news/news01011.php. Accessed on June 3, 2009.

Sunstein, Cass R. 2001. *Designing Democracy: What Constitutions Do.* New York: Oxford University Press.

Sunstein, Cass, David Schkade, Lisa Michelle Ellman. 2004."Ideological Voting in Federal Courts of Appeal. A Preliminary Investigation." *Virginia Law Review* 90(1): 301–354.

Sunstein, Cass, David Schkade, and Lisa Michelle Ellman, and Andreas Sawicki. 2006. *Are Judges Political? An Empirical Analysis of the Federal Judiciary.* Washington, DC: Brookings Intitution Press.

Svåsand, Lars and Nadini Patel, eds., 2007. *Government and Politics in Malawi.* Zomba: Kashere Books.

Tate, C. Neal and Torbjorn Vallinder, eds., 1997. *The Global Expansion of Judicial Power.* New York: New York University Press.

Taylor, Matthew. 2008. *Judging Policy: Courts and Policy Reform in Democratic Brazil.* Stanford: Stanford University Press.

Taylor, Michelle M. 1992. "Formal versus Informal Incentive Structures and Legislative Behavior: Evidence from Costa Rica." *Journal of Politics* 54(4): 1055–1073.

Times of Zambia Reporter. 2007. "Zambia: Magistrate's Court Orders Resumption of Chiluba, Two Others Trial." *Times of Zambia.* June 1. Available at http://allafrica.com/stories/200706010931.html. Accessed on June 3, 2009.

Tribune Reporter. 2008. "Malawi: Political Arrests Punctuate President's Leadership." *The Tribune.* December 26. Available at http://allafrica.com/stories/200812300650.html. Accessed on June 3, 2009.

Trinidade, João Carlos and João Pedroso. 2006. "The Judicial System: Structure, Legal Education and Legal Training." In Boaventure de Sousa Santos, João Carlos Trinidade and Maria Paula Meneses, eds., *Law and Justice in a Multicultural Society: The Case of Mozambique*, edited by B. de Sousa Santos, Dakar, Senegal: CODESRIA, pp.113–143.

Tsebelis, George. 1990. *Nested Games: Rational Choice in Comparative Politics.* Berkeley and Los Angeles, CA: University of California Press.

Tsebelis, George. 1995. "Decision Making in Political Systems: Veto Players in Presidentialism, Parliamentarism, Multicameralism and Multipartyism." *British Journal of Political Science* 25(3): 289–325.

Tsebelis, George. 2002. *Veto Players: How Political Institutions Work.* Princeton, NJ: Princeton University Press.

United Nations. 1985. "Basic Principles on the Independence of the Judiciary." Seventh UN Congress on the Prevention of Crime and the Treatment of Offenders. August 26–September 3. Milan, Italy. Available at http://hrli.alrc.net/pdf/UNBasicPrinciplesontheidependenceofthejudiciary.pdf Accessed on October 20, 2009.

United Nation's Development Programme (UNDP). n.d. "Human Development Index." Available at http://hdr.undp.org/en/statistics/. Accessed on June 3, 2009.

United Nation's Development Programme (UNDP). 2005. "Human Development Report 2005. International cooperation at a crossroads: Aid, Trade and Security in an Unequal World." Available at http://hdr.undp.org/en/media/hdr05_complete.pdf. Accessed on June 3, 2009.

United Nation's Development Programme (UNDP). 2006. *Human Development Report 2005. International Cooperation at a Crossroads: Aid, Trade and Security in an Unequal World*. Oxford: Oxford University Press.

United Nation's Development Programme (UNDP). 2008. "Human Development Indices: A statistical update 2008—HDI rankings." Available at http://hdr.undp.org/en/statistics/. Accessed on June 3, 2009.

Uprimny, Rodrigo. 2004. "The Constitutional Court and Control of Presidential Extraordinary Powers in Colombia." In Siri Gloppen, Roberto Gargarella, and Elin Skaar, eds., *Democratization and the Judiciary: The Accountability Function of Courts in New Democracies*. London: Frank Cass, pp. 46–69.

Uprimny, Yepes Rodrigo. 2007. "Judicialization of Politics in Colombia: Cases, Merits and Risks." *Sur—Revista Internacional de Derechos Humanos* 3(6): 53–69.

Uprimny, Rodrigo, Cesar Rodriguez, and Mauricio García Villegas. 2002. "Más allá de la oferta y la demanda: Análisis sociojurídico de la justicia colombiana a comienzos de siglo." Unpublished Manuscript. Bogotá, Colombia.

Uprimny, Rodrigo, and Mauricio García Villegas. 2002. "Corte Constitucional y emancipación social en Colombia." Unpublished Manuscript. Bogotá, Colombia.

Urcuyo Fournier, Constantino. 1995. "La Sala Constitucional: Necesarios límites al poder." *Revista Parlamentaria* 3(3): 17–50.

USAID. 2005. *Corruption Assessment: Mozambique. Final Report*. Washington DC: MSI.

Vargas Cullell, Jorge. 2007. "Costa Rica: Fin de una era política." *Revista de ciencia política*. 27:113–128.

Velasco, Eugenio. 1976a. "The Allende Regime in Chile: An Historical and Legal Analysis." *Loyola of Los Angeles Law Review* 9(1): 480.

Velasco, Eugenio. 1976b. "The Allende Regime in Chile: An Historical and Legal Analysis." *Loyola of Los Angeles Law Review* 9(2): 711.

Velasco, Eugenio. 1976c. "The Allende Regime in Chile: An Historical and Legal Analysis." *Loyola of Los Angeles Law Review* 9(3): 961.

Venegas Campos, Ismael. 2000. "Archivada la reelección." *La Nación*. September 13. San José, Costa Rica. Available at http://www.nacion.com/ln_ee/2000/septiembre/13/pais4.html. Accessed June 3, 2009.

Vizcaíno, Irene. 2004. "Sala IV anuló apoyo oficial a invasión en Iraq, Ordenó a Gobierno gestionar retiro de lista de aliados." *La Nación*. September 9. San José, Costa Rica. Available at http://nacion.com/ln_ee/2004/septiembre/09/pais4.html. Accessed June 3, 2009.

VonDoepp, Peter. 2002. "Are Malawi's Local Clergy Civil Society Activists: The Limiting Impact of Creed, Context and Class." In Harri Englund, ed., *A Democracy of Chameleons: Politics and Culture in the New Malawi*. Uppsala: Nordiska Afrikainstitutet, pp 123–139.

VonDoepp, Peter. 2005. "The Problem of Judicial Control in Africa's Neopatrimonial Democracies: Malawi and Zambia." *Political Science Quarterly* 120(2): 275–301.

VonDoepp, Peter. 2006. "Politics and Judicial Assertiveness in Emerging Democracies: High Court Behavior in Malawi and Zambia." *Political Research Quarterly* 59(3): 389–399.

VonDoepp, Peter. 2008. "Context-Sensitive Inquiry in Comparative Judicial Research: Lessons From the Namibian Judiciary." *Comparative Political Studies* 41(11): 1515–1540.

VonDoepp, Peter. 2009. *Judicial Politics in New Democracies: Cases from Southern Africa*. Boulder, CO: Lynne Rienner.

VonDoepp, Peter and Rachel Ellet. 2008. "Strategic Models of Executive-Judicial Relations: Insights from New African Democracies." Paper presented at the Annual Meeting of the American Political Science Association, August 27–31, Boston, MA.

Weyland, Kurt G. 2002. "Limitations of Rational-choice Institutionalism for the Study of Latin American Politics." *Studies in Comparative International Development* 37(1): 57–85.

Wickeri, Elisabeth. 2004. "Grootboom's Legacy: Securing the Right to Access to Adequate Housing in South Africa." Working paper Series No. 05 at Center for Human Rights and Global Justice, New York University Law School. Available at http://www.chrgj.org/publications/docs/wp/Wickeri%20Grootboom%27s%20 Legacy.pdf. Accessed October 16, 2009.

Widner, Jennifer A. 1999. "Building Judicial Independence in Common Law Africa." In Andreas Schedler, Larry Diamond, and Marc F. Plattner, eds., *The Self-Restraining State: Power and Accountability in New Democracies*. Boulder, CO: Lynne Rienner Publishers, pp. 177–194.

Widner, Jennifer A. 2001. *Building the Rule of Law*. New York: W.W. Norton & Company.

Williams, J. Michael. 2004. "Democracy and Constitutionalism in Southern Africa." Unpublished manuscript.

Wilson, Bruce M. 1994. "When Social Democrats Choose Neoliberal Economic Policies: The Case of Costa Rica." *Comparative Politics* 26(2): 149–168.

Wilson, Bruce M. 1998. *Costa Rica: Politics, Economics, and Democracy*, Boulder, CO: Lynne Rienner Publishers.

Wilson, Bruce M. 2005. "Changing Dynamics: The Political Impact of Costa Rica's Constitutional Court." In Rachel Sieder, Line Schjolden, and Alan Angell, eds., *The Judicialization of Politics in Latin America*. New York: ISA/Palgrave Macmillan, pp. 47–66.

Wilson, Bruce M. 2007a. "Costa Rica's General Election, February 2006." *Electoral Studies* 26(1): 712–716.

Wilson, Bruce M. 2007b. "Observación de las elecciones generales del 2006 en Costa Rica: Un ensayo fotográfico." *Revista de Derecho Electoral* 3(1): 1–15.

Wilson, Bruce M. 2009. "Rights Revolutions in Unlikely Places: Colombia and Costa Rica." *Journal of Politics in Latin America* 1(2): 59–85.

Wilson, Bruce M., Juan Carlos Rodríguez Cordero, and Roger Handberg. 2004. "The Best Laid Schemes…Gang Aft A–gley: Judicial Reform in Latin America—Evidence from Costa Rica." *Journal of Latin American Studies* 36(3): 507–531.

Wilson, Bruce M., Juan Carlos Rodríguez Cordero. 2006. "Legal Opportunity Structures and Social Movements: The Effects of Institutional Change on Costa Rican Politics." *Comparative Political Studies* 39(3): 325–351.

Wilson, Bruce M. and Roger Handberg. 1999. "From Judicial Passivity to Judicial Activism: Explaining the Change within Costa Rica's Supreme Court." *NAFTA: Law and Business Review of the Americas* 5(4): 522–543.

World Bank. 2004. "Mozambique: Legal and Judicial Sector Assessment, Legal Vice Presidency." Available at http://web.worldbank.org. Accessed June 3, 2009.

Yamin, Alicia Ely, and Oscar Parra Vera. 2008. "How Do Courts Set Health Policy? The Case of the Colombian Constitutional Court." *PLoS Med* 6(2): 147–150. Available at http://www.plosmedicine.org/article/info:doi/10.1371/journal.pmed.1000032. Accessed on October 16, 2009.

Index